AF873798

CTR
CRASH TEAM RACING
NAUGHTY DOG
SONY
PAL
SUPER NINTENDO
ENTERTAINMENT SYSTEM
8 MB
MEMORY CARD
MagicGate
PlayStation 2
NINTENDO 3DS
ZELDA
Frei ab 12 Jahre
LNA-CTR-AJRP-EUR
BACK
START
Microsoft
18
www.pegi.info
105310

Welcome to

THE HISTORY OF VIDEO GAMES

Congratulations! You have just picked up a time machine. This isn't one of those 88mph DeLoreans or ramshackle phone booths made by hucksters and charlatans, though, this is a special time machine: it will take you through the history of videogames. As you flick through these pages, you'll be transported to the computer labs of the Sixties, where videogames were born, through to the modern era of the Twenties where games are a billion-dollar industry. Along the way, you'll learn how the likes of Atari and Space Invaders took over the world, delve into exciting hardware like the PlayStation and Xbox, and marvel at landmark titles such as Jet Set Willy, World Of Warcraft and more. So what are you waiting for? Turn the page and begin this fantastic voyage through time!

FUTURE

THE HISTORY OF VIDEO GAMES

Future PLC Quay House, The Ambury, Bath, BA1 1UA

Editorial
Editor **Drew Sleep**
Designer **Emma Wood**
Compiled by **Aiden Dalby & Jon Wells**
Senior Art Editor **Andy Downes**
Head of Art & Design **Greg Whitaker**
Editorial Director **Jon White**

Contributor
Nick Thorpe

Photography
All copyrights and trademarks are recognised and respected

Advertising
Media packs are available on request
Commercial Director **Clare Dove**

International
Head of Print Licensing **Rachel Shaw**
licensing@futurenet.com
www.futurecontenthub.com

Circulation
Head of Newstrade **Tim Mathers**

Production
Head of Production **Mark Constance**
Production Project Manager **Matthew Eglinton**
Advertising Production Manager **Joanne Crosby**
Digital Editions Controller **Jason Hudson**
Production Managers **Keely Miller, Nola Cokely, Vivienne Calvert, Fran Twentyman**

Printed in the UK

Distributed by Marketforce, 5 Churchill Place, Canary Wharf, London, E14 5HU
www.marketforce.co.uk Tel: 0203 787 9001

The History of Videogames Fourth Edition (GAB5753)
© 2023 Future Publishing Limited

We are committed to only using magazine paper which is derived from responsibly managed, certified forestry and chlorine-free manufacture. The paper in this bookazine was sourced and produced from sustainable managed forests, conforming to strict environmental and socioeconomic standards. The paper holds full FSC or PEFC certification and accreditation.

All contents © 2023 Future Publishing Limited or published under licence. All rights reserved. No part of this magazine may be used, stored, transmitted or reproduced in any way without the prior written permission of the publisher. Future Publishing Limited (company number 2008885) is registered in England and Wales. Registered office: Quay House, The Ambury, Bath BA1 1UA. All information contained in this publication is for information only and is, as far as we are aware, correct at the time of going to press. Future cannot accept any responsibility for errors or inaccuracies in such information. You are advised to contact manufacturers and retailers directly with regard to the price of products/services referred to in this publication. Apps and websites mentioned in this publication are not under our control. We are not responsible for their contents or any other changes or updates to them. This magazine is fully independent and not affiliated in any way with the companies mentioned herein.

FUTURE

Connectors. Creators. Experience Makers.

Future plc is a public company quoted on the London Stock Exchange (symbol: FUTR)
www.futureplc.com

Chief executive **Zillah Byng-Thorne**
Non-executive chairman **Richard Huntingford**
Chief Financial and Strategy Officer **Penny Ladkin-Brand**

Tel +44 (0)1225 442 244

Part of the retro GAMER bookazine series

Widely Recycled

ipso. For press freedom with responsibility

CONTENTS

8 The Big Bang
Steve Russell on his highly influential creation, *Spacewar!*

12 The Seventies
Gaming moves out of the labs and into the world

14 Hardware Of The Seventies
Take a look at the iconic games machines of the era

16 Atari: King Of The Seventies
Learn how this legendary company ruled the decade

22 Retro Revival: Pong
You can't get more 'videogames' than this classic

24 Baer's Odyssey
We remember the father of modern gaming

30 The Impact Of Space Invaders
Discover how an army of pixellated aliens took over the world

38 The Eighties
Return to the era where gaming really hit its stride

40 Hardware Of The Eighties
Marvel at this roster of diverse computers and consoles

42 Rise Of The Bedroom Coder
Take a look at how hobbyist coders made games from their homes

46 Jet Set Willy
Matthew Smith takes you inside Miner Willy's eccentric mansion

50 The Rise Of Nintendo
How the Kyoto-based games company started its supremacy

52 The History Of Videogame Magazines
From *Amstrad Action* to *Edge*, we look at all of the best print mags

58 Retro Revival: Tetris
Why this puzzler has been wearing out your thumbs for decades

60 The Complete History Of Mario
Delve into the story of gaming's most celebrated hero

70 The Nineties
Travel back to the time where 3D became a hot topic

72 Hardware Of The Nineties
Witness the huge leap in power across this decade

74 The Rise Of The World Wide Web
Today it's everywhere, but learn about its humble beginnings here

76 A New Dimension: 3D Games Take Over
How developers adapted to the switch from pixels to polygons

82 Sony's Game Changer
The story behind the ultra-stylish PlayStation

86 *Retro Revival: Super Mario 64*
It's many people's favourite game, learn why here

88 *The Story Of Sonic The Hedgehog*
Discover how this Blue Blur brought attitude to the Nineties

98 *The Noughties*
Drop back in time to when Microsoft entered the console fray

100 *Hardware Of The Noughties*
An exciting decade of ambitious consoles and handhelds

102 *World Of Warcraft*
Journey to Azeroth and discover this mind-blowing MMORPG

108 *Online Gaming Gets Huge*
How the internet shaped gaming during the Noughties

110 *Brave New Open Worlds*
This decade ushered in a brand-new genre, learn more here

114 *Retro Revival: Wii Sports*
Revisit this Wiimote-waggling modern classic

116 *Inside The Xbox*
Seamus Blackley on making Microsoft's debut console

126 *The Tens*
Is this where gaming went truly mainstream? Let's find out

128 *Hardware Of The Tens*
This decade brought in a lot of gimmicky machines...

130 *The Retro Revolution*
How old school cool became big money

134 *Virtual Reality Blows Up*
The future of gaming has arrived! Explore it right here

136 *Retro Revival: Minecraft*
Why Mojang's sandbox is a perfect game for everyone

138 *The Twenties*
An amazing year of games, new consoles... and a virus

140 *Hardware Of The Twenties*
Examine the new kids on the block, and some retro machines

142 *Gaming In A Pandemic*
How videogames helped us through a tough year

THE BIG BANG:

STEVE RUSSELL AND THE CREATION OF SPACEWAR

Words by Paul Drury

Take a journey back in time to where it all began and hear from the man who coded the very first 'true' videogame

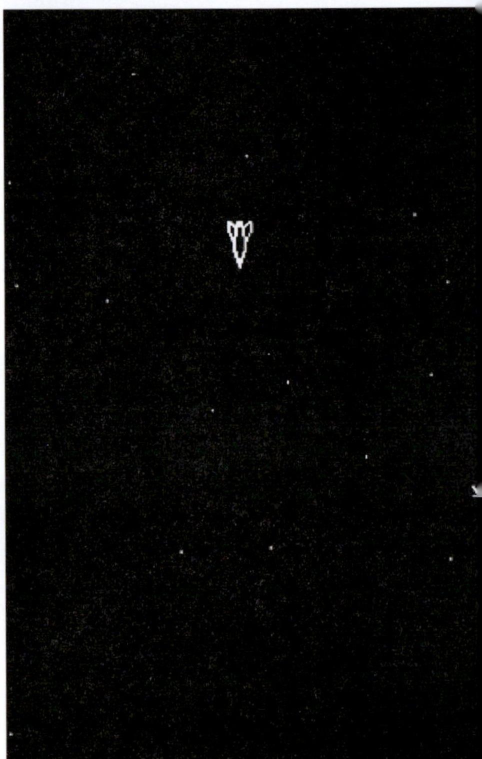

» The ships were nicknamed the Needle and the Wedge for obvious reasons.

***S**pacewar!* **was released way back in 1962 on the PDP-1 and usually has the honour of being acknowledged as the first true videogame.** You could certainly play games on computers before *Spacewar!*'s creation – versions of traditional games such as *Noughts And Crosses* and *Draughts* existed on mainframe computers as early as the Forties, and Willy Higinbotham's famous technical demo *Tennis For Two,* which was created in 1958, hinted at the shape of games to come. Steve Russell's *Spacewar!* was something entirely new, however, something which could only exist in digital form, and its 'deep space deathmatch' theme is still a mainstay of the industry it helped birth over half a century ago.

The late Ralph Baer, the creator of the Magnavox Odyssey console, has been frequently called 'the father of modern videogames'. So does this make you the grandfather?

I'm reasonably comfortable with that [laughs]. Mostly what I did was demonstrate you could play an interesting game on a computer at a time when computers were very expensive and so no one could possibly have got one just to play games. When computers did become cheap enough [for that], some of the people who made those early arcade games remembered *Spacewar!* and tried to do something like it… or better!

You arrived at the prestigious Massachusetts Institute Of Technology (MIT) during September 1958 to work with the computer scientist professor John McCarthy…

I'd worked with him at Dartmouth the summer before, and after I graduated he offered me a job working on AI, a term he'd recently coined. I was 21 years old and it was a great opportunity. I had access to the fastest and most powerful computer of the day – the IBM 704, which was cranky and annoying but could be very satisfying to program as well.

When a PDP-1 arrived at MIT in the autumn of 1961, did you immediately see the potential for writing a game?

Not straight away. Professor Marvin Minsky had written a demonstration program which everyone called 'Minskytron', which produced a kaleidoscope effect on-screen. You could use switches to change the pattern, and it was kind of interesting to play with for a while but it wasn't really engaging. Here was this new computer with some new features, which had a typewriter that worked relatively well, so the impetus for me to write *Spacewar!* was to get some experience with the PDP-1, to do a better demo program and to build a spaceship trainer.

Wait a second, what do you mean by a 'spaceship trainer'?

The space race was very much in the news at the time, so having a spaceship you could control seemed like a relevant demonstration program and it might teach people something [about astrophysics]. By making it a game, it might increase their motivation. We were all fond of science fiction. 'Doc' Smith's writing had these space battles that excited the imagination and so we decided to give the spaceships torpedoes. You could blow up the other ship so now you had a two-player game. We'd been calling it '*Spacewar*' for some time and I put the exclamation point at the end when it was working well enough to demonstrate!

You began coding the game in late 1961. Did it become your main job?

Oh, it was very much a 'spare time' project and not official in any sense. Remember, software was considered worthless back then and was still considered worthless right up until the Eighties. I really mean that! You couldn't copyright it, no one sold it and no one saw any value in it. MIT was charging 'real' projects for using the PDP-1 so the agreement was we could use the computer if no one else wanted it. No authorised user was going

1960
APRIL
Sega is founded by Martin Bromley and Richard Stewart and is initially known as Nihon Goraku Bussan.

1961
A Digital Equipment Corporation PDP-1 is installed at MIT. The minicomputer catches the attention of all, including one Steve Russell.

1961
FEBRUARY
William George Daly Jr submits a thesis to MIT of a computer program based on *Qubic* (*3D Tic Tac Toe*) for the TX-0.

1962
Sega publishes an electromechanical game called *Punching Bag*. It promises operators to be 'time-tested' for proven top profits.

1962
This year also sees Elwro engineer, Witold Podgórski create the mainframe puzzle game, *Marienbad* (an adaptation of *Nim*) for the Odra 1003.

» Nolan Bushnell (right of the *Pong* cabinet) says *Computer Space* wouldn't exist with *Spacewar!*.

» Hyperspace was always an option if you were in a tight spot, but it was made deliberately unreliable.

to turn up at 11pm at night so that was usually when I worked on *Spacewar!*.

The graphics for the spaceships are rather stylish. Did you draw them on graph paper first?
That's exactly what I did and I can even tell you the prototypes! The Needle – the long spaceship – is my cartoon of a Redstone rocket, the first the US put into space. They were essentially tubes with tail fins which was good because they were easy to draw! The other ship, which we called Wedge, was based on a *Buck Rogers* design from the Thirties.

Is it true you wanted the missiles you shoot to be unreliable?
Not only did I want it, I put it in! I just added a small random number to the X and Y velocities of the torpedoes so it might make them miss sometimes, especially at long range. It was when *Spacewar!* was more or less working but without gravity, and boy did I get some feedback! Nobody liked weapons that don't fire straight! [Laughs]. By popular demand, I withdrew it.

You mention gravity was added later on…
I'd always wanted to implement gravity but I'd not figured out how to do it. The problem was that the gravity calculation involved a couple of square roots and so is relatively time-consuming. Remember, the program was constructed as a big loop. You went through all the displayable objects, displayed them and the background, and then you did it again. The repetition rate was determined by how long it took to get through that loop and that governed the ▶

NOLAN BUSHNELL
FOUNDER OF ATARI

"*Spacewar!* was massively important in the creation of *Computer Space*. I distinctly remember a November evening in 1966 when I played it for the first time at the computer lab at the University Of Utah. I was reintroduced [to it] at the AI lab at Stanford University, probably in October 1970, after a night of playing *Go*. In some ways that was more important because my skills had grown and the price of components had dropped, making it seem feasible to build a coin-op unit for the first time. I started on the project the next day."

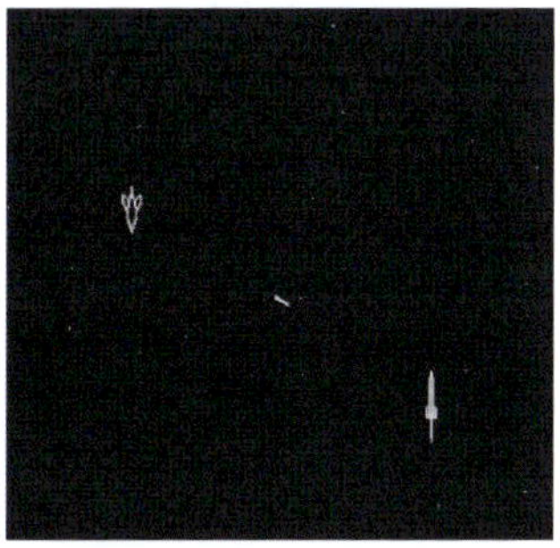

» The sci-fi novels of EE 'Doc' Smith were a big inspiration for *Spacewar!*.

1962 APRIL *Spacewar!* is created by Steve Russell at the Massachusetts Institute Of Technology. It's for the institute's PDP-1.

1964 The PDP-7 is added to Digital Equipment Corporation's range of computers. A total of 120 systems are sold – big numbers back then!

1964 APRIL IBM announces the first of its computer family, the IBM System/360. It will go into production next year.

1964 MAY John G Kemeny and Thomas E Kurtz create the programming language BASIC at Dartmouth College.

1965 Namco releases an electromechanical game called *Periscope* in Japan. It is actually designed by Masaya Nakamura, the founder of Namco.

» Steve takes on Chris Garcia, curator of the Computer History Museum in California. We were too polite to ask who won...

» *Spacewar!* received many tweaks and improvements through the Sixties, including better explosions and on-screen scoring.

» Feeling gravity's pull, *Spacewar!* style. Adding this mechanic gave Steve developmental headaches.

AL ALCORN

CREATOR OF PONG

"*Spacewar!* was the first time a computer was used for interactive fun and Nolan saw the potential. He had also worked at an amusement park in Utah in the summer and he started to connect the dots... 'How can we translate a game on a million-dollar computer to the arcade?' I believe that *Spacewar!* was the spark that started the industry. From Steve Russell to Nolan to me and beyond – we found something truly useful for computers to do!"

ED LOGG

CREATOR OF ASTEROIDS

"I did some work at the Stanford AI Lab from 1971 to the spring of 1972, and I saw *Spacewar!* being played on the local machine. It was four-player and each player held a little box with controls on it. I thought it was an amazing game. It certainly influenced *Asteroids* because I was familiar with the options and gameplay, like the wraparound of the shots and the way your ship flies, as well as the shape of the player's ship itself."

» Steve Russell's game has had a huge impact on the industry.

▶ number of torpedoes you could display at one time – well, that and memory. At the end of 1961, we had a version with no sun and no gravity and could barely keep up the display when they were a bunch of torpedoes.

How did you speed things up?

Dan Edwards figured out how he could make my display code much faster. We think what he did was the first example of what we now call a 'just in time' compiler and his code ran the display at a speed which gave us the time to calculate the square roots to deal with the gravity calculation. That made it a much more interesting game! Pete Samson figured out a way to display a very 'low overheads' starfield and he put that in instead of my random stars. It displayed stars in their actual position in the night sky and at their approximate brightness, and that made it much easier to imagine you were a real space pilot, which was great for those of us who read science fiction.

Spacewar! keeps track of your score. Was that feature added to stop people playing for too long?

[Laughs]. When we were polishing the 'gravity' version of the game in spring 1962, I had put in some scoring because we realised the problem was that people would play and play, and not give other people a chance to have a go. That version showed the score in the lights [on the PDP-1 front panel itself rather than on-screen] which was fine for us because we could do binary-to-decimal conversion but it's not very user-orientated! On-screen scoring was added later, in 1963 I think.

You even added a 'hyperspace' option.

We saw that if someone had a few games' experience and the other didn't, he would win quickly and it was pretty boring. We figured if we added hyperspace, which is a standard feature in sci-fi, that would allow the inexperienced player to escape when they were surrounded by torpedoes and so have chance to learn a little more. We put that in, and it worked – sort of. We saw a lot of inexperienced players constantly hitting hyperspace and not learning anything more. So we made hyperspace unreliable. No ship has been known to survive seven trips into hyperspace!

The addition of bespoke controllers must have made things easier for players, too.

It was a no-brainer! Using the switches on the front panel of the console to control your ship was very uncomfortable because your elbow is resting on the console table and gets sore quickly, plus you have to turn your head to look at the display. Also *Spacewar!* players kept wearing out the switches on the PDP-1, which annoyed the maintenance people. They were a bitch to replace. These were all good reasons not to play the game using switches. We discovered you could wire in more switches [to the rear of the PDP-1] and Bob [Saunders] and Alan [Kotok] connected them to a wooden box and that was much better. They lasted almost a year!

1965 MARCH
The PDP-8 minicomputer is released by Digital Equipment Corporation. Its chief engineer is Edson De Castro.

1966
Nintendo releases the Ultra Hand. The device itself is created by Gunpei Yokoi, who will go on to help create several key Nintendo systems.

1966
Ralph Baer, the inventor of videogames, begins work on The Brown Box. It will go on to sow the seeds for the modern videogame console.

1967
Sega publishes *Rifleman*, an electromechanical game with a distinctive western theme where the player must get five ten-point shots.

1967 FEBRUARY
Nutting Associates, an arcade manufacturer, is formed in Mountain View, California by William Gilbert Nutting.

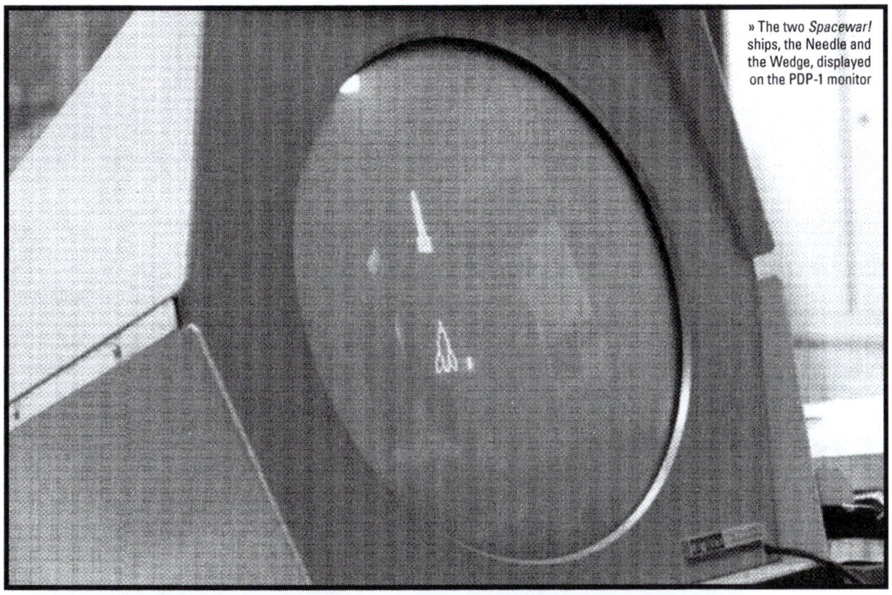

» The two *Spacewar!* ships, the Needle and the Wedge, displayed on the PDP-1 monitor

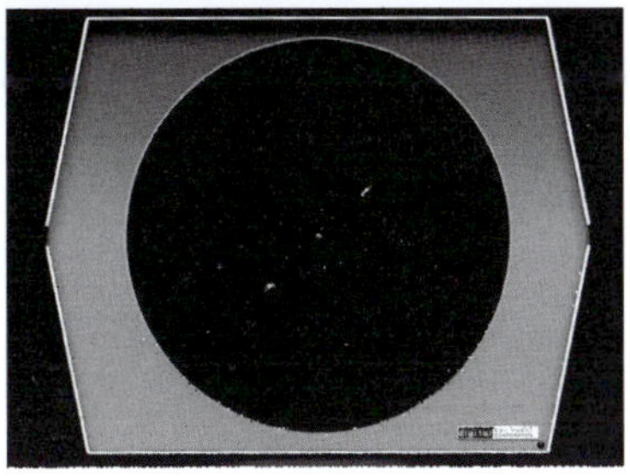

» Unless you live next door to the Computer History Museum in California, the easiest way to play *Spacewar!* is via the handy emulator at masswerk.at/spacewar.

You have mentioned several other people involved with the creation of Spacewar! there...
Lots of people added improvements. It was a collaborative effort though there weren't that many people. We had a reunion [in 2018] of everyone who made a significant contribution and there were eight of us there – sadly Alan has passed away.

Were you at the 'official' presentation of* Spacewar! *at the MIT Science Open House?
No, I was tied up with some Army Reserve training. Martin 'Shag' Graetz [part of the dev team] did a short paper for the Digital Equipment User Group, which was a loose association of PDP owners, and he put the game in their library so everyone who wanted a copy of *Spacewar!* could have it. That was as close as we got to a release. As I said before, software was worthless.

Did you have any sense that you had produced something which would grow into the billion-dollar videogame industry?
No! I had been in the business for four years by then and I'd learned that predicting what was going to come next was almost impossible. I was just interested in my next project. I mean, was anyone gonna hire me to create fancier versions of *Spacewar!*? Nah! Remember it was another decade till things got cheap enough to make machines dedicated to playing games.

When that did happen in the Seventies, there were several early arcade games like* Computer Space *and* Space Wars *which borrowed heavily from* Spacewar!*. Did you resent your work being used like that without permission?
What's to resent? *Spacewar!* was open source. Here it is. Give me credit if you like. And have fun!

Did you ever kick yourself for not patenting any of the innovations introduced by* Spacewar!*?
I told you, I couldn't! How many times do I have to tell you? Software was worthless! Copyrighting software was not even on the horizon…

You must have a sense of pride, though, at what you and your colleagues achieved back then?
Yes I do and I'll give you my boast. The emulated version you can play on the web at Norbert Landsteiner's website [visit masswerk.at/spacewar] or the one we demonstrate on the PDP-1 at the Computer History Museum in California uses the original code from 1962 and as far as I can tell, it hasn't crashed once in over 50 years! ✱

SPACE PIRATES

FOUR EARLY ARCADE GAMES THAT OWE A DEBT TO SPACEWAR!

COMPUTER SPACE (1971)

Nolan Bushnell has always acknowledged *Spacewar!* was the inspiration for the first commercial arcade game. Bill Pitts and Hugh Tuck's *Galaxy Game*, released the same year, was an even closer copy.

SPACE WARS (1977)

Author Larry Rosenthal was an MIT graduate and a big *Spacewar!* fan. This Cinematronics release uses a vector display and allows ships to take damage without being destroyed.

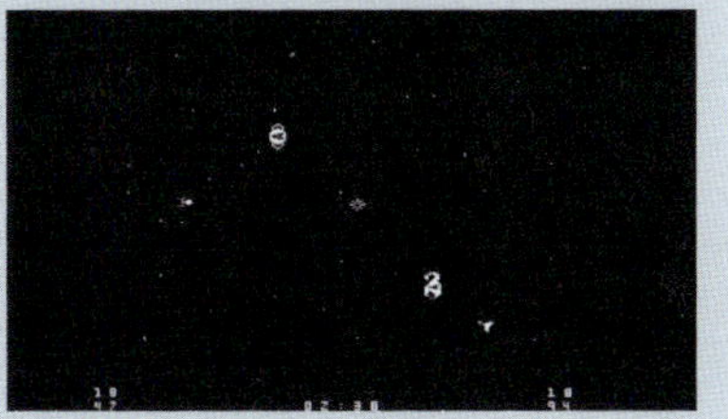

ORBIT (1978)

Owen Rubin's version allows a huge number of options to be selected in-game, from adding black holes to offering space stations for refuelling, via the 22 buttons on the cabinet – a record, we believe.

ASTEROIDS (1979)

Ed Logg took some of the key features of *Spacewar!*, such as ship rotation and hyperspace, and added in a load of space rocks to create Atari's biggest-selling coin-op title.

Images supplied from *From Bedrooms To Billions: The Evolution Of Video Games* TV series, with thanks to Anthony and Nicola Caulfield and Rebellion.

1968 Ralph Baer creates a Golf Game accessory for The Brown Box. It's a golf ball mounted on a joystick, it won't be released commercially, sadly.

1968 Strategy game, *Hamurabi* is developed by Doug Dyment and was created specifically for Richard Merrill's FOCAL coding language.

1969 Ken Thompson creates *Space Travel*, initially for the Multics operating system. The game simulates travel across our solar system.

1969 *Lunar* (or the *Lunar Landing Game*), a text-based game written by Jim Storer, is created, continuing this decade's love of space.

1969 Sega releases an electromechanical game, *Duck Hunt*, which features moving and flying ducks against a realistic backdrop.

THE 1970s

OUT OF THE LABS AND INTO THE WORLD

This is it – the beginning, the decade where humanity gained the ability to go out into the world, drop a coin in a machine and play a videogame. And that's largely what they did, as the arcades hosted many of the decade's most famous games and accounted for most of the industry's revenue. However, that wasn't the whole story. Home consoles entered the market and rapidly grew in sophistication, eventually becoming capable of hosting any game you might choose to throw at them. Computer games were important, but the hardware remained expensive until late in the decade, limiting their impact.

Games of the decade

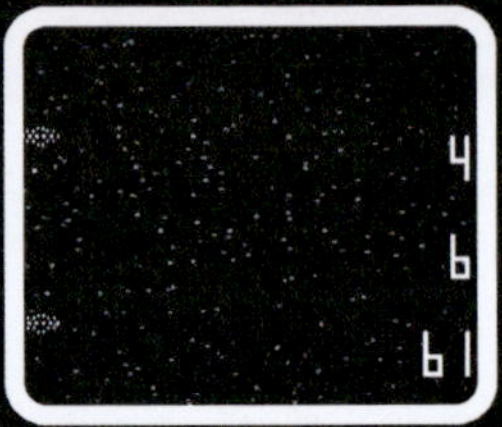

1971 COMPUTER SPACE

This is the big one – the first commercially available videogame. This adaptation of *Spacewar!* wasn't the hit that was needed to inspire any imitators and give the medium a real start, nor did it convince Nutting Associates to carry on with videogames, but in terms of historical importance, it's absolutely massive.

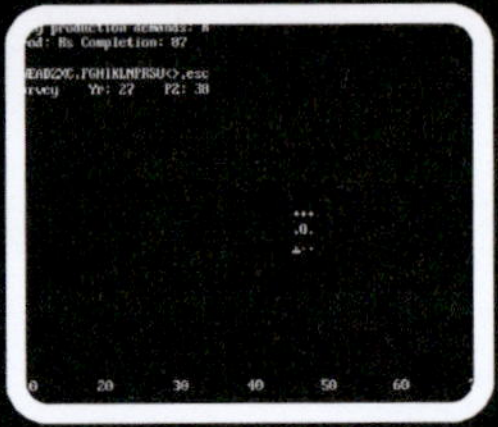

1972 EMPIRE

This mainframe game, written by Peter Langston, is a multiplayer 4X wargame that is an early precursor to today's turn-based strategy games. The original version, which was named after a board game, was lost when the HP2000 computer it ran on was retired, but it was popular enough to spawn a variety of new versions from other authors.

1973 SPACE RACE

Sometimes, you just need to take a concept and run with it, literally. Two players control competing rockets in an attempt to travel the length of the screen as many times as possible within the time limit, while avoiding asteroids. Atari's second game wasn't too popular with audiences, but it did at least move the industry past countless *Pong* clones.

1974 TANK

Steve Bristow's combat game was a big step up in complexity over other efforts at the time, as players navigated a maze filled with deadly mines and a foe that's keen on killing you. Notably, this was manufacturer Kee Games' only title that wasn't a clone of an existing Atari product – the company was a surreptitious Atari subsidiary.

1975 GUN FIGHT

Taito's Wild West-themed arcade game by Tomohiro Nishikado is notable for a couple of reasons. Firstly, it introduced the use of modern CPUs to arcade games, moving the medium away from the discrete logic boards that had been used. Secondly, it's a thematic advance as this is the first videogame to depict humans in combat with one another.

1971
The original text-only version of *The Oregon Trail* is created in a high school by Don Rawtisch, Bill Heinemann and Paul Dillenberger.

1971
Don Daglow creates the first game that's based on baseball using a PDP-10 computer. The game will be updated over the next few years.

1971 NOVEMBER
Bill Pitts and Hugh Tuck create the space dogfighter *Galaxy Game*. The initial prototype costs the dev duo $20,000.

1971 NOVEMBER
Nutting Associates' *Computer Space* is released. The machine is created by Nolan Bushnell and Ted Dabney.

1972
Don Daglow beavers away on the PDP-10 once again and this times creates a fascinating homage to *Star Trek*. He gets lots of fan mail as a result.

The Seventies...

AS TOLD BY DAVID BRABEN

FRONTIER DEVELOPMENTS' FOUNDER AND ELITE CO-CREATOR REMEMBERS THE TECHNOLOGY THAT HOOKED HIM ON CODING

Though we look back to the Seventies as the start of our own technological revolution, David's personal memories are of a childhood relatively free of the devices that have become ubiquitous in the modern world. "Compared to today, there was remarkably little technology about," he recalls. "Not only were there no mobile phones, but hardly any TVs or screens (compared to now) – and those that there were had small screens and were big and boxy and almost entirely black and white."

With early developments being both expensive and often not suitable for the home, it's the latter half of the decade that really set the wheels in motion. "Various home games consoles started to appear in the mid-to-late-Seventies, which played variants of *Pong*, *Breakout* and a few others, using simple rotational controllers," says David, before getting on to the formats with which he's more widely associated. "When home computers first appeared, right at the end of the decade, it was an amazing change." A brief conversational detour takes place here to discuss arcade games. "At around the same time, *Space Invaders* appeared. It had a colour screen – but on closer inspection it was strips of coloured plastic stuck to the front of a black and white screen!"

David quickly returns to the computer scene, though. "Those home machines were amazing in contrast to the home games consoles," he remembers. However, David found himself admiring machines like the TRS-80 and Apple II from afar, as he didn't have access to one. "Magazines appeared with type-in listings, and I used to look at these with interest, executing them on paper – long before I actually had a computer (they were too expensive)."

The fascination David developed during the Seventies persisted into the early Eighties and led him to his first computer – though it wasn't quite what he'd expected. "Before I got a computer of my own I imagined they were a lot faster than in fact they were. One of my first programs was flying through a 3D starfield (I had worked out how to do it before I even had a computer), which I wrote in BASIC on the Acorn Atom. I could see it drawing the stars one by one, then clearing the screen and doing it again – it took over a second so there was no visual continuity or sense of movement. I was terribly disappointed, but started learning machine code straight away. A few months later my starfield ran at 60 frames per second, and I was hooked."

Of course, many of you know what David did next. "The 3D starfield changed into the bones of a simple 3D space fighter game over the next few months before I went to university... but that's another story."

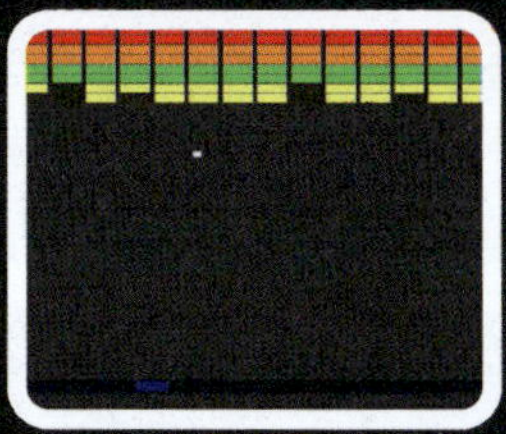

1976 BREAKOUT

This block-busting blockbuster was a successful solo spin on the established *Pong* formula, and came from Apple founders Steve Wozniak and Steve Jobs. *Breakout* was a highly influential arcade game, with *Arkanoid* iterating on the design in the Eighties and even games like *Puchi Carat* adopting its template in the Nineties.

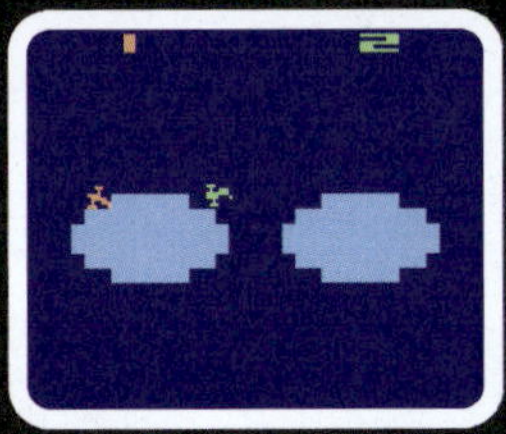

1977 COMBAT

The pack-in game for early Atari 2600 (or Atari VCS, depending on who you ask) consoles is so much more than just a home version of *Tank* – it's an early demonstration of the flexibility that console games could offer over their arcade rivals. With a roster of extra modes featuring jet fighters and biplanes, *Combat* offered real choice and variety.

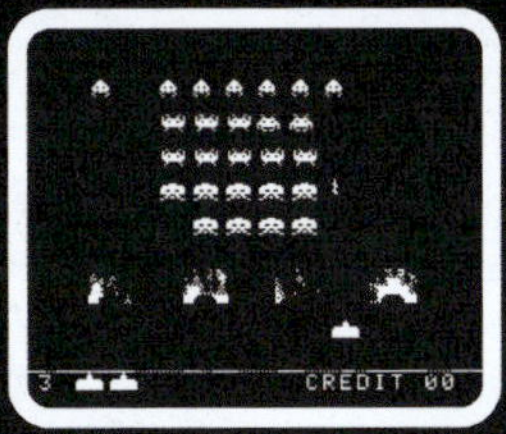

1978 SPACE INVADERS

Taito's arcade hit was such an enormous deal that even now, those distinctive space invaders are used as an icon for videogames as a whole. In 1981, MP George Foulkes told UK parliament that young people "play truant, miss meals and give up other normal activity to play *Space Invaders*" – yes, it was that good.

1979 GALAXIAN

Namco's first major arcade hit took the *Space Invaders* shooter formula and enhanced it, allowing the enemies your spaceship faced to break rank and attack alone, bringing the-then burgeoning shoot-'em-up genre forward. The game also popularised RGB colour graphics, which became the standard in arcade games going forward.

1979 ASTEROIDS

Yes, we've included two 1979 entries on this list – blame the sheer lack of releases in 1970. And if we had to choose a year with a second game, 1979's *Asteroids* justifies this one. Between the mesmerising vector graphics that still enthrall us today, the simple, oppressive background music and the compelling game design, it's really something special.

1972 JUNE
Atari Inc is founded and videogames as an industry takes its first tentative steps. Turn to page 24 for more Atari.

1972 SEPTEMBER
Magnavox releases the first home console, the Odyssey. It's based on Ralph Baer's Brown Box prototype.

1973
Kee Games is formed by Atari as a subsidiary. It's headed by its namesake, Joe Keenan who is a long-time friend of Nolan Bushnell.

1973
The business simulation game *Lemonade Stand* is created. It's based on the popular American tradition of kids selling lemonade in the suburbs.

1973
Nintendo releases its lightgun shooter *Laser Clay Shooting System*, which is masterminded by Hiroshi Yamauchi and Gunpei Yokoi.

THE FUTURE STARTS HERE

1

The Seventies is the decade that saw computer technology finally becoming viable for home use, due to the small size and low cost of machines – at least relative to the past. Alongside general-purpose computers, dedicated videogames consoles were introduced. At first they played only preloaded games, but by the end of the decade had shifted to using ROM cartridges for game distribution, allowing for a potentially infinite number of games to be released. By the end of the decade, the first true console war was underway, with Mattel Electronics fighting an underdog battle against the industry's first giant, Atari.

2

3

1. MAGNAVOX ODYSSEY

Magnavox, 1972

The Magnavox Odyssey was the first ever home videogame console – the final commercial result of Ralph Baer's 'Brown Box' prototype, developed at defence contractor Sanders Associates. The system was extraordinarily simple, capable of displaying just a few dots on the screen, with users manipulating them using dials and a single button. As a result, the console had to be packaged with plastic TV overlays and board game pieces, to expand the possibilities of the games. The system could only support the PCB cartridges that were supplied with it, which modified the internal logic of the system, and it didn't feature a CPU of the kind we use today.

The system was a modest commercial success, selling 350,000 units, but it's the wider impact of the system that earns it recognition today. Lawsuits over the Odyssey patents made Magnavox over $100 million, and the company soon began to manufacture dedicated consoles. However, these were designed in-house at Magnavox and Philips, which had acquired the company in 1974. The creators of the Magnavox Odyssey would go on to different projects, with the most notable being Ralph Baer's popular electronic toy Simon, which tests your memory with a sequence of button inputs and is still released in various forms today.

2. APPLE II

Apple, 1977

One of the first home computers to offer colour graphics was a big hit with American computer buyers, and marked the beginning of a long-lived dynasty for the fledgling Apple Computers. The machine was enormously expensive, retailing for over $1,000 at launch, but it was adopted by businesses and, particularly, schools, ensuring that many youngsters would become familiar with the machine over time. The success of the computer caused Apple's success to soar, ballooning from $774,000 per year in September 1977 to $118 million per year three years later. A revised Apple II Plus was released in 1979.

3.PHILIPS VIDEOPAC G7000

Philips, 1978

The major follow-up to the Magnavox Odyssey, known as the Odyssey 2 elsewhere in the world, was a curious device. Outwardly it looked more like a computer than a console, thanks to its bulky size and membrane keyboard, which could be used for edutainment games. However, the system was largely intended for entertainment purposes and delivered on that with games like *KC Munchkin*, a maze game similar to *Pac-Man*, and the *Master Strategy Series* hybrid video/board games including *Quest For The Rings*. The console couldn't keep pace with Atari's sales and even lagged behind the Intellivision, and its successor – the Videopac+ G7400 – withered due to the 1983 market crash.

1973
Taito creates *Soccer* and *Davis Cup*. They're designed by Tomohiro Nishikado and focus on, you guessed it, football and tennis.

1973
Over at the NASA Ames Research centre, the first-person *Maze War* is created by Steve Colley, who will go on to establish nCUBE in 1983.

1973
Text adventure *Hunt The Wumpus* is created by Gregory Yob and has gamers tracking down the titular creature and dodging 'super bats'.

1973 MAY
Hudson Soft Ltd is established in Japan with the aim to sell telecommunication devices and art.

1973 JULY
Atari releases its second game after *Pong*, *Space Race*, into arcades. Sadly, it is not commercially successful.

4. ATARI 2600
Atari Inc, 1977

The impact that Atari's home console had on videogames cannot be overstated. The system was the first smash hit console, fuelled by Atari's arcade conversions and classic original games, as well as licensed games like *Space Invaders*. The single-button joysticks became iconic and set a standard for game controllers that followed, and ROM cartridges were popularised as a game distribution media for decades to come. The success of the system propelled Atari to enormous profits, and at one point it was one of the fastest-growing companies in America, comfortably fending off all challengers in the marketplace.

Of course, the Atari 2600's legacy isn't entirely rosy. Atari's dismissive attitude towards its developers ultimately caused the rift that gave birth to Activision, gaming's first third-party publisher. Atari's own mismanagement of projects and stock, as well as the glut of products from external developers, contributed to a North American market crash that caused global ripples, and caused businesses to lose faith in videogames as a business. But when the industry rebounded, the cheap and abundant games, combined with a new hardware revision, made Atari's ageing console a wallet-friendly alternative platform, a status that kept the system on shelves right through to the early Nineties.

5. ATARI 8-BIT
Atari Inc, 1979

Having firmly established itself at the top of the videogames industry over the course of the Seventies, Atari looked to move into the general purpose computer market at the end of the decade. The machine's graphical capabilities were considerably ahead of the competition, making it a great machine for gaming, and its key early game, *Star Raiders*, offered genuinely amazing space exploration and combat. However, many of its users came to own it in the Eighties, after a brutal price war with the similarly capable Commodore 64 dragged the cost of the revised XL series hardware down to near-wholesale levels.

6. INTELLIVISION
Mattel Electronics, 1979

Toy giant Mattel had already experienced success in the Seventies, with handheld electronic games such as *Mattel Auto Race* and *Mattel Football*, so its attempt to join the rapidly developing console scene made a lot of sense. The Intellivision became a rival to the Atari 2600, with early games boasting superior graphics, and a great range of sports games as well as licensed properties such as *Dungeons & Dragons*. However, it was more expensive than Atari's machine and couldn't match the branding power of its arcade hits, so it ultimately fell behind. The machine still has a cult following today, though.

4

5

6

OTHER SYSTEMS FROM THE SEVENTIES

Fairchild Channel F • Fairchild, 1976

This was the first console to use a CPU and ROM cartridges, essentially making it the first console in the modern style. It was soon toppled by the Atari 2600.

Interton VC 4000 • Interton, 1978

This system's hardware and software showed up in a variety of different guises throughout Europe, and was popular but naturally had little legacy. Its use of analogue joysticks as standard was pioneering.

Microvision • MBC, 1979

This innovative handheld achieved reasonable success for Milton Bradley, but was severely limited by a 16x16 display. The system did inspire the creation of Nintendo's Game & Watch series, though.

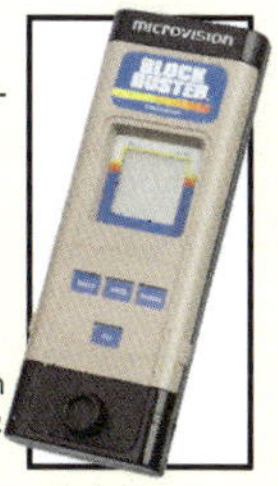

1973 OCTOBER
Allan Alcorn creates *Gotcha*, the industry's first maze game for Atari. It receives a lukewarm reception.

1974
Namco acquires Atari's Japanese coin-op division, enabling the company to bring the US hits over to Japanese arcades.

1974 MAY
Via its subsidiary Cyan Engineering, Atari revs up with arcade racing game *Gran Trak 10*. The coin-op is well received.

1974 NOVEMBER
Tank is developed by Atari subsidiary Kee Games. The game is a success and gives Atari a vital cash injection.

1974 DECEMBER
With the arcade scene gathering more and more traction, an arcade-focused magazine, *Play Meter*, is launched.

Nolan Bushnell

Allan Alcorn

Atari birthed the modern videogame industry. It cracked the code of coin-op success, pioneered games marketing and successfully invaded the living room. But before its mainstream hits turned Atari into a household name, the company began as a scrappy group of Silicon Valley hippies making it up as they went along

Atari of the Seventies was a different animal to the corporate juggernaut that captured worldwide attention and became the fastest growing company in US history in 1980. This coin-op-focused Atari was chaotic and flew (and grew) by the seat of its pants. It broke new ground, buttressed by engineering smarts and Nolan Bushnell's gutsy management, while attracting the notice of Wall Street and the general public.

Nolan Bushnell was an engineer at the Silicon Valley stalwart Ampex when he recruited his friend and coworker Ted Dabney to form a company to design video display-powered games. Nolan envisioned a consumer-focused version of the game *Spacewar!* he had played as a student at the University Of Utah. The duo created their first game, *Computer Space*, for Nutting Associates, a maker of quiz and electromechanical games. It was a modest success, selling 1,500 units and netting nearly $3 million in sales, which paved the way for future projects. But more importantly, it proved that there was a market for video-driven, hardware-based consumer games.

With the earnings from *Computer Space*, the two hired their first employee: engineer and fellow Ampex alum, Allan Alcorn. While he wasn't enamoured with *Computer Space*, Allan was intrigued by its engineering and the potential challenge of a startup. "It was really, really insane to quit a good job and start a company," Allan says. He points out that startup culture and entrepreneurship weren't as common or as glamorised as they are now. "Today, everybody is doing it," he says. But Atari was self-funded. "We had no backing," Allan

1975
Cinematronics is founded in El Cajon, California. The company will become known for its string of vector-display arcade games.

1975
Magnavox follows up on its pioneering Odyssey games console by launching revised editions, the Odyssey 100 and Odyssey 200.

1975
Don Daglow creates the RPG *Dungeon* for the PDP-10 mainframe computer, based on his enjoyment of *Dungeons & Dragons*.

1975
Another dungeon-crawling role-playing game pops up this year with *Mora*, which is created for PLATO computer systems.

1975
Influential microcomputer magazine *Byte* is launched by UBM Technology Group. The publication will soldier on all the way to July 1998.

ATARI
King Of The Seventies

Words by Tim Lapetino

explains. "It wasn't like somebody was giving us money. We had nothing!"

Allan left the security of Ampex and took a pay cut, though he gained 10% of the company stock as part of his hiring package. He considered that benefit worthless at the time, but it would prove valuable when Atari was sold to Warner Communications in 1976. "I figured it would be more fun than Ampex. I would see a much broader view of business. When you start a company, you're doing everything. I figured it would fail, as most startups do, and I'd go back to work at Ampex after a few years," Allan says. He threw his lot in with Nolan and Ted, impressed by both of them. By Allan's account, Ted "was very wise in analog circuit design, and really helped a great deal. He was kind of a mentor to me". Nolan had different strengths. "Nolan never impressed me for his technical expertise," Allan says, "but he was quite the entrepreneur, always driven to beat things. He was the spark plug. He had this grand vision when he pitched me."

Nolan leaned heavily on this early team. "Al was a very good engineer, no question about it," he recalls, "and he was curious and capable. Ted was a multiskilled person. He was as good with table saws as he was with the soldering iron. And he was very, very capable in the video display world. But more than that, Ted was a guy who could just solve problems."

Armed with some success after *Computer Space*, the three set out to create another original videogame and a pinball machine, both of which were part of a contract they had with industry titan Bally. But before those efforts started in earnest, Nolan wanted Allan to hone his skills on a practice project, the game that became *Pong*. "*Pong* wasn't really a test as much as it was an exercise," Allan says. Nolan believed a more successful game would need to be more elaborate than *Computer Space*, potentially a driving game. *Pong* was intended as a warm-up.

Atari's contract with Bally was based on the strength of its new technology – coin-operated amusement games in the vein of *Computer Space*. But once the *Pong* prototype proved to be wildly successful, the team pivoted. Or, more accurately, Nolan did. He presented *Pong* to Bally as required by contract, but then proceeded to talk the company out of selecting it ▶

1975 SEPTEMBER
Epoch releases TV Tennis Electrotennis, a dedicated home videogame machine. It's the first of its kind to arrive in Japan.

1976 APRIL
Exidy creates *Death Race* for arcades, which courts controversy thanks to its then-violent depiction of killing other humans.

1976 APRIL
Steve Jobs, Steve Wozniak and Ronald Wayne start Apple Computers in the garage of Jobs' Los Altos home.

1976 APRIL
Apple Computers launches its first product, the Apple I home computer, which is designed entirely by Steve Wozniak.

1976 MAY
Breakout is released in arcades by Atari. It's also designed by Steve Wozniak,who's having a pretty busy year.

» One of the things that really stands out with the Atari of old is its now-iconic marketing. It created plenty of desirable adverts for many of its products, particularly its first home console (look how happy these people on the left are). This advertising became even more aggressive as newer competitors entered the market as the advert far left shows.

so that his own team could design, manufacture and sell it. He believed the game would be a major hit, and pushed Ted and Allan to move from pure engineering and game design to becoming a full-fledged manufacturer. Over his partners' objections, Nolan pressed forward, and *Pong*'s success in 1972 changed the company forever.

The game's incredible reception "felt like getting hit in the ass by lightning!" Allan says. "What does a company that has no equity and no revenue – what does it need?! It needs something to sell, and all of a sudden – boom! We had something to sell! We stumbled our way into making a couple thousand of these *Pong* machines. They were so popular we could sell them cash up front. We were retaining profits quickly. There was no investment. The bank wouldn't even give us a line of credit!"

> "It was a really interesting thing. People wanted to come work for Atari because of the culture"
> **Nolan Bushnell**

Atari avoided the mistakes of larger competitors like Bally, which failed to see the coming revolution of videogames in the home. Allan believes that Bally couldn't escape its own identity as a coin-op company, and missed the bigger picture. But Nolan was adamant about avoiding the same narrow thinking. "'We are innovative leisure! We are not just defined by coin-op!'" Allan recalls Nolan stating. "We were going to disrupt every market we could in entertainment," he adds.

But it wasn't just expansive thinking that gave Atari an edge. In its incredible growth, the company had retained its unusual creative, free-thinking environment. "Our corporate culture gave us the ability to hire anyone we wanted to," Nolan says. "It was a really interesting thing. People wanted to come work for Atari because of the culture. Steve Jobs worked for me. He took it to Apple, and when the companies looked around and saw the success of Apple [and] saw the success of Atari. So, it started to be adopted by other companies that were more stable. I think it slowly permeated."

It wasn't just the casual atmosphere of beer Fridays, hot tub meetings and flexible hours. The difference was more foundational to Atari's operation. "We basically did not care about process," Nolan explains. "We didn't care if our employees came to work in their bathing suits or naked, or showed up at midnight and worked until two. As long as they got their jobs done. If you totally focus on outcome and not process, it turns out that you create a very, very egalitarian structure."

That Atari ethos came partially from Nolan's experience managing the Lagoon Amusement park in Salt Lake City, Utah, and the influence of the San Francisco hippie movement. His carefree-yet-calculated leadership was an essential ingredient, according to Allan. "You need a madman driving you with this thing," he says. "A Larry Ellison. A Steve Jobs. And I'm the Wozniak to Nolan's Steve Jobs. So, I was dragged along, screaming and kicking, into the future.

"As it grew, we made mistakes," Allan recalls. "We got ripped off. But I guess the attitude was lighthearted, because we were all young – an open environment of treating people well, because we didn't know any different. When you hire bright people and trust them to do their job, you get more out of them. It was just a crazy, crazy growth period, which had its own series of obstacles in growing that fast."

Not content with breaking the rules of innovation, Atari bucked industry practices as well. It tried to increase game sales and gain leverage by double-dipping with distributors. Each city typically had two large, competing coin-op distributors, each with their own exclusive contracts. But the company wanted to sell to both sides. To do so, Atari created a fictitious competitor, Kee Games, run by Nolan's friend and neighbour Joe Keenan. They would then slightly alter hit games, rename and then sell them to the distributors Atari didn't work with – claiming the new games were Kee knockoffs! Atari planted rumours, complained about the 'competition', and made money on both ends. After the charade ended in 1978, Kee Games dissolved and Joe Keenan returned to officially become president of Atari.

In 1974 Atari continued to wrestle with cashflow and an ill-fated expansion into international markets. It needed a large infusion of cash to push into the home market and launch the

1976 OCTOBER
Sega releases its monochromatic boxing game, *Heavyweight Champ* in arcades. A remake will launch a year later.

1976 OCTOBER
Warner Communications buys Atari for $28 million. You can read a little more about that in this very feature.

1976 NOVEMBER
Fairchild Semiconductor launches the Video Entertainment System (also known as the Fairchild Channel F).

1977
Vector graphics arcade game *Space Wars* is released by Cinematronics. It's designed by Larry Rosenthal, who was inspired by *Spacewar!*.

1977 JANUARY
The unique-looking Commodore PET home computer launches into the market and becomes a landmark success.

Atari VCS. An IPO was a possibility, but in the end, the team looked at acquisition. "Atari had been a real struggle because we never had enough money," Nolan says. "We never had enough capital to sustain our growth."

Atari discussed selling to Disney, Quaker Oats and others, but Warner Communications made the most sense. "Warner seemed like a decent fit," Allan says, "because they were in the music and movie business, where they understood that you have a flop and you have a hit. That's very important, because at lots and lots of companies, like Proctor and Gamble, you don't have a flop. If you have a flop, your career is over! So, we had a partner that understood that nobody ever set out to make a bad movie, but they are made. Same thing with videogames."

The deal was consummated and Warner purchased Atari for $28 million. It seemed like an ideal scenario and signalled that the videogame industry was growing up, with established corporations like Warner taking a serious interest in the developing medium. It worked out very well for Nolan and Allan, too. "All of a sudden we were offered more money than I ever thought I was going to make," Nolan recalls. "I always thought of myself as a farm boy from Utah. All of a sudden, actually becoming a multimillionaire was kind of attractive to me."

But the post-sale reality never lived up to expectations. "The big promise was that they were used to dealing with creatives," Nolan says, "and that they left them alone. Those were the promises and that didn't match the reality."

"It was a difficult fit because the cultures were completely different," Allan recalls. "Maybe the people back east thought we were frauds. They were really nervous. This was a very, very risky, bold thing to purchase this startup, this crazy Silicon Valley company. The massive culture clash had to do not so much with Warner itself, but with the people who were directly tasked with managing the Atari investment." Nolan elaborates: "They were New York financial analysts. They had this New York bias to the way they thought business worked. They thought you came to work every day in a coat and tie, and you showed up at eight o'clock, left at five, and had an hour lunch with a martini." ▶

Designing out of the box at Atari: Regan Cheng

In the Seventies, Atari pioneered coin-op videogames. Its games could be found in bowling alleys, bars and arcades, enticing gamers to insert a coin into their slots. If you encountered one of those games, there was a good chance that it reflected the design handiwork of Regan Cheng.

Regan was an industrial designer at Atari who made a significant impact on the look and feel of Atari – first in the company's wildly successful arcade games, and later within its consumer console division. In 11 years Regan worked alongside artists, marketers and programmers to ensure that Atari products possessed the company's signature look and feel.

Along with fellow industrial designer Pete Takaichi, Regan started work for Atari while still an undergrad at San Jose State University. The two roommates were hired on back-to-back days in 1972. "It really was kind of a dream job," Regan says. "At that time, industrial design was very much about styling, and it was a luxury for a company to have industrial designers on board." He joined a team still wrestling with how to make coin-op games – a wooden cabinet, TV and control panel – stand out in arcades and bodegas around the country. "About a year into it, I really felt we were doing something different. Videogames were still new. I felt like we were the kings of this type of technology."

Hired by Atari industrial engineer George Faraco, the pair worked on early games like *Space Race*, *Gotcha* and others, bringing unlikely inspiration to their work. "We studied European architecture and interior design," Regan explains. The designers drew influence from that era's high-end product design and interiors, "Things like appliances, furniture, chairs, lamps."

While a game was still in-progress, a team would convene for a 'blue sky' brainstorming session, with art director George Opperman, graphics team members, the industrial designers and marketing representatives working together to find a way to tell the game's story in a small space and quick glance. "The real estate in an arcade is very expensive," Regan explains. "You basically just have your two-foot-by-two-foot footprint."

After a game's release, Atari designers counted on feedback from arcade operators and technicians to understand how people played the games, incorporating those insights into future designs – in replay value, controller strength or service access. "Our in-house guys held the key to making it look like an Atari product," Regan says. The team would deploy its arsenal to differentiate a game, including graphics, lights, controllers or anything else they could manage.

While Atari didn't invent the amusement game cabinet, it surely reimagined it, bringing early ergonomics research into the industry. "I look back now," Regan said, "and I'm really proud of it. We did the best we could, making new designs based on all the restrictions of the industry – materials, cost, timeframes and everything else."

» The Atari VCS was a huge success, with its packaging promising the owner plenty of great games to enjoy.

1977 JUNE Apple Computers steps up its game and releases its follow-up to its debut Apple I computer, the Apple II.

1977 JUNE In Japan, Nintendo launches its Color TV-Game series, a line of home videogame machines.

1977 AUGUST Tandy launches the TRS-80 Model I desktop microcomputer. It will go on to outsell the Apple II five-to-one.

1977 SEPTEMBER Atari releases its console, the VCS (and will later be renamed 2600). Again, you can read more about that right here!

1978 Ed Logg creates *Super Breakout* after hearing that Nolan Bushnell wanted Steve Wozniak's original game updated.

The movers and shakers of Atari

The people that turned the company into a juggernaut

NOLAN BUSHNELL
COFOUNDER

Nolan was the cofounder of Atari and its driving force in its earliest days. His grand visions, freewheeling culture and moxie helped Atari create a series of enduring games, while also birthing a new industry. Following his departure from Atari, Nolan went on to found the Chuck E Cheese chain of restaurants.

TED DABNEY
COFOUNDER

A founding engineer, Ted's expertise made Atari work with his deep knowledge of video display. With Nolan Bushnell, he designed *Computer Space*, proving they could create an inexpensive TV-based game. But Ted's management inexperience and distaste for Nolan's self-promotion led to his departure in 1973.

GEORGE OPPERMAN
ART DIRECTOR

George designed the iconic and distinctive Atari logo and joined the company in 1976. He professionalised the design during the firm's early years, bringing modern graphic sensibilities to the company while borrowing from editorial design and illustration to tell the visual stories of videogames in their infancy.

ROGER HECTOR
HEAD OF R&D

Roger led research and development at Atari, managing its advanced products from 1976 to 1981. As head of that department, he helped push the boundaries of what Atari was doing – in ways that harmonised with its current videogames, and also for the electronic entertainment of the future.

MANNY GERARD
CEO

Hired to run Atari after its acquisition by Warner Communications, Manny's New York management style was an ill fit for the laid-back, creative culture he inherited in Atari. His regular clashes with Nolan and disagreements on the fate of the Atari 2600 eventually led to him firing Atari's original founder.

Building an industry

How Atari shaped the games business

BRINGING VIDEOGAMES INTO THE LIVING ROOM

While Atari wasn't the first to release a home videogame console, it was the most successful. For better or worse, Atari provided a blueprint for competitors and successors, though others (like Nintendo) would learn important lessons from its first-mover mistakes.

INADVERTENTLY CREATING THE THIRD-PARTY MODEL

When four Atari engineers grew frustrated with their lack of recognition and commensurate pay for designing bestselling videogames, they quit and founded Activision. After a lawsuit with Atari, Activision became the first competitor to create games for a manufacturer's system, ushering in a model that provided a greater diversity of games for future consoles.

PIONEERING THE ARCADE TRANSLATION

Today it seems obvious that converting popular arcade games into home releases would be a successful strategy, but it wasn't a foregone conclusion in gaming's early days. The technological challenges of translating arcade hits on the Atari 2600 weren't small, but once Atari got a taste of incredible success with the 2600 version of *Space Invaders*, the practice never ceased.

PROFESSIONAL MARKETING, ART AND DESIGN

Atari employed high-calibre graphic designers and artists to communicate the power and stories behind its game releases. It took great pains to produce great artwork, tell compelling stories and use visual media to bolster the company's distinctiveness and brand story.

1978 Atari subsidiary Kee Games launches *Ultra Tank*. This version features the ability to select multiple maps, along with invisible tanks.

1978 Interton launches its Video Computer 4000. A whopping 40 games will be released over its lifespan (look, it was a lot back then!).

1978 Raph Baer, the father of videogames, follows up on his Magnavox Odyssey console with the 'Simon' electronic memory game.

1978 Konami decides it wants a slice of that sweet, sweet videogame money pie and debuts its first arcade game, *Block Game*.

1978 JUNE Taito launches *Space Invaders* to critical acclaim. It soon becomes visual shorthand for the term 'videogame'.

ALLAN ALCORN
ENGINEER

Allan was hired as Atari employee number one in 1972, after working with both Nolan and Ted at Ampex. He designed the arcade game *Pong* as an engineering test, which was intended as a prelude to a real game, but it was so popular that the team launched it to incredible success.

FRED THOMPSON
INDUSTRIAL DESIGNER

Fred was the industrial designer behind Atari's 2600 console. His design helped it blend into the living room environment of the Seventies, and set standards which still echo in console design today. His background in audio helped Atari make a smooth transition from arcade business trading to consumer products.

CLIFF SPOHN
ILLUSTRATOR

As the illustrator behind the artwork of nearly 20 Atari 2600 games, Cliff had a huge impact on how the new console was first perceived in the marketplace. His iconic illustration style and use of montage provided energy, emotion and separated Atari from other videogame companies as the gold standard in the industry.

» Atari creative director George Opperman (left) talks through arcade design concepts with illustrator Bob Flemate, who was also instrumental in helping define Atari's early visual style.

COMMITMENT TO R&D

Atari spent significant resources considering the future of games and 'innovative leisure'. Whether in arcade games, consoles or moonshot ideas, Atari's engineers knew that obsoleting the company's own products was the only way to remain competitive. It dabbled in holograms, voice-activated controllers, and other ideas that never came to life, all true to that innovative spirit the company was known for.

The sale signalled the beginning of the end for Atari's Seventies startup era, now a juggernaut with an established corporation and marketing muscle behind it. This became particularly important for the final development and release of the Atari VCS (Video Computer System, later renamed the 2600), Atari's effort to bring cartridge-based videogaming into the living room.

While the VCS sold respectably in its 1977 launch, it didn't set the world on fire. The initial games were solid, but Atari programmers had yet to unlock the flexibility of the system's architecture that led to its long shelf life and massive games library. While Atari wasn't the first to market with a cartridge-based home console (that was the lackluster Fairchild Channel F system), it did manage to optimise and popularise the idea, cementing videogames' place in the home.

"We knew it was going to be a good product," Allan says, "because the games were good and because of the architecture that Steve Mayer and Ron Milner created. It was a fraction of the cost to build it compared to the other competing systems. It was brilliant! Inadvertently, it was more flexible than the other systems."

After a modest first year, VCS sales began to taper off. Allan explains that he and the rest of the original Atari team thought it was time to move on and create a replacement console. "In Silicon Valley," he says, "the way things work is that if you don't obsolete your successful product, somebody else will. So you've got to create a product that will knock off your own product, and that's what we wanted to do. But Warner – more conservative, traditional – said, 'No, we're going to pour a lot of money into marketing and advertising for the product.' They did it and it was the right move. God, it was the right move! But that created a lot of friction between Warner and Nolan and those guys."

> *"The way things work is that if you don't obsolete your successful product, somebody else will"*
> **Allan Alcorn**

Warner's decision to double down on the VCS paid off in spades when Atari's home version of *Space Invaders*, became the platform's first killer app in 1980. It supercharged VCS sales and made Atari the darling of the industry and the console to beat. Warner won that argument with entrenched Atari management, but the philosophical disagreement beneath it persisted.

Nolan, occupied with his new wealth and R&D, remained at loggerheads with Warner's leadership. Atari's handlers wanted a good return on their investment, and it seems that they were more comfortable marketing and extending product lines than innovating. This mentality rankled many Atari employees, and would eventually erode the creativity that made Atari successful in the first place. It subsequently led to Nolan's ousting in 1978.

"After 1978, under Warner management, not one new product got released by Atari," Allan says. All of the products they released were already in development at the time of the company's purchase. "There were new cartridges and games, but Warner did not have the guts to release anything new. You have to obsolete your own product. They learned that lesson the very hard way." Warner-led Atari would create some standout games and usher in a new era in games, but the company was irrevocably changed.

Despite the videogame market crash of 1983 and subsequent tumult, Atari left a lasting imprint. "We were the catalyst to introduce a whole new form of technology," Allan says. "What we did in the early days was to figure out how to make an appliance in the home – called a television set – become an interactive entertainment device. That was a big change! We figured out how to put games out around the world, creating a whole new form of entertainment that – for good or bad – has absolutely changed the world, and I guess we're not going to go back."

Atari ushered in a new era in electronic ubiquity. "Videogames have turned out to be a kind of the training wheels of computer literacy," Nolan says. "I know no programmer who didn't cut their teeth on videogames early on, and most of them were still big gamers. I think videogames themselves eased the transition into a computer-literate society." *

1978 OCTOBER
Pinball and block-breaking game *Gee Bee*, Namco's first arcade game to be designed in-house, is released.

1978 DECEMBER
Magnavox launches its Odyssey 2 console. Over on European shores it's known as the Philips Videopac G7000.

1979
Sega releases *Monaco GP* in arcades in three different styles: upright, 'cocktail' table and sit-down deluxe. It becomes a roaring success.

1979
British software publisher Quicksilva is formed by Nick Lambert. The name was inspired by the band Quicksilver Messenger Service.

1979
Capcom is founded by Japanese businessman Kenzo Tsujimoto. While founding his new venture, Tsujimoto was still president of Irem.

Pong

EVERY SAGA HAS A BEGINNING

» RETROREVIVAL

» ARCADE » 1972 » ATARI INC

If there's one game that defines the Seventies then it's surely Atari's *Pong*. While you can make plenty of arguments for *Space Invaders*, Atari's breakthrough game feels far more influential and it's arguably one of those transcendent moments when people suddenly realised that videogames had the potential to make a lot of money.

Pong's influences are many and obvious. Trip Hawkins paid tribute to it by saying, "The first casual game and the first social game. Everyone played it. I mean everyone." Philip Oliver remembered that his and Andrew's early programming events "were to rewrite *Pong* on our brother's ZX81", and Ocean's Jim Bagley just remembered it being "bloody good fun".

And *Pong* was bloody good fun, particularly if you were playing against another person. Even today rallies on *Pong* can be tremendously satisfying to take part in, and there's nothing more enjoyable than watching that ball slip past your opponent's bat. *Pong* wasn't just huge in arcades, it was massive in the home, too, and virtually every family I knew owned a *Pong* machine of some kind, official or otherwise (we had an orange Binatone system, in case you're wondering). You can argue that most of *Pong*'s success was down to it being fun to play, easy to find and (perhaps most important of all) extremely simple to pick up. This last thing is important because that entry level is something shared by most of the other Retro Revivals this bookazine.

Without *Pong* it's arguable that the gaming landscape would be a very different place today. Nintendo, Coleco, Namco and Konami are just a few of the companies that entered the videogame market due to the success of *Pong*, while countless budding programmers copied the Olivers' attempts to recreate the game. *Pong* is a phenomenon and it highlights that great game mechanics will always win out over flashy graphics. *

1979 JUNE
Text adventure specialist Infocom is founded in Cambridge, Massachusetts and becomes known for its *Zork* games.

1979 AUGUST
The dungeon-crawling role-playing game *Temple Of Apshai* is launched by Automated Simulations.

1979 OCTOBER
Activision is established by a group of Atari developers who are dissatisfied with the company's new management.

1979 NOVEMBER
Arcade shooter *Galaxian* is released by Namco in Japan. Midway will pick up distribution rights for the US in April 1980.

1979 NOVEMBER
Space debris shooter *Asteroids* is launched by Atari and becomes a runaway success in arcades.

1979 NOVEMBER
The Atari 8-bit is launched. It comes in two flavours: the 400 or 800, the latter sports a membrane keyboard.

1979 NOVEMBER
Milton Bradley unleashes is unique Microvision handheld videogames console – the first of its kind.

1979 NOVEMBER
Namco releases its block-breaking video pinball game hybrid, *Cutie Q*, in arcades – the third game in the *Gee Bee* trilogy.

1979 DECEMBER
Nintendo releases *Radar Scope*, an arcade shooter, with Shigeru Miyamoto in an early career role as codeveloper.

1979 DECEMBER
Warren Robinett creates *Adventure* for the Atari 2600 and credits his own name as an in-game Easter egg.

BAER'S ODYSSEY

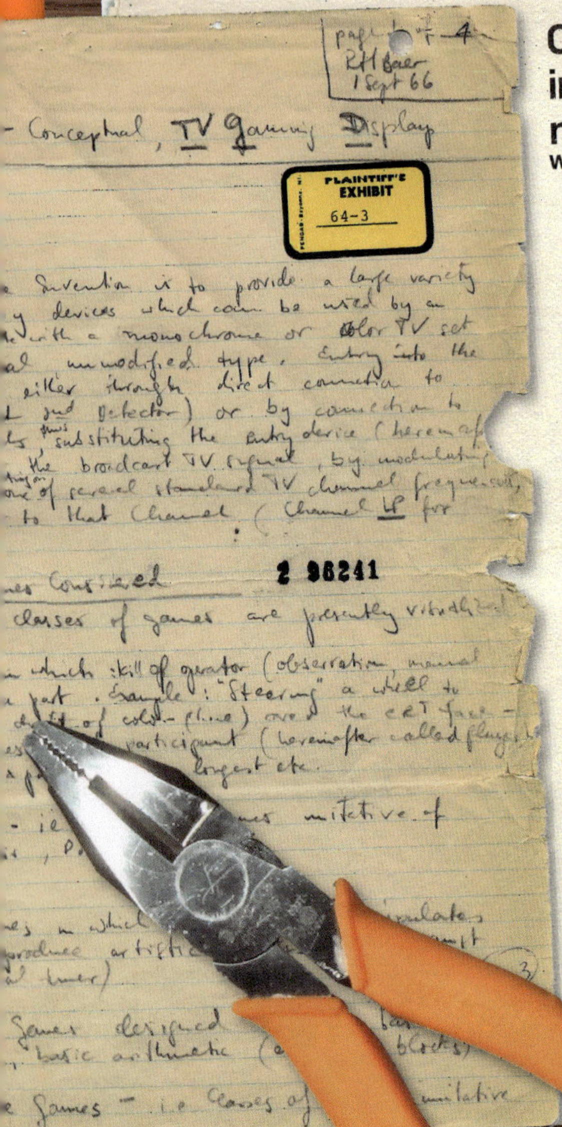

Considered the father of videogames, Ralph Baer's impact on the industry spreads far and wide. We remember our meeting with the late, great pioneer

Words By Paul Drury

"It was a nice sunny day," recalled Ralph Baer, of 2 June 1976. "He was with his lawyer. We shook hands, exchanged a few pleasantries and that was it. A smile, a hello and a goodbye. That was the first time I met Nolan Bushnell."

It was a brief encounter outside the Chicago Federal District Court Building, yet a momentous one in the history of videogames. Not only was Magnavox, the manufacturer of the first videogame console, about to sue Atari over *Pong*-related patent infringement, this was the first meeting of the two founding fathers of the industry. Nolan, who with Atari had made arcade games a part of popular culture, and Ralph, whose pioneering work in the Sixties led to the creation of the Odyssey games console in 1972, which turned our TVs into playfields. Here, we remember Ralph's journey, and salute the father of home videogames who sadly passed away in 2014 aged 92.

1946 – First serve?

"My brother-in-law, Walter, swears I had a bouncing ball on my oscilloscope back in 1946," Ralph began. "I have zero recollection of it but I bet you dollars to doughnuts that I wasn't the only one playing with their 'scope at that time, making spots bounce back and forth on the X-Y display. If he saw it or if he didn't, it really doesn't make any difference in the history of videogames."

So we'll sadly never know for certain whether a very primitive *Pong* ever played out on Ralph's tiny oscilloscope screen, 12 years before Willy Higginbotham's *Tennis For Two* briefly wowed visitors to Brookhaven National Labs in 1958. His brother's memory did, however, demonstrate Ralph's keen interest in electronics. Coming from a Jewish background, he and his family fled Germany in 1938, just two months before the Nazi's savage anti-Semitic Kristallnacht pogrom. They settled in New York, and Ralph spent three years serving in the US Army, both stateside and overseas. He put his electronics expertise to good effect: "When I was with military intelligence, one of the first things I did when we got to Europe was build a radio for the guy who I shared a bunk with. I managed to convert German mine detectors so we could pick up the American Forces Radio Station and listen to Glenn Miller."

After the war ended, Ralph took advantage of the GI Bill Of Rights and went to college in Chicago. Graduating in 1949 with a Bachelor Of Science in Television Engineering (the first degree available of this kind at the time), he would soon get the chance to make a TV set of his own.

1951 – 'That's kind of neat'

In 1951, Ralph was gainfully employed at Loral, an electronics company based in the Bronx, working on a high-class projection television set. "Part of the test equipment we used as we built the set was a pattern generator," he told us. "You could put a pattern on-screen, like a chequerboard, so you could test the height, width, contrast, brightness, that kind of thing… I said, 'That's kind of neat, you can fiddle with these controls and things happen on the screen. Couldn't we build something like this into a television set and make it into some kind of game?' I took the idea to my supervisor and he said, 'You're already behind schedule, just get the damn TV set built!' And that was the end of that!"

The name of Ralph's supervisor? Sam Lackoff. We couldn't help wondering, if it weren't for his lack of vision could we have been playing

» The famous Brown Box and rifle, with the tangle of wires within that made the magic happen.

» Ralph with his Telesketch console in 1975.

games on our televisions in the Fifties instead of the Seventies? "No question about it," Ralph stated, emphatically. "Technically, no problem whatsoever. If it would've resulted in a saleable product that did enough for whatever it would cost, well, that's a question I can't answer."

Just imagine if the industry had started 20 years earlier than it did. Where would we be now?

1966 – Do The Bus Stop

15 years had passed since Ralph first toyed with the notion of playing games on a television. Since then, he'd moved to Sanders Associates and risen up the ranks to chief engineer, working mainly on military defence electronics projects, but his inner 'TV gamer' had never died. "I was waiting at a New York bus terminal for a colleague and it just came back to me," Ralph smiled at us. "The idea of playing games on a television set had always been just under the surface. I remember sitting on a cement step outside the terminal, scribbling notes on a small pad. I got that feeling of being on to something..."

When he returned to his office in New Hampshire the following day, he wrote up his New York notes into a four-page document that laid out his ideas for playing games on a conventional television set. It's a fascinating piece of videogaming history because not only does it contain talk of oscillators, modulators, 'free-running raster techniques' and the numerous practicalities of actually getting images on-screen, it talks about games. Action games, card games, sports games, even *"Auto Racing* using the screen as a roadway". Before a spot was even displayed, Ralph was planning what we might actually be playing in this brave new gaming world.

"What's wrong with looking ahead?" he laughed. "I was thinking of what I could do with this thing! I knew there were 40 million TV sets in the United States. If I could hook up some kind of box to a TV set that did something that people would want to pay for and I could sell that to just 1% of TV owners, that's 400,000 right there! I got a business! Then there's the rest of the world. That's gotta be another 40 or 50 million, right?"

Ralph was thinking big, which might explain why he clearly stated in the document that development should take place 'in a guarded and otherwise inaccessible room', with 'disclosure confined to a minimum of personnel'. He also had the presence of mind to get the seminal document signed and dated by a trusted colleague, Bob Solomon, to establish a legal record of his eureka moment, a highly prescient move given the slew of lawsuits that would follow over the following decades. Ralph, you must have instantly realised this was an important breakthrough. Something big, something worth protecting?

"There was no question in my mind," he confirmed to us. "Of course, I could never have known how big it would really get...."

Realising the potential was one thing; making it become reality was to be an arduous, elongated struggle. It began by Ralph assigning a technician,

"I bet you dollars to doughnuts that I wasn't the only one playing with their 'scope at that time, making spots bounce back and forth on the X-Y display"

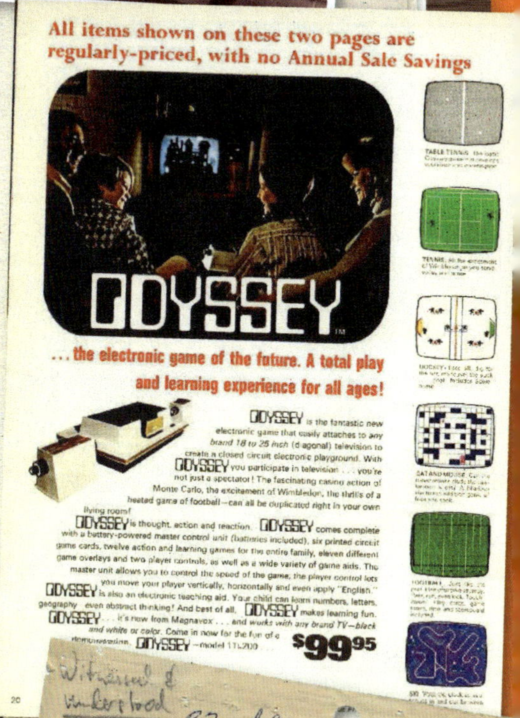
All items shown on these two pages are regularly-priced, with no Annual Sale Savings

ODYSSEY™

... the electronic game of the future. A total play and learning experience for all ages!

ODYSSEY is the fantastic new electronic game that easily attaches to *any brand 18 to 25 inch* (diagonal) television to create a closed circuit electronic playground. With ODYSSEY you participate in television ... you're not just a spectator! The fascinating casino action of Monte Carlo, the excitement of Wimbledon, the thrills of a heated game of football—can all be duplicated right in your own living room!

ODYSSEY is thought, action and reaction. ODYSSEY comes complete with a battery-powered master control unit (batteries included), six printed circuit game cards, twelve action and learning games for the entire family, eleven different game overlays and two player controls, as well as a wide variety of game aids. The master unit allows you to control the speed of the game; the player control lets you move your player vertically, horizontally and even apply "English." ODYSSEY is also an electronic teaching aid. Your child can learn numbers, letters, geography—even abstract thinking! And best of all, ODYSSEY makes learning fun. ODYSSEY ... it's new from Magnavox ... and *works with any brand TV—black and white or color*. Come in now for the fun of a demonstration. ODYSSEY—model 1TL200

$99.95

20

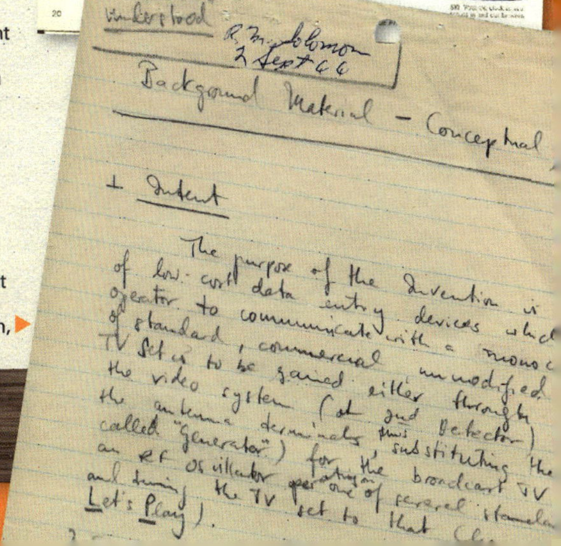
Witnessed & understood

R. M. Solomon
2 Sept 66

Background Material – Conceptual

1 Intent

The purpose of the invention is ...

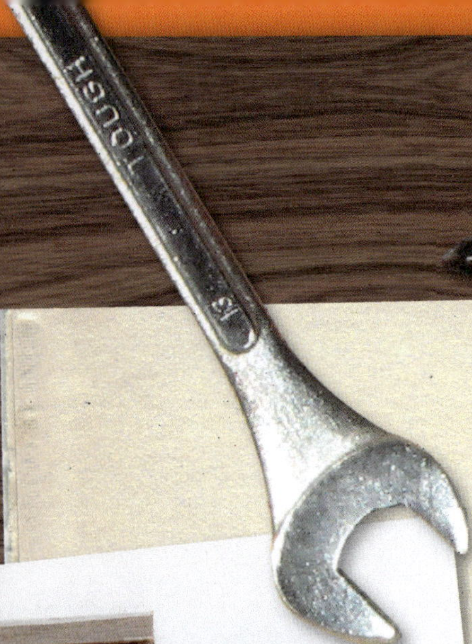

Bob Tremblay, to his secret project. Ensconced in the former company library on the fifth floor, out of sight from any curious eyes, Bob (under Ralph's direction) created a vacuum-tube circuit, which was christened 'TV Game Unit 1'. So, we wondered, did tense games of ping-pong between the two engineers?

Ralph laughed out loud at the thought. "No, no, it couldn't do a hell of a lot! It could put a spot on the screen and stretch it vertically, horizontally, move it around and change its colour. It wasn't meant to be a product but it proved we could get symbols on-screen and that was the purpose of the exercise…"

That tiny tangle of wires and tubes was the 'proof of concept' that Ralph needed. He approached the company's corporate director of research and development, Herbert Campman, and gave a demonstration of the unit. This time, Ralph's superior had vision, and on 22 December 1966, he agreed to fund further development: $2000 for direct labour and $500 for materials. Now that he project had a little cash, and some credence from the company's management – it was game on.

» An overlay for *Prehistoric Safari* – the *Dino Crisis* of the early Seventies.

1967 – A Tale of Two Bills

The new year brought two additions to Ralph's team. Two very different men that would in very different ways play vital roles in the creation of the first games console. "Bill Harrison was my kind of guy," Ralph highlighted. "He was a really good technician. He became an engineer later on, and he designed all the circuitry. He was on the bench, while I was out there running a division of five hundred people. I'd stick my head in a couple of times a day for 15 minutes to see how things were going. He worked under my direction but he did the work and came up with stuff that we could manufacture and was inexpensive. For example, to generate a spot to move around a screen like for a ping-pong game, to do that in discrete logic typically takes four transistors. He did it in two. Once you need three spots, for two bats and a ball, that's a lot fewer transistors and resistors and that's saving you money."

"For the first time in human history, we had a videogame running with verbal instructions coming out of the TV set"

So on 12 February 1967, Ralph took Bill to the same secretive room where Bob Tremblay had put together TV Game Unit 1, and he began working on what would become the second iteration of their console adventure.

Meanwhile, Ralph began sharing his game ideas with one of Herb Campman's engineers, Bill Rusch. "He was an MIT graduate," Ralph explained to us. "Very bright, very creative and very eccentric. He'd go out at lunch to play his guitar to people I thought were groupies. He was very independent and wouldn't take direction, but I tolerated it because he was very useful. A million times I would've cheerfully let him go if he wasn't such an important contributor to the effort."

That contribution can be clearly seen in a memo dated 10 May 1967. It detailed 21 different videogames, a culmination of conversations between Rusch and Ralph over the previous three months about what their TV game unit might be able to deliver. It reads like a manifesto for future game genres; there's a top-down racing game where circuit-crashes or rear-ending the race leader are penalised; a baseball game where the speed of the pitch can be controlled and the batter must time their swing perfectly to make a hit; a maze game in which a white rat must traverse a labyrinth; various target-shooting

» Ralph demonstrating the Odyssey 200 console, released in 1975.

» Ralph taking aim using a Brown Box rifle.

The Big Guns Come Out

"What do you do with a single spot on a screen?" Ralph mused to us. "It's pretty boring, right? So you shoot it! As soon as that idea came along, I sent Bill Harrison out to buy a plastic rifle. Opened it up, found room to put some electronics in – a sensor, some amplification, a little coincidence circuitry – so when you pull the trigger, and you're lined up with that source of light on the screen, the spot, you get a hit and you make that hit turn off the spot so it disappears."

Thus in 1967, a lightgun game was implemented for TV Game Unit 2, and another long-running videogame genre was established. We wondered whether the idea of adding a gun to the project might have come from the fact that Sanders was involved primarily in the defence industry, or perhaps it was a reflection of America's well-established gun culture?

Ralph was quick to respond. "This comes up so often. You see these documentaries on the history of videogames and they make a big deal about this relationship with the military. I don't think it had a damn thing to do with it. A kid that goes to a carnival, does he have a go at skeet shooting because his dad was in the army? No, it's because it's freakin' fun!"

games (see right); and an idea for an aerial World War One dogfighting duel, preempting Atari's ubiquitous *Combat* cartridge by a decade. There are even plans for an intriguing golf game that resulted in a bizarre peripheral.

"We built joysticks for Game Unit 2," said Ralph, speaking about the practical aspects of implementing some of their game ideas. "What's more obvious to an engineer like me than to drill a hole in a golf ball and stick it on a joystick? Put it on the floor and hit it with your putter. Get it right and you get a hole in one!"

Mid-1967 – Summer Of Games

Full of ideas and with an encouraging number of incremental technical breakthroughs, the group prepared to showcase their progress to the president of the company, Royden Sanders, and the board of directors. "I knew I couldn't blow this," Ralph explained to us, "so I recorded the instructions for the games on Game Unit 2 on audio tape and I had Bill Harrison build a little 4.5MHz oscillator and modulator so the sound came through the television set. I switched it on and, for the first time in human history, we had a videogame running with verbal instructions coming out of the TV set."

Seven games were demoed to the board that day. *Fox and Hounds*, a two-player chase game, had a single red spot for a 'fox', pursued by three white 'hounds', while *Target Shooting* allowed one player to move the bullseye with the joystick, as a second tried to blast it with his rifle. Most intriguing was *Pumping Game*, in which the player took on the role of a firefighter frantically trying to extinguish the flames in a burning house, success being achieved by pumping a handle on the console. This primitive button-basher was accompanied by a charming hand-drawn overlay, featuring a determined fireman gripping his hose. The windows of the building were transparent, allowing the player to see the opposing levels of red (fire) and blue (water) colour on screen, which indicated success or failure.

So, did the board see the germ of a multi-billion dollar industry in those seven videogame vignettes? "They said I was nuts!" exclaims Ralph. "We were a military electronics company building very complex, very expensive equipment, like anti-aircraft to ground missile protection. This was a long, long way from that. The reception was actually pretty cold. Out of the whole group, only two were smiling after the demo was done and they became supporters. The rest looked pretty dumb. But I guess they trusted me. I had been around a while..."

The truth was Ralph and his team were also starting to have doubts. Their games were fun, but their lasting appeal was questionable. There was only so much entertainment you could squeeze out of two spots chasing each other across the screen, however cleverly you dressed it up. Then in November came a major breakthrough. Bill Rusch designed some novel spot generator circuitry on paper, Bill Harrison implemented it and now a third spot could be displayed on screen. This spot was different; it was machine controlled, and therefore, most excitingly, it could be a 'ball'.

"It was obvious we finally had something worth going after," Ralph enthused, warming to the subject. "I mean, the other games, we were dragging them in by the hair just to have something to do but as soon as we had a ping-pong game, that was of a totally different order."

And so the first 'killer app' was born. All that had to be done was to turn the game into something they could sell to the world.

1969 – Boxing Clever

Videogame Unit 7 was given the name of the 'Brown Box', so called because the aluminium chassis containing the game circuitry was now covered with brown, self-adhesive wood-grain vinyl. This box of tricks could play various kinds of ping-pong, all developed by the team over the previous year. Volleyball, soccer and hockey all played around with the same basic 'two bats, one ball' formula, some utilising overlays to add goals and other little touches of 'realism' to proceedings. The light-gun and golf-putting games also made the final cut, along with a version of checkers. Herb Campman's response confirmed the team's hopes: "This looks like it's for real."

"No question it was ready to produce," said Ralph, "but we had to figure out who was going

» A selection of the many games and toys Ralph had worked on over the years.

to put it into production! We had been trying to get cable companies interested but they just didn't have the guts.

"I can't believe it took us a whole year to realise all the parts we were using were the same parts used by TV and radio manufacturers. Those were who we needed to be talking to! And they came, one by one, and all of them said, 'Gee, this is great, but did any of 'em move off a dime?' No. RCA was the only one who put together a contract and that took three months and it was so onerous to us that we walked away. But we got lucky. One of the RCA guys left to join Magnavox and told them they should take another look at us. We presented [the Brown Box] to them and their manager said, 'Go!' That's how it all started."

then, like $300,000 in today's dollars. It was like someone had turned a switch on in me. In a microsecond I went from depression to elation!"

That three-foot photocopy of the first royalty cheque received by Sanders for sales of the Odyssey console was tangible proof of what Ralph and his tiny team had always believed: people would love videogames. That Christmas, 100,000 consoles were sold and the Magnavox Odyssey went on to sell 350,000 units over the next few years.

"In terms of selling a brand new product it was an unqualified success," beamed Ralph. "It didn't matter that by the time it came out it was old technology. It worked and it was fun. And you know, it owed much of its success to the fact that Atari had brought out their copy of it, *Pong*, in the

"You can't compare the technology I had back in the sixties with what we have today. I look at my iPad and it's magic! Bloody magic!"

Simon Says

Of Ralph's numerous post-Odyssey creations, the most commercially successful was the iconic handheld Simon. The simple 'follow the notes' gameplay, and stylish, circular design led to sales of several million units and versions of the handheld still remain in production today, more than 30 years after its launch in 1978.

"It was just serendipity that *Close Encounters Of The Third Kind* was out," Ralph told us. "The mothership was round and made sounds like Simon. When I saw the movie I said, Hey it's Simon coming in! I'm sure, subliminally, it helped sales."

Simon had a special place in Ralph's heart, and it's not just due to its lasting popularity. The idea for the game originated after he had played an old Atari arcade game called *Touch Me* at a trade show, a game that was supposedly born from a concept by Nolan Bushnell himself.

"We managed to make a real success of Simon and so, unintentionally, I managed to upstage Nolan for once," chuckled Ralph.

You can read the full Simon story in **Retro Gamer** issue 73.

1972 – The Best Medicine

It was the summer of 1972 and Ralph was lying in a hospital bed, recovering from a routine operation. The high of 1969 seemed a long time ago. Since his TV game was given the greenlight, things had been moving slowly. A year to sort out the legal contracts and another for the Brown Box prototype to be manufactured into the Magnavox Odyssey, which finally hit the shelves in the summer of 1972. Worse still, Sanders was hit badly by a severe slump in the defence industry, resulting in large-scale job losses at the company. Ralph was in a 'deep funk'.

"You can read all the books on psychology you want, the reason people get depressed is that they lose confidence in themselves," he reasoned to us. "My division in the company had shrunk by a few hundred people, employees were hiding behind storage cabinets to avoid getting on the layoffs list and I was in hospital for this operation. Then in walks Herb Campman with a giant cheque for $100,000! That was substantial money back

arcades. You wanna play that at home, you go buy a Magnavox Odyssey game. And that's what people did..."

Success inevitably breeds imitation. Atari had built their arcade business from the huge profits generated by *Pong*, which did indeed bear an uncanny resemblance to the Odyssey's ping pong game. Countless other Johnny-come-latelys also jumped on the bandwagon and produced home and arcade versions of the game. In 1975, Atari decided to produce a home version of its arcade hit and so we return to those courthouse steps in Chicago, where Ralph first met Nolan.

1976 – Who's the Daddy?

"I felt confident from the start," Ralph told us. "Nolan had played our game at a Magnavox dealership in Burlingame, California, in May 1972. No-one can tell me that wasn't the inspiration for him to tell Al Alcorn to build *Pong*. That's fine. I've been in the toy and game business long enough to know everyone bases their ideas on other people's. Nothing comes from a vacuum. But we

» The Magnavox Odyssey, the world's first console debuted in 1972.

An innovative inventor to the end

From Computer Perfection to Coleco's Telstar and Kid-Vid series, Ralph was involved in literally hundreds of innovative projects, ranging from interactive toys for children to talking greetings cards. And despite living into his nineties, he had no intention of stopping. "As we're speaking, my marketing guy is on his way to California to present two products we've just finished to a company in the Bay area," Ralph explained proudly to us. "I've got better at doing at my own software and I've done dozens of games over the last few years. One of the projects is a talking book, where a kid can store their own voice and play around with it, and the other is a tricycle with electronics added in that turn it into a games machine!" Mobile gaming the Baer way. His soldering iron and endless imagination will always be a source of inspiration.

had issued patents that had clearly been infringed by Atari and others."

The judge agreed and Magnavox – and by extension, Ralph – won on all counts. Well, all but one, perhaps. For many years, as the videogame industry boomed, and occasionally busted, into the billion-dollar business it is today, it was Nolan who was referred to as the 'father of videogames'. Ralph's role was largely ignored and his huge contribution to the birth of our favourite hobby went unacknowledged for several years. Thankfully, the wonderful web helped put the story straight.

"I was a no-show before the internet," sighed Ralph. "Then I got a website and that put me on the map. Since then, I've received the National Medal Of Technology from President Bush, the original Brown Box is in the Smithsonian Museum and I've been awarded so many prizes and medals, I don't know what to do with them all. They're cluttering up my desk here! The amount of emails I get from students with yards of questions to help them with a paper they're writing on the history of videogames, maybe that's an indication that I've finally arrived!"

Before we left Ralph to get back to work at his bench in his basement lab (at the time of us meeting him in the early Tens, he was approaching 90 and was still inventing new products), we explained that this article is for an edition of **Retro Gamer**, and wondered whether he ever looked at what videogames have become, both commercially and culturally, and think, 'Did I really start this?' He thought for a short while before answering our question.

"Well, obviously, yes, but I'm very conscious that though I might have started it, there are thousands of creative people that made it all happen. And you can't compare the technology I had back in the Sixties with what we have today. I look at my iPad and it's magic! Bloody magic! And everything's getting more magical!"

So gamers, raise your joysticks to the wizard that cast the first spell. To Ralph Baer, the true Father Of Videogames. *

Make sure to check out Ralph Baer's book *Videogames: In The Beginning*, and find out more about his incredible career at www.ralphbaer.com. Additional images courtesy of David Winter of www.pong-story.com.

» Ralph with one of the latest versions of his ever-popular handheld, Simon.

» This overlay for the early *Pumping Game* was hand drawn by Stew Gregory, a draftsman at Sanders.

THE IMPACT OF

SPACE INVADERS

THEY DIDN'T COME FROM OUTER SPACE BUT A COLLECTION OF ALIENS MADE JUST AS BIG AN IMPACT HERE ON EARTH WHEN THEY BOUNDED INTO ARCADES IN 1978. CREATOR TOMOHIRO NISHIKADO JOINS A HOST OF DEVELOPERS AND CULTURAL ARTISTS IN DISCUSSING THE WIDE-RANGING EFFECTS OF SPACE INVADERS

Words by David Crookes

Throughout the best part of the Seventies, game developer Tomohiro Nishikado looked towards America with aspiration in his eyes. In turn, the US peered back at Japan with a dollop of suspicion.

But that was symptomatic of the state of these nations during that period — a decade in which post-war America, in line with much of the western world, suffered economic stagnation while the Far East enjoyed rapid growth.

Nishikado was a talented young developer, an engineering graduate who had been employed by the Japanese vending machine manufacturer Taito since 1969. He'd had reasonable success with a variety of games, starting with the *Pong* clone *Elephong* in 1972, followed by *Davis Cup* and *Soccer* in 1973, again inspired by the classic game from Atari.

TIMELINE

Charting over 40 years of repelling invaders

- *Space Invaders* released in the arcades
- Yellow Magic Orchestra samples *Space Invaders* sounds in the single *Computer Game*

-1978-

- Gamers could pop their name on the high score table in *Space Invaders Deluxe*
- A cocktail table follow-up, *Space Invaders II*, appears

-1979-

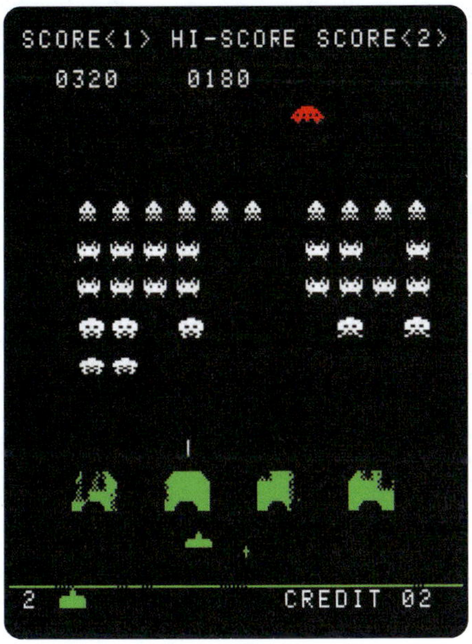

» [Arcade] The game mirrored your own anxiety: the more successful and palm-sweaty you were, the faster it became.

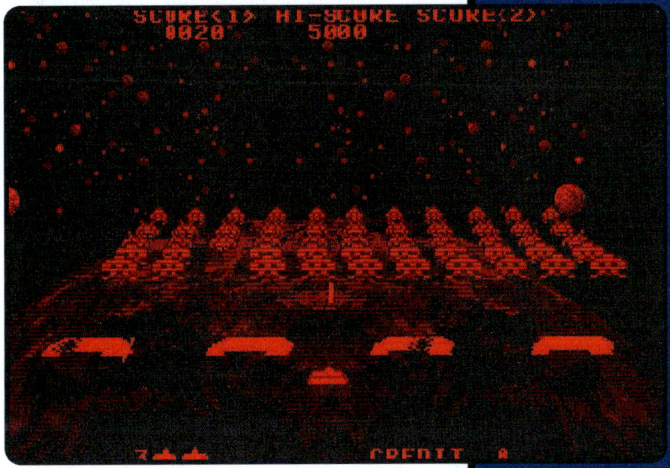

» [Virtual Boy] You'd be seeing red if you played *Space Invaders* on the Virtual Boy but that was entirely down to the screen.

The titles he worked on would show great promise and innovation. *Speed Race* in 1974 had scrolling graphics, a racing wheel controller and a choice of beginner or advanced play; *Western Gun*, or *Gun Fight* in the US, was the first to bring human-against-human violence to videogames the following year.

Yet at that time America was dominating the videogame industry. Atari in particular had seized the market and it was leading in arcades – and homes, too, thanks to the launch of the 2600 console. Nishikado became hooked on Atari's *Breakout* and the more he played, the more determined he became to better it.

"My goal at that time was to catch up with the United States," he tells us. But in that aim, he was not alone. For throughout the Seventies (and going into the Eighties), Japan had been snapping at the heels of key American businesses, most notably the automobile industry. American manufacturing had been in decline and power was swinging.

As such, there was rising discrimination and an increase in what has been dubbed 'Japanophobia' – a revival of anti-Japanese sentiment that predated the Second World War. "There was this interesting tension as the rise and strength of the Japanese economy really made an impression on the US national identity as the great country of innovators and inventors," says the academic game designer professor Lindsay Grace.

» Tomohiro Nishikado is the creator of *Space Invaders*.

With that in mind, Nishikado's next game, *Space Invaders*, would face multiple battles. Alien invasions aside, it had to fight against a fear of Japanese influence on American culture. And, there were worries the game was proving too distracting for children.

On the issue of Japanophia, however, Lindsay contends *Space Invaders* "gave more fodder or proof for not being afraid". Indeed, it opened up gaming and its huge potential right across the world. "It's hard to know what would have happened to gaming without *Space Invaders*," says Mark Cutmore, head of commercial enterprises at the Science Museum Group.

Space Invaders landed with impeccable timing. "Videogames were in the ascendent, a new form of entertainment with untold promise," explains Iain Simons, director of culture at the British Games Institute. As such, it was a time of great experimentation, of pushing the available tech and creating new genres.

To that end, Nishikado began work on *Space Invaders* in 1977 and he created a microcomputer from scratch to do so. It was the first Japanese game to use microprocessors and it became the most advanced arcade game available. Built around Intel's 8080 8-bit processor rather than using discrete logic chips, it made for a better performance.

Perhaps more importantly, *Space Invaders* also anchored itself to the predominant themes of mainstream culture at the time. "This era was the dawn of the space age – both in reality with the Apollo moon landings, the launch of the space shuttle, communications and spy satellites, interplanetary probes, and with science fiction such as *Star Wars*, *Star Trek*, *Dune* and *Aliens*," says Eugene Jarvis, who went on to produce his own sci-fi shooter, *Defender*, in 1981. ▶

Super Invader becomes an early clone

Funny Stuff releases the song *Disco Space Invaders*

The Pretenders release the hit song *Space Invader*

Space Invaders lands on the Atari 2600

10,000 players compete in the National *Space Invaders* Superbowl run by Atari

Bally Midway releases a pinball version

1979 — 1980

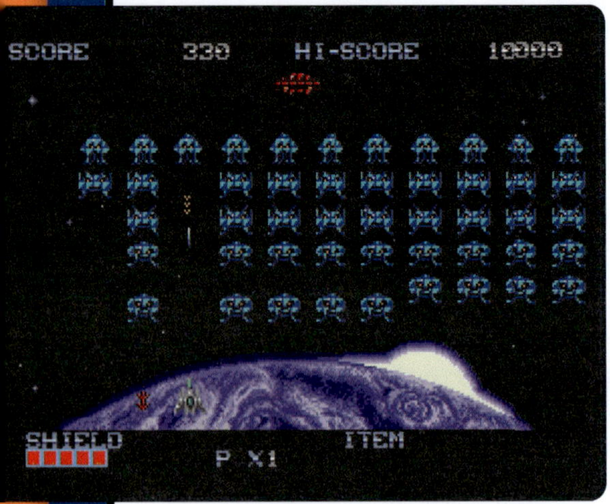

» [Mega Drive] A rather faithful rendition of the original game, *Space Invader 90* nevertheless had enhanced sound and graphics.

It wasn't always going to be that way. Initially, Nishikado considered aeroplanes as the enemy, but he switched to humans for technical reasons. Taito wasn't happy and felt it would be too immoral to have gamers blasting away at people so Nishikado chose to set the game in space instead. It was, he tells us, "a convenient theme for videogames unlike sports that are bound by specific rules". He chose well, as history demonstrates.

"*Star Wars* had just captured the imagination of the entire world, not just as a movie, but as a universe," Iain continues. "We didn't just buy a ticket to watch the film, we bought the action figures and the lunchbox to take our sandwiches to school in. *Space Invaders* arrived at the peak of that first wave of a new, popular science fiction explosion. It was a new, aspirational technology that shackled itself to the moment."

» [Arcade] *Space Invaders Part II* allowed gamers to add their names to their high scores, making for a more competitive, social experience.

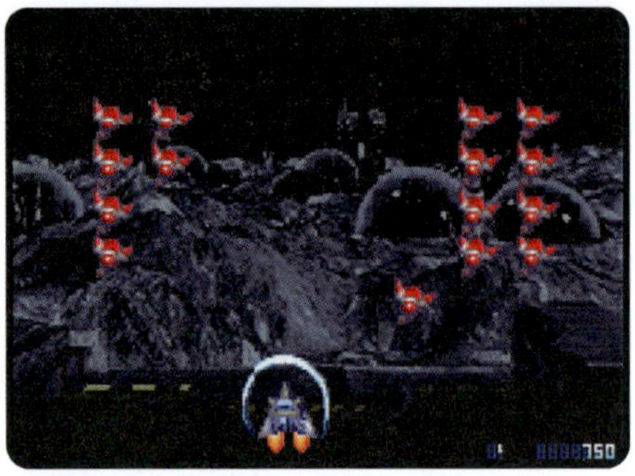

» [GBA] *Space Invaders* is such a simple, casual game that it works perfectly well on smaller screens.

Even so, *Space Invaders* still had to be attractive in itself and that was always at the forefront of Nishikado's mind. It meant that when *Space Invaders* was released in the arcades in Japan in 1978, its impact was immediate, with some pachinko parlours and bowling alleys soon rebranding themselves as *Space Invaders* arcades, filled to the brim with coin-op machines.

"I was surprised by media reports saying that pachinko parlours – a leading industry in Japanese entertainment at that time – were being invaded by the game," Nishikado says. He was also astonished to read that the game was causing a shortage of 100 yen coins.

"It is true that newspapers reported *Space Invaders* caused the shortage of 100 yen coins and, consequently, Nippon Ginko's increased production of 100 yen coins, but I didn't feel that much at the beginning of the boom," Nishikado explains. "One day, I happened to see the tyre of a truck weighed down by a load of collected 100 yen coins in the car park at Taito's headquarters. This surprised me and I realised that *Space Invaders* had become a phenomenon."

Although many a gaming expert have since dispelled the yen shortage as fake news, *Space Invaders*' popularity was very much true. But even though it was eating up cash, there were fears in Japan that the game was leading to delinquency and children playing truant.

"It was an unanticipated fad for the amusement industry and so rules or regulations were not able to catch up with that instant phenomenon," Nishikado says. "But if I, as a games creator, was to look back in a positive way, I'd say it heralded a new era of entertainment in Japan."

There is no denying that. When Nishikado visited the Amusement and Music Operators Association show in 1978 when the game was introduced, he was astounded. "I saw a lot of people waiting in the queue in front of the *Space Invaders* cabinet and, at that moment, I felt that our games might be overtaking the videogame giant." The US had competition.

» Mark Cutmore works at the Science Museum Group.

"IT HERALDED A NEW ERA OF ENTERTAINMENT IN JAPAN"

Tomohiro Nishikado

It was 1981 and a number of parents in the affluent village of Irvington in the state of New York were waging a war of sorts against their children. They were incensed at the plethora of coin-op machines which had been invading their space for a few years and they'd manage to convince the authorities to do something about them.

The proposal was dramatic and involved banning anyone under the age of 17 from playing. It also sought to impose a $100 licensing fee for machines and restrict the number that any single establishment could have to two. "I hear they're addictive," said mayor Reginald F Marra, as the village prepared to vote on the issue.

Marra was against the age limit, but he sympathised with the concerns. Just as in Japan, the games were eating up pocket money and while that was good news for the owners, they were being blamed for kids going without lunch or arriving late at school.

The coin-op had been brought to America by Midway and it had quickly appeared in cafes and pizza parlours in cities across the US. But although arcade machines had been making in-roads into American culture for the best part of ten years, they had not attracted quite the same level of attention as the Japanese newcomer.

"I found a *Pong* machine in a landromat in Kent, Ohio, in 1975 and I decided that I preferred spending my quarters on drying clothes," scorns games developer Matt Householder, who went on to develop *Moon Patrol*, for the ColecoVision. "*Space Invaders* was the first videogame (coin-op or otherwise) that I found was truly fun to play." He wasn't alone.

"Suddenly, videogames had some character," Iain says. "Sure, they were two dimensional and rudimentarily animated but the aliens in *Space Invaders* had enough character to make themselves feel like characters. *Pong* was an astonishing achievement, but it didn't provide videogames with a figurehead. *Space Invaders*' marauding, oceanic aliens delivered such a powerful character design that they're still used to symbolise videogames to this day."

As it proved, 1978 was a turning point both for the videogame industry and the growing backlash against it. The

1982 – Acclaimed author Martin Amis writes *Invasion Of The Space Invaders*

Space Invaders grosses $2 billion

1983 – *Pepsi Invaders* is commissioned by Coca-Cola

1985 – *Return Of The Invaders* is released

Taito releases the game on the NES in Japan

1987 – KP Snacks sells Space Raiders crisps

same happened in the UK, the rest of Europe and other markets around the world. One of the main problems was that *Space Invaders* was so attractive and addictive, although some people found other, more bizarre reasons to outlaw this particular invasion.

» Iain Simons works at the British Games Institute.

In *Japanamerica: How Japanese Pop Culture Had Invaded the US*, author Roland Kelts writes of *Pac-Man* creator Toru Iwatani's "bafflement when discussing the banning of Space Invaders in several southern states in the Eighties – allegedly because aliens are not in the Bible, and because of the game's violence towards them". Unlucky for them, *Space Invaders*' success only led to more shooters. In the Eighties, Japanese arcades were dominated by them.

"As the most popular game of the era, *Space Invaders* became the target of fear but the cause was that people didn't understand the emerging trend for gaming or recognise the positive aspects of it," argues Mark. "The same fears had been levelled at television in its early days and at new genres of music like punk and hip-hop."

As it happens, the proposed ban on children in Irvington was thrown out and the planned restrictions on cabinet numbers were loosened to three machines per establishment. Yet arcade games – *Space Invaders* in particular – continued to attract as much negative attention as it did positive. In 1981, George Foulkes, Labour MP for South Ayrshire in Scotland tried to push the Control Of *Space Invaders* And Other Electronic Games bill through the UK parliament.

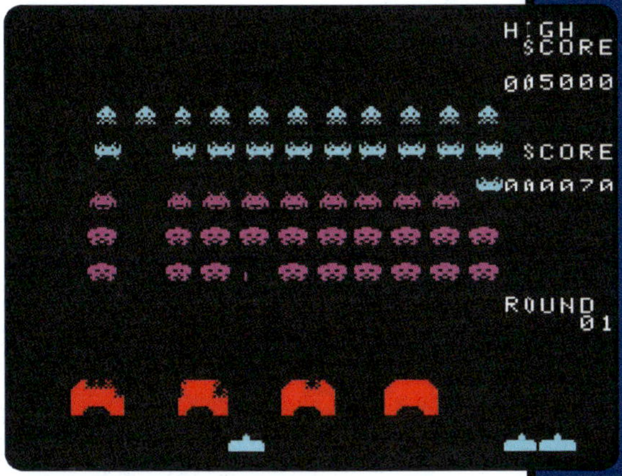

» [PC Engine] With better weapons and lovely backdrops, Taito's porting of *Space Invaders* to the PC Engine in 1990 was a success.

WORLD DOMINATION

How Space Invaders made its way into the zeitgeist

MUSIC

■ Musicians were inspired by *Space Invaders* after its launch and, even putting aside the sampled audio in the messy medley that was Yellow Magic Orchestra's hit, *Computer Game*, fans could enjoy *Disco Space Invaders* by Funny Stuff in 1979, *Space Invader* by The Pretenders in 1980 and *Space Invaders* by Player One.

TELEVISION

■ *Space Invaders* has had an impact on the small screen in a variety of ways. Not only was a BBC series by celebrity builder Tommy Walsh called *Space Invaders*, there have been numerous references to the game in *Futurama*, *Scrubs*, *Chuck*, *Danger Mouse* and *Black Mirror* among many others.

FILM

■ Whether it's *Spaced Invaders* or appearances in sci-fi films such as *Terminator 2: Judgement Day* and *Cherry 2000*, Hollywood hasn't been immune to the classic title. *Space Invaders* has a role in *Pixels* and there's talk of a movie directly based on the series.

LITERATURE

■ It may seem odd that Martin Amis' wrote the guide, *Invasion Of The Space Invaders*, in 1982 but he's not the only author to reference the game. Terry Pratchett's *Only You Can Save Mankind* saw invader-style aliens surrendering and seeking help. Characters in *Discworld* play *Barbarian Invaders*.

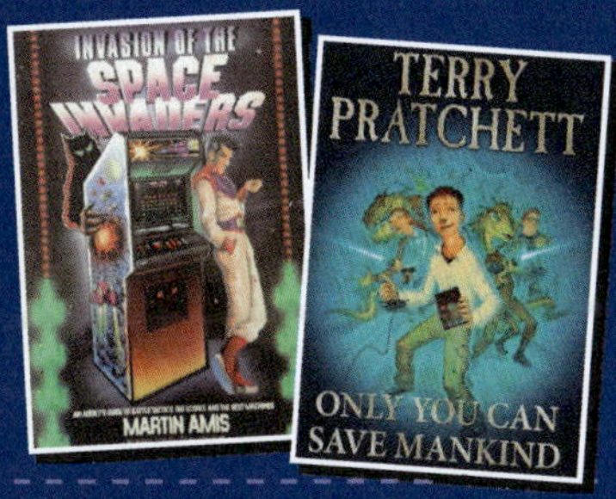

ART

■ The urban artist Invader has decorated cities across the world with *Space Invaders* ceramic tile mosaics, some of which were stolen in Paris in 2017. The game has also featured in many exhibitions and gallery spaces, with one single alien invader sprite becoming a design icon.

©KylaBorg

ARCHITECTURE

■ Many home interior design companies are called 'Space Invaders'. But does the game's influence spread to blueprints? Yes, if NL Architects' proposed *Space Invaders* alternative tower block is anything to go by. It was earmarked for South Korea.

Majestic Twelve: The Space Invaders Part IV launches

Versions of the game hit the Game Boy and Mega Drive

A prize-winning riff on the game offers a £20 jackpot

1990

Super Space Invaders offers non-arcade action for home computers

Space Invaders appears in the film Terminator 2: Judgement Day

1991

The remake Space Invaders DX for arcades is released

1993

OUT OF THIS WORLD

Key games that define the series

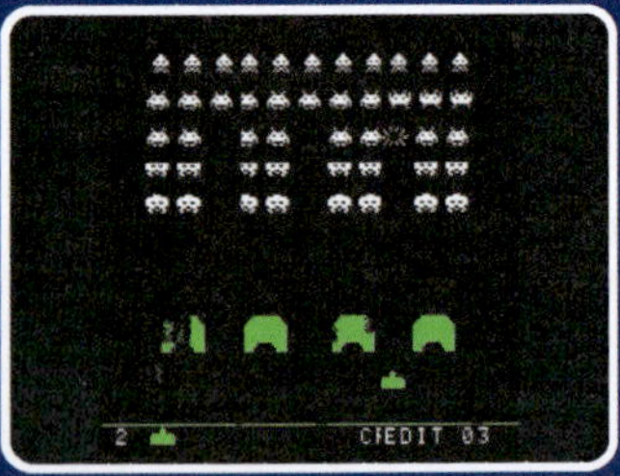

SPACE INVADERS

1978, ARCADE

■ The original was entirely black and white and was released in Japan by Taito as a sit-down cocktail table. An upright cabinet was introduced in the west by Midway, reflecting the graphics on to a painted backdrop. Gamers soon became acquainted with the need to blast away five rows of 11 aliens.

SPACE INVADERS 95: ATTACK OF THE LUNAR LOONIES

1995, ARCADE

■ This is a wacky, upbeat, cartoony rendition of *Space Invaders* which allowed you to play as various characters. It has many Earth-based settings and gives you five bosses to battle making it familiar and unique at the same time.

SPACE INVADERS

1980, ATARI 2600

■ Atari bagged the home licence from Taito and created the 2600's must-have title. It only had 36 aliens and three (rather than four) defence barriers, but there were a staggering 112 game variations along with an assortment of shots, difficulty levels and a two-player modes. It sold very well indeed.

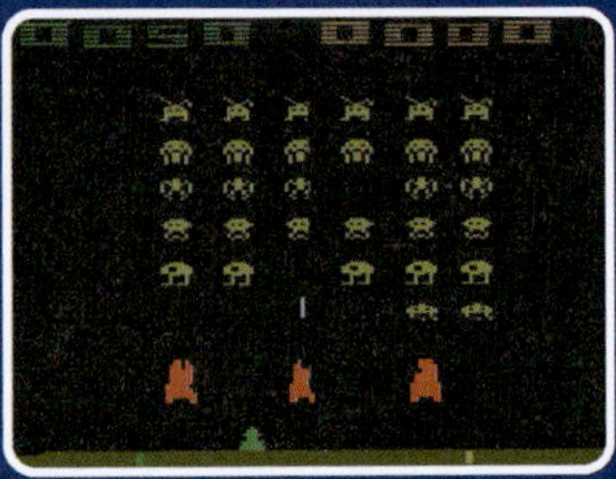

SPACE INVADERS

1999, PLAYSTATION

■ This was one of a glut of *Space Invaders* variants at the turn of the millennium but it puts a fresh spin on the design. Modelled in 3D and with a blistering soundtrack, players have to hit four aliens of the same colour in a row to receive different power-ups. There are nods to 1978 in the intro, too.

RETURN OF THE INVADERS

1985, ARCADE

■ The true colour sequel launched seven years after the original and it unleashed the invaders like never before. The blocks of old were supplemented by patterned waves of aliens that proved increasingly difficult to see off. Deflector invaders had to be shot right in the centre otherwise your fire would bounce back.

SPACE INVADERS EXTREME

2008, NINTENDO DS/PSP

■ Produced to coincide with *Space Invaders'* 30th anniversary, *Space Invaders Extreme* stands as one of the finest remakes in the series' history. Four-hit combos would earn power-ups and it was possible to control when the UFO appeared. A sequel arrived in 2009.

MAJESTIC TWELVE: THE SPACE INVADERS PART IV

1990, ARCADE

■ Also known as *Super Space Invaders 91*, this version was ported to 8-bit and 16-bit computers and consoles. As well as introducing boss invaders, the CG30 cannons could take more than one hit, and it was possible to play with a friend.

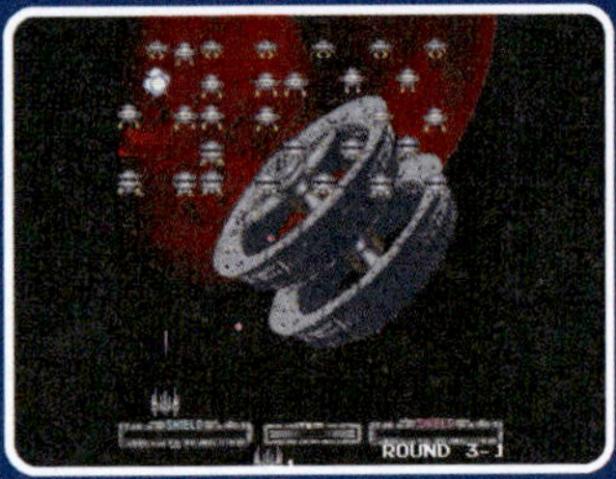

SPACE INVADERS INFINITY GENE

2009, iOS/ANDROID

■ As another reimagining, Infinity Gene brought *Space Invaders* up to date with charming simplicity, making the most of the touchscreens of mobile devices. It also added the ability to unlock better weapons and rewarded the chain destruction of enemies.

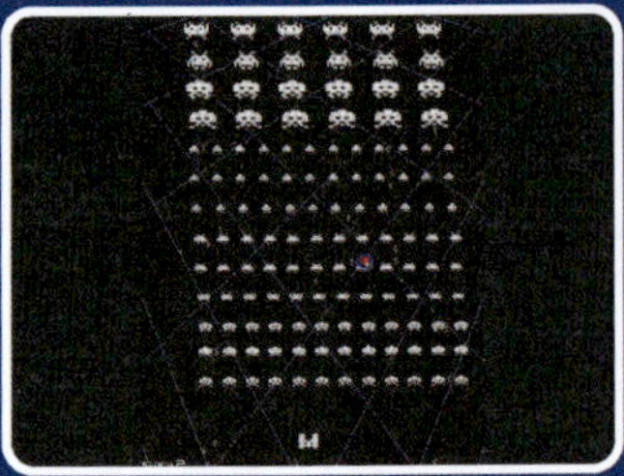

SPACE INVADERS DX

1993, ARCADE

■ A number of games make up this classic: there are colour, monochrome and cellophane versions of the original. The most fun of all is the parody game: this replaced the iconic *Space Invaders* sprites with characters from nine of Taito's games including *Bubble Bobble* and *Arkanoid*.

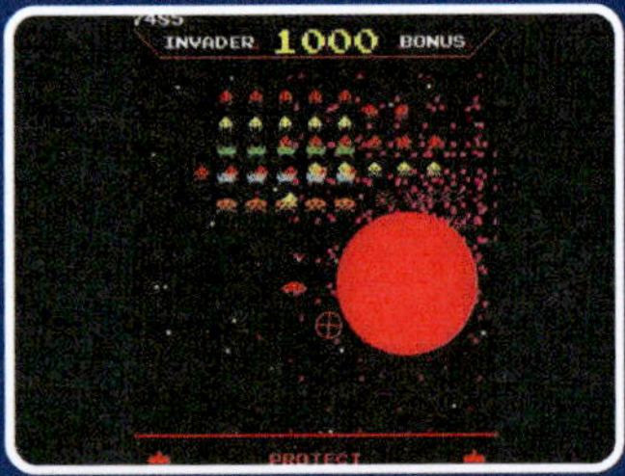

SPACE INVADERS FRENZY

2017, ARCADE

■ You can't miss Raw Thrills' *Space Invaders Frenzy*. It plays on a nine-foot screen, uses lightgun cannons as controllers and allows you to identify and blast at individual aliens regardless of where they may be.

- **1995** – Players can enjoy a Virtual Boy *Space Invaders* experience
- **1999** – *Space Invaders* looks very different on the PlayStation
- **2003** – *Space Invaders Anniversary* celebrates 25 years of the series
- **2005** – *Space Invaders Revolution* is launched on the Nintendo DS
- **2005** – The PSP is blessed with the interesting *Space Invaders Evolution*
- **2006** – The game is chosen to represent Japan by the country's Agency For Cultural Affairs

"IT WAS ONE OF THE FIRST TIMES I HAD SEEN 'ADVANCED GRAPHICS'"

Graeme Devine

"A Sheffield mother is quoted as saying that a Jekyll and Hyde change came over her 14-year-old son when he became hooked on *Space Invaders*," he told MPs. "In London, a 13-year-old vanished from his home for ten days, visiting arcades to play the machines. Also in London, a 17-year-old boy was so desperate for money to feed the machines that he turned to blackmail and theft, demanding £900 from a clergyman with whom he had previously had sexual relations."

For those who were playing *Space Invaders* however, there was nothing better on Earth. It proved inspiring and it created a social scene for young people to hook into. "The game was being enjoyed by all ages due to its simple gameplay," explains Nishikado. "Having said that, the game is not that easy to win. The enemy aliens shoot at the player, which makes the players feel frustrated and nervous. On the other hand, the game gives exhilaration when the player defeats all the enemy aliens and clears a level. A blend of these feelings urged the players to insert another coin for next challenge. I suppose this is the reason for the success of *Space Invaders*."

» [Arcade] If the characters here look familiar it's because they've come from various Taito games. How many can you name?

» [PlayStation] Sony's PlayStation received a number of upgraded arcade classics, and *Space Invaders* was no exception.

Scores of players and wannabe developers agreed and there was no getting around the fact that *Space Invaders* was hugely innovative. "It was one of the first times I had seen 'advanced graphics', and the novelty of controlling something on a screen was still really new," says Scottish game designer and programmer Graeme Devine, who went on to create *The 7th Guest* and *The 11th Hour*. "*Space Invaders* was also a watchable game: you'd understand the rules after watching a friend play a few games and you'd want to have a go."

Some of videogaming's key figures over the years were influenced by the game, not only in Japan but in the US, UK, the rest of Europe and beyond. John Romero cites it as a key influence, as does Eugene.

"It was the first fully formed videogame with real enemies, incredible audio, ever-increasing difficulty and tension with infinite play time as long as you can stay alive," he tells us. "It also created the first videogame addicts and launched the worldwide videogame revolution. By allowing expert players to set record scores limited only by skill, endurance and bladder capacity, *Space Invaders* also became the first esport."

Dona Bailey, who was working as an assembly language programmer for microprocessors in Cadillac engines at a GM-Delco plant in Santa Barbara, California, clearly recalls her first encounter with videogames and the impact it had not just on her but other media. "It was April 1980 and my best friend was very interested in new music," she says. "He played the first Pretenders' album constantly and it had an instrumental song called *Space Invader* on it. I didn't typically like instrumentals but I heard that one so much, I started really liking it."

» Graeme Devine created *The 7th Guest* and *The 11th Hour*.

One night she asked a friend what the song was about and what the title meant. "He got wildly excited and explained it was about this great arcade game called *Space Invaders*," she says. "He said there was a game in a bar close to where we worked, and I should go there with him at lunch some day to check it out. We went, he put in quarters, I got killed before I could figure out what I was supposed to do but I recognised how much the game display looked like the climate control display I programmed on the car back at work, and that's how I fell in love with videogames."

Dona ended up moving to Sunnyvale in May 1980 without a job or much of anything else, but she was soon hired at Atari where she devised and worked on the popular track ball arcade game *Centipede*. *Space Invaders* had taught her much

Space Invaders is included in the Game On exhibition at the Barbican Centre, London

Space Invaders Get Even appears on WiiWare

Taito releases an album called Space Invaders 2008

An art game Invaders! is included at the GH ART exhibition at the Games Convention, Leipzig

Space Invaders launches on iOS

Space Invaders Infinity Gene launches on PS3 and Xbox 360

2006 – 2008 – 2009 – 2010

» [PS2] Known as *Space Raiders* in Japan, this was rebranded here as *Space Invaders: Invasion Day*. It's not particularly memorable, either.

about gameplay and she thrived. The same was true of other developers.

"Skill, risk and strategy," affirms David Perry of the lessons taught. "The feeling that each time you play, you feel you're getting better; the rewards for taking risks. *Space Invaders* really was ahead of its time."

David draws attention to the fact that players could not hide the whole game. They had to keep popping out into danger or risk being exposed when the barriers were destroyed or killed if the aliens got too close. "The fact that you could attack in any order and use bases for cover allowed for strategy and the two most clever parts were that things sped up, forcing you to rethink your strategy of how to handle the last invaders," he says. "And that was before you saw the glorious strategy disrupter – the spaceship."

» [PlayStation] The intro to *Space Invaders* on the PlayStation made multiple knowing references to the original game.

» [Wii] Made available as WiiWare, *Space Invaders Get Even* allowed players to control the aliens.

The coin-ops themselves were another disrupter. The emergence of the arcades proved crucial in getting people interested in videogames and it could be argued that gaming and *Space Invaders* may not have become so big had they not been introduced in such a way.

"The immense success of the *Space Invaders* arcade cabinet saw competitive gaming enter new and often unexpected locations for its time, such as shops and restaurants," argues Marie Foulston, curator of the V&A's Videogames: Design/Play/Disrupt Exhibition. Jason Fitzpatrick, curator and chief executive officer of the Centre For Computing History in Cambridge, agrees, "They didn't have a strong barrier to entry – players could put 10p in a machine and play without having to invest in expensive home computers or consoles. The arcades had a feel about them and an atmosphere that people enjoyed. Games were instantly social."

Even so, *Space Invaders* did land in people's homes. In 1980, Atari had grabbed an exclusive licence for the game, making it the first arcade game to be ported on to a console. It appeared on the VCS, later known as the 2600, and became a hit, helping to quadruple sales of the machine three years after it was launched.

"Probably the biggest masterstroke was cementing *Space Invaders* into people's homes by porting it to the 2600," Iain says. "By bringing a half-decent version of an arcade experience onto the first truly popular home videogame console, it embedded itself into living rooms as well as arcades."

» David Perry cofounded Shiny Entertainment.

For Atari cofounder Nolan Bushnell, it was another feather in his cap. Already successful in the arcades himself thanks to *Pong*, he had pulled off a coup, even though he was initially sceptical of it. "*Space Invaders* gave me further humility on how to judge a good game," Nolan tells us. "When I first played it I didn't think much of it but clearly I was massively wrong. It made me realise that you have to be careful of quick judgments about a game – you need to play it enough to make an accurate judgment. It became one of my favourite games."

> "IT HAD THE CORRECT BALANCE BETWEEN RISK AND REWARD"
>
> Nolan Bushnell

Suddenly a Japanese-made game was propelling an American-created console to great heights and *Space Invaders* began to enjoy a second wind. "It was probably the first videogame that had both dynamic and narrative development," Nolan continues. "It had the correct balance between risk and reward."

Just as with the arcade coin-op, the home console version proved encouraging. "It inspired a new generation of people to get into games development and coding," Mark says. "The music and sound effects in *Space Invaders* were influential on the future of games development, showing what a background score which reacts to development within the game can do for the experience. People recognise that these developments had a huge impact and *Space Invaders* is held in high regard as a creative turning point."

It had a big effect on people such as Jenna Seiden who was eight years old when *Space Invaders* launched on the Atari 2600. She eventually became the former vice-president of content development and strategic partnerships at Microsoft Studios, and then the head of content acquisition at the gaming distribution platform Ultra. "*Space Invaders* hit all the right notes and it became iconic the moment it landed on the shelf," she says, "It combined the successful shoot and destroy mechanics of previous titles with more intense graphics, and it was an inspiration for gamers like me."

Jenna says the game became an icon because it moved the industry into one of the first examples of storytelling in videogaming. "I did love the double bullets if you held the reset button while you turned the 2600 on, and I liked getting my phalanx-narrowing on, but it was truly the fact that *Space Invaders* spawned the next phase of iconic titles like *Galaga* and *Asteroids* that also resonated with the marketplace."

Space Invaders also impacted on the Japanese development scene. "*Space Invaders*' success stimulated many companies in Japan to embark on game developments," says Nishikado. "The rapid growth of the game industry threw up some masterpieces and developed the consumer game

A new species of arachnid is named 'Taito spaceinvaders' — 2014

Space Invaders appears in the Adam Sandler movie *Pixels* — 2015

The *Space Invaders Frenzy* coin-op dwarfs gamers in the arcades — 2017

field from which the Famicom, or NES, was born. When the Famicom became a global hit, it was clear Japanese videogames were taking the world by storm." As for *Space Invaders*, its legacy was set in stone.

» Marie Foulston curated the Design/Play/Disrupt exhibition.

The game grossed $2 billion in less than four years and, as Mark argues, "it demonstrated that the emerging entertainment industry was big enough to rival film and music". Big companies were keen to associate themselves with the game. But unlike those who worked in rival industries, Nishikado did not achieve personal fame for a few years, with Taito's policy being to hide the creators.

» Atari cofounder Nolan Bushnell.

"I don't think that I felt frustrated at the time, but I had some small sad and envious feelings when I encountered the individual names of videogame creators of other manufacturers later on in magazines," Nishikado says. "I feel happy that nowadays disclosing their individual names is quite natural and common sense."

French street artist Invader has peppered cities across the world with depictions of the *Space Invaders* aliens that he creates out of square ceramic tiles. People also often use pseudonyms to take part in *Space Invaders* competitions (although Frank Tetro was more than happy to be named when, aged 14, he hit the headlines for achieving an incredible 110,125 points in the National *Space Invaders* Superbowl of 1980).

Crucially, the name *Space Invaders* has become ubiquitous and it remains on the tip of people's tongues. "The visual design of space invaders is a universal iconic shorthand for 'videogames'," says Iain. "Even if only by that measure, it's hugely relevant." *

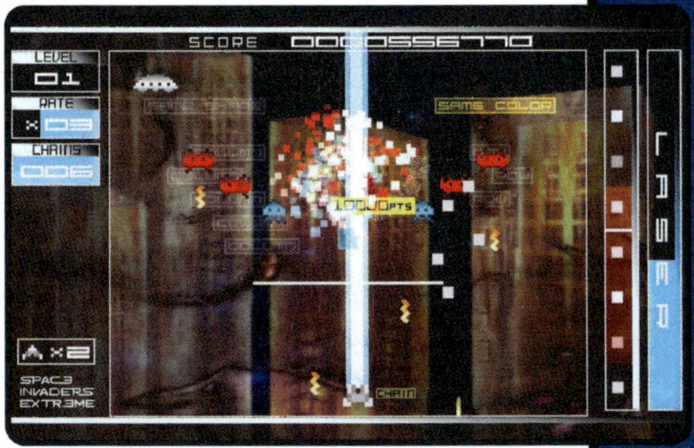

» [Xbox 360] Launched for Xbox Live Arcade, *Space Invaders Extreme* saw revamped graphics as well as new visualisers created by Jeff Minter.

MARKING 40 YEARS

How Taito and Square Enix celebrated four decades of Space Invaders

To celebrate the 40th anniversary of *Space Invaders* in 2018, Taito's parent company Square Enix planned and developed four attractions. They brought the game to life like never before, starting with the amazing *Play! Space Invaders* Exhibit in January which took place at in the Roppongi district of Tokyo, Japan.

» *Space Invaders* being projected against a backdrop of the night sky is an no-brainer, really.

The highlight was *Space Invaders Gigamax*, an impressively huge, wide installation that projected the game onto the windows of a building and allowed up to ten players to enjoy the classic title against the backdrop of Tokyo. It proved to be a sight to behold, with the invaders making their way towards the city's streets as gamers sought to blast them away.

Another exhibit created by Square Enix was *Arkinvaders* which projected the game onto the floor and introduced elements of *Arkanoid*. Here, players attempted to destroy the aliens by kicking digital circles at them while trying to prevent the weapons falling off the playing field. It was energetic and fun and an artistic spin on age-old gameplay that feels fresh.

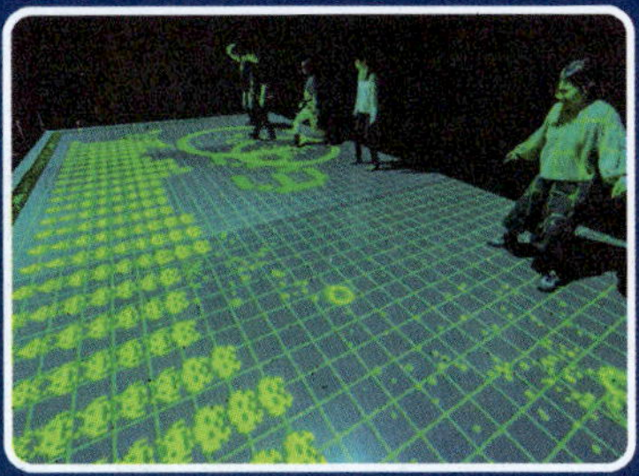

» The simple design of *Space Invaders* invites many innovative ideas on how to play the game.

More sweat-inducing was *Noborinvaders* which was projected against a climbing wall. As the players climbed, invaders appeared on the various boulders, meaning players had to position themselves close and reach out to touch them, thereby removing the aliens from the playing area and racking up the points.

Finally, there was *Bahamut Disco*, a mind-bending experience which projected the game onto a 360-degree screen. Four players picked a colour of alien and used Vive VR controllers to swat them away as they appeared, all soundtracked to a disco beat. Since it didn't need a virtual reality device, Square Enix said it offered a new way of playing with VR hardware.

» The art and iconography of the arcade classic lends itself perfectly to a unique art exhibit.

THE 1980s

A DECADE OF EXPANDING HORIZONS AND ARTISTIC AMBITION

Over the course of the Eighties, games began to flourish as a rounded creative medium. As hardware capabilities increased, the depth and storytelling possibilities of text-based games became available to graphical games. Meanwhile, companies created more compelling characters, birthing a generation of popular mascots like Bomberman, Dizzy and Mega Man. Where game presentation at the beginning of the decade was often functional, often showing just enough to ensure the game functioned, by the end of the decade we were treated to rich, detailed 2D scenes with animated backgrounds, and musical accompaniments that would linger in the memory for decades.

GAMES OF THE DECADE

1980 PAC-MAN

As one of the first ever gaming mascots, *Pac-Man* achieved fame and inspired music, cartoons and all manner of merchandise. But Namco's game design deserves praise, too – the act of munching a power pellet and turning the tables on your aggressors felt magnificent back then, and still feels fantastic today.

1981 DONKEY KONG

Nintendo's arcade hit pioneered the platform game as we know it, and also introduced a couple of characters you may have heard of: Donkey Kong and Mario. The fierce challenge of the game is famous, and despite its age, the battle for high scores ensures that it maintains a fierce competitive scene.

1982 PITFALL!

David Crane's platform game was a smash hit, and deserved the success it received for making fantastic use of the Atari 2600 hardware. But it was also vindication for Activision, which was formed by ex-Atari coders who felt that they deserved recognition for their skill and creativity as game developers.

1983 DRAGON'S LAIR

This LaserDisc arcade game was stunning, combining amazing Don Bluth animation with player interaction. Players were bowled over by the game's visuals and more LaserDisc games followed, but the trend waned as the Eighties progressed. You can feel echoes of its game design in modern quick time events sequences.

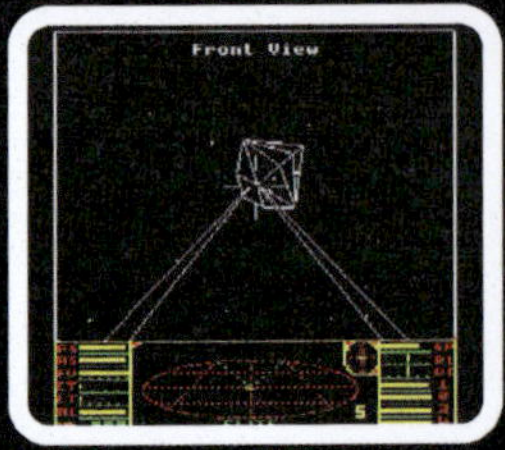

1984 ELITE

When David Braben and Ian Bell put this space trading game together, they gave many players their first taste of freedom in videogames – *Elite* enabled you to choose where you went in the galaxy, who you attacked and how you made your money. Many youngsters did just that, for hours and hours at a time.

1980
Doug and Gary Carlston start Brøderbund Software. Its first game is *Galactic Empire* for the TRS-80. The studio will become known for its 8-bit games.

1980
Phoenix drops into arcades and is one of the first videogames to showcase boss battles. A home conversion will surface in 1982.

1980
The dungeon-crawler *Rogue* launches. It will inspire scores of similarly styled videogames that become known as 'roguelikes'.

1980 JANUARY
The Sinclair ZX80 is released by Science Of Cambridge and is one of the first computers to be sold for less than £100.

1980 FEBRUARY
HAL Laboratory is founded by Mitsuhiro Ikeda. While it will stay independent, it will be known for its close work with Nintendo.

THE EIGHTIES…

AS TOLD BY TRIP HAWKINS

THE ELECTRONIC ARTS FOUNDER OPENS UP ON A PIVOTAL DECADE FOR GAMING AS AN ART FORM AND A BUSINESS

For Trip, the Eighties was defined by a drive towards videogames as an art form. But the high cost of arcade games kept them out of the home, and the low cost of consoles limited their power – in both cases, limiting the depth that could be offered. "Even then, an 8-bit home computer like the Apple II was way more powerful and could offer legitimate artistic expression and detailed simulations," he explains. "I was at Apple when the Eighties began and we were making even more amazing 'art' with our 16-bit system prototypes. This is when I realised software would become an art form and go well beyond being just a way to kill time. I knew the industry would follow in the footsteps of Hollywood and I set out to create a 'New Hollywood'." With so many systems in competition, Trip built his new Hollywood on the foundation of two key CPUs. "The 6502 was in everything from the Apple II to the C64 to the NES, doing huge volumes. The 68000 was in the Mac, Amiga, Atari ST, Sega Mega Drive and many coin-op machines," he explains. "The PC clones were an important market but for EA, the 6502 carried the revenue while the 68000 bridged the technology to the next leap, which was the Sega Mega Drive."

In those early days, there was still plenty of trendsetting to be done. "Electronic Arts' biggest risk was in pioneering its own distribution network – no software publisher had ever done that and it almost killed us," explains Trip. This had a knock-on creative effect, though. "It got me to think more outside the box because we needed more games to cover the overhead. We got into more game genrés, began the affiliated label program, acquired other brands and began to build internal studios. Tim Mott ingeniously noticed that our development tool, Deluxe Paint, could be a great consumer paintbox product, and that led to a big line-up of creativity tools and helped pioneer that new category."

Of course, there was plenty of other groundbreaking software coming from all sources. "Pinball Construction Set was the first big source of inspiration because it had one of the first 'what you see is what you get' interfaces, stunning interactive art, it allowed players to be creative and gave birth to the concept of user-generated content. I loved *Archon* and *MULE* because they were the birth of social gaming, and are still classics. Flight simulators and *Sim City* proved that games have powerful, interactive educational value," says Trip, though his heart lies with EA's biggest brand. "EA Sports was the most meaningful breakthrough for me personally, as it was my true passion."

1985 SUPER MARIO BROS

Nintendo's platform adventure was an incredible first game for any NES owner. The level design was challenging but fair, the graphics and music conveyed an excellent sense of place, and it was filled with secrets. But what was best was how Mario controlled – with a little weight and surprising agility, but always precisely.

1986 OUT RUN

Sega's masterful driving game was one of the finest of the simulator-style arcade cabinets that emerged during the mid-Eighties. But even in a standard cabinet, the scaling sprites were amazing and the music was so good that rather than being simple background accompaniment, it was a featured aspect of the game.

1987 DUNGEON MASTER

FTL Games' pioneering RPG combined atmospheric 3D dungeons with real-time elements rather than traditional turn-based battles, making for one of the most engrossing experiences of the 16-bit era. A wave of clones followed, including *Bloodwych, Chaos Strikes Back, Black Crypt* and *Eye Of The Beholder.*

1988 DRAGON QUEST III

Enix's JRPG series is one of the genre's elder statesmen, and this sequel improved on its forebears with day/night cycles, the ability to choose your party composition and greater openness. The game was a cultural phenomenon in its homeland, with players picking up over a million copies on the first day of release.

1989 POPULOUS

Bullfrog's spin on strategy gaming saw you trying to create hospitable conditions for your followers, so that they might grow in number, fuel your divine powers and eventually wipe out the followers of a rival deity. This innovative template was the first real example of the 'god game' genre we know today.

1980 APRIL
Ball, the first game for the Game & Watch range of electronic handheld toys is released by Nintendo. More will follow.

1980 MAY
Oxford graduates Tony Milner and Tony Baden establish the 8-bit developer Bug-Byte Software.

1980 MAY
Namco releases *Puck-Man* in Japan. It will arrive in the US in October this year with the more familiar name of *Pac-Man*.

1980 JUNE
Commodore releases its 8-bit VIC-20. In Germany it's renamed the VC-20 as 'VIC' can be interpreted as an expletive.

1980 JULY
Dave Theurer's *Missile Command* hits arcades and draws comparisons with the real-life Cold War that is taking place.

THE WILD WEST

1

4

5

2

3

Image by Ruben de Rijcke

The Eighties was a time of enormous diversity in videogames, as distinct regional markets and market turbulence allowed a multitude of companies to experience local success, with few truly global trends to be found. Consoles were dismissed as a passing fad in North America following a market crash, but the ruin of domestic companies allowed Japanese competitors to fill the void. In Europe, microcomputers rose to prominence instead, giving rise to a generation of creators. As the decade came to a close, console manufacturers began to introduce handheld devices, doing for videogames what the Walkman had done for music.

1. MASTER SYSTEM

Sega, 1985

Although Sega's 8-bit console was named Mark III in Japan, reflecting its position as an evolution of the SG-1000 line, it was really a generational leap. Though some players in Japan and North America remember it fondly, primarily for conversions of arcade games like *Out Run* and *Shinobi*, it struggled due to difficulty in attracting third-party developers. However, strong regional support made the Master System a favourite of European and South American players, where its lifespan continued into the *Sonic* era.

2. PC

IBM, 1981

IBM's hardware specification for the original PC was open – so open, in fact, that it was incredibly easy for rival manufacturers to create clone systems, which used Microsoft's MS-DOS operating system to run compatible software. The only proprietary component of the PC was its BIOS, which was soon reverse engineered. However, IBM's loss was gaming's gain, as rapidly improving graphics capabilities allowed the format to catch up to and overtake other home computers, eventually gaining dominance in the Nineties. The emergence of an open platform for both hardware and software vendors birthed today's PC market, and the PC has essentially become an 'eternal' platform – though hardware and operating systems change, the lineage can easily be traced back to IBM's original machine.

3. ZX SPECTRUM

Sinclair Research, 1982

Sir Clive Sinclair's earlier home computers had achieved success due to their low price, and the introduction of colour graphics really put the ZX Spectrum over the top. The system became popular in the UK and elsewhere in Europe, where children convinced their parents that a computer would help with school work, and even achieved a rare feat by surviving the demise of its parent company. The system remained popular until the early Nineties, when more powerful systems finally supplanted it.

4. COMMODORE 64

Commodore, 1982

After innovating in the low-cost home computer market with the popular VIC-20, Commodore developed a machine that became the bestselling single computer model of all time. Chip manufacturer MOS Technology developed the system's VIC-II graphics chip and renowned SID sound chip with games in mind, and Commodore's ownership of the company allowed it to build the C64 very cheaply. Commodore was therefore able to drop prices to levels many competitors couldn't match. Fuelled by the boom in bedroom coding, the games market exploded and the system was a popular platform for players until the early Nineties. The computer was discontinued in 1994, just prior to Commodore's bankruptcy. Sales estimates vary, between 12.5 million and 17 million units sold.

5. MEGA DRIVE

Sega, 1988

Sega's 16-bit console had a slow start in the market, with limited popularity in Japan and a slow release schedule. It gained an early audience in the west for its great arcade conversions and sports games, but aggressive marketing and *Sonic The Hedgehog* really helped the Mega Drive to break through. However, the Mega-CD and 32X hardware upgrades were expensive and under-supported, damaging consumer trust. Over 30 million Mega Drives were sold, of which over 85% were bought outside Japan.

6. AMIGA 500

Commodore, 1987

Although Commodore's 16-bit Amiga platform was introduced in 1985, this revision was the first model targeted at home users. It still wasn't as cheap as its rival, the Atari ST, but it had top class multimedia capabilities that made it better for games. As the price came down and strong bundles like the *Batman Pack* hit the market, the Amiga 500 gained ground and became Commodore's best-selling model of the computer. The system's primary popularity was in European markets.

7. AMSTRAD CPC

Amstrad, 1984

The design philosophy behind the debut computer from Alan Sugar's company was simple: get everything into one unit, make it simple to set up and make it affordable. It achieved

1980 OCTOBER
Andrew Hewson forms publisher Hewson Consultants which goes on to work with many prolific British coders.

1980 NOVEMBER
The wireframe vector graphics arcade tank shooter *Battlezone* rolls into arcades courtesy of Atari.

1980 DECEMBER
Infocom's innovative text adventure *Zork* is commercially released. More games in the series are planned.

1981 FEBRUARY
Konami's iconic *Scramble* makes its arcade debut and inspires many aspiring shoot-'em-up developers worldwide.

1981 MARCH
Sinclair follows up its ZX80 with the ZX81. It goes on sale in kit form to be put together by the buyer or preassembled.

6

7

8

9

those goals, and the hardware was capable of wonderfully colourful, chunky graphics. However, it never overcame the head start that the Commodore 64 and Spectrum had in the marketplace, and frequently received underwhelming Spectrum ports as both systems used a Z80 CPU. Over 2 million computers were sold in Europe.

8. NES

Nintendo, 1983

The first major home console from Nintendo was introduced to Japan as the Famicom and sold well there, and basically revived consoles in the North American market. Though the system was technically rather limited, cartridges often expanded its capabilities, allowing the system to remain viable well into the Nineties. Popular series like *Zelda* and *Metroid* began here, not to mention the *Super Mario Bros* franchise. 61.9 million consoles were sold, over 85 per cent of which were bought in Japan and North America.

9. LYNX

Atari Corp, 1989

The Lynx was an astonishingly capable piece of hardware designed by ex-Amiga engineers at Epyx – the first ever full-colour handheld console, capable of advanced graphical techniques like sprite scaling. The system's innovative ability to run with the d-pad on either side was also welcome. Unfortunately, the system was large and ran through batteries at an astonishing rate, and Atari struggled to attract external developers, leading to frequent barren release schedules. Just 3 million units were sold.

10. GAME BOY

Nintendo, 1989

With its monochromatic graphics, Nintendo's handheld didn't have the benefit of dazzling presentation. What it did have was the right technology for the job – it was cheaper than the colour rivals it would compete with, and offered considerably better battery life. The system hosted numerous early classics, including the compelling pack-in *Tetris* and *Super Mario Land*. The Game Boy would later host the likes of *Kirby's Dream Land* and *The Legend Of Zelda: Link's Awakening*, but its portable nature was best exploited by *Pokémon*, a truly social role-playing game that swept playgrounds across the world in the late Nineties. 64.4 million systems were sold before the introduction of the Game Boy Color, solidifying handheld gaming as a viable market.

10

OTHER SYSTEMS FROM THE EIGHTIES

BBC Micro • Acorn, 1981

Though many used it in schools, the high price of Acorn's computer made it a less popular choice for home users.

ColecoVision • Coleco, 1982

This system promised a generational leap over the likes of the Atari 2600, but was cut down in its prime by the market crash.

Vectrex • GCE, 1982

A built-in vector monitor allowed this console to deliver authentic arcade experiences, but the videogame crash killed it. It's still popular with collectors, though.

Atari ST • Atari Corp, 1985

The first truly affordable 16-bit computer was popular in Europe, but lost steam as the rival Amiga's price dropped.

PC Engine • NEC, 1987

Boasting strong graphical performance and a tiny form factor, NEC's console was popular in Japan and spawned the UK's import market.

1981 JUNE
Origin's role-playing game *Ultima* is released on Apple II and Konami's classic *Frogger* debuts in arcades.

1981 JULY
Nintendo's *Donkey Kong* bounds into arcades and kicks off a score chase that will persist for decades after its release.

1981 AUGUST
International Business Machines launches its 5150 IBM Personal Computer. Solidifying what will become a 'PC'.

1981 SEPTEMBER
Muse Software's *Castle Wolfenstein* creeps to market showing stealth and World War II can be harnessed in games.

1981 NOVEMBER
Computer & Video Games becomes the first British games magazine. *Space Invaders* features on the first issue's cover.

» Eighties bedroom coder David Jones (right) donating his development system to the Centre For Computing History.

1981
NOVEMBER
Computer Gaming World magazine launches in the United States, kicking off a long run which will last up to 2006.

1981
DECEMBER
The BBC Micro home computer is released in the United Kingdom. Developer David Braben pays attention.

1982
Jeff Minter forms his software house, Llamasoft. The studio would make a name for itself by producing outlandish, arcade-style games.

1982
Programmer Sid Meier and ex-pilot Bill Stealey set up MicroProse. Three games debut: *Floyd Of The Jungle*, *Chopper Rescue* and *Hellcat Ace*.

1982
Arcade game designers Tim and Chris Stamper start up their own company, Ultimate Play The Game, in Ashby-De-La-Zouch.

RISE OF THE BEDROOM CODER

Home coding began in the early Seventies and continues to this day, but the indie developers of the Eighties were special. Discover how a generation of young computer enthusiasts rebuilt the games industry from their bedrooms

WORDS BY RORY MILNE

By 1983, the golden age of US arcade gaming was waning, and the videogame crash had decimated America's slice of the industry. The meagre output of UK and European coin-op and console developers did little to negate this implosion, and the Japanese games industry was largely focused on its home market. But as seasoned developer David Perry explains, an unlikely solution to this seemingly hopeless situation lay in the hands of youthful home computer owners. "I grew up in the middle of nowhere, and it was freezing cold outside!" David says of his northern Irish childhood. "So I got a ZX81, and I had a little black-and-white TV in my bedroom. I was making these little games, and I sent one to *Interface* magazine. As a kid I was just so excited to be in a magazine, but I didn't understand that I was going to be paid. I think my first cheque was for £450. That was something that I wasn't expecting, and it turned me into a bedroom coder."

Industry legend John Romero tells a similar story, although he grew up in the States and favoured a US computer to a British one. "When my parents finally got an Apple II at home I was basically *done* going outside," John recalls. "The only place I had to code was my bedroom. Publishers were just people in their houses, they didn't have internal teams, and the games they were publishing were made by indies from their bedrooms."

Like David Perry, John's first published game appeared as a type-in listing in a magazine. More followed, and soon the schoolboy developer was coding around the clock to the detriment of his studies. "I made 60 games in the Eighties, plus I had to go to high school!" John laughs. "I was writing code on paper in class, and I barely got out of school because I didn't do any school work. Bedroom coding was all about self-motivation and learning on your own, and the only thing that I could use to judge how well I was doing was the commercial games I was playing."

Budget game specialists Philip and Andrew Oliver took a similar approach to their educations as John Romero when they first started making games, and their hours spent programming only increased after they left school. "When we were at school it was juggling coding and schoolwork, doing the bare minimum of homework and just scraping through exams," Philip remembers. "The minute we left school it was alarm clocks on at seven o'clock in the morning and working through to one or two in the morning. That was every day, seven days a week, 365 days a year – including Christmas."

Rather than creating magazine type-ins, like John Romero and David Perry, or posting games off to publishers, like the Olivers, acclaimed developer Steve Crow had his early efforts released by a family friend's commercial software firm. "I started writing videogames at school, and I had a friend called Justin Whisker," Steve reminisces. "His dad was a banker, and he was going to set up this company where I would get 49%. My dad said: 'Let me run this by one of my friends,' and his friend said: 'You don't want to do that, because you won't have any ownership of it.' But this friend did business software, and he said: 'Me and my partner will fund Steve.'"

While Steve was still at school, a slightly older David Jones had started work as a trainee surveyor, although a subsequent redundancy saw him turn his coding hobby into a profession. "I'd moved back to living ▶

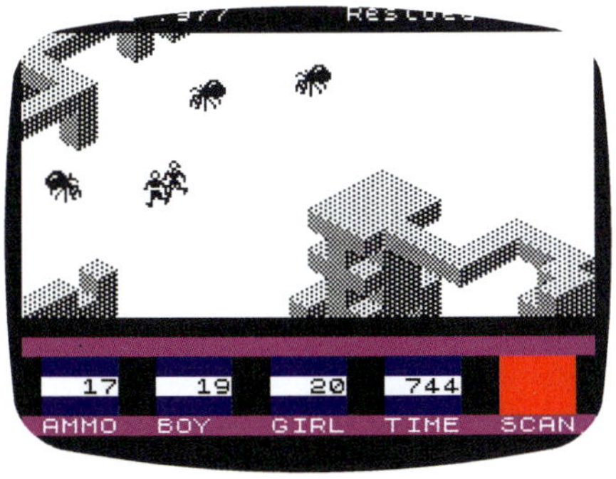

» [ZX Spectrum] The hero of Spectrum bedroom coder Sandy White's *Ant Attack* scarpers having rescued his girlfriend.

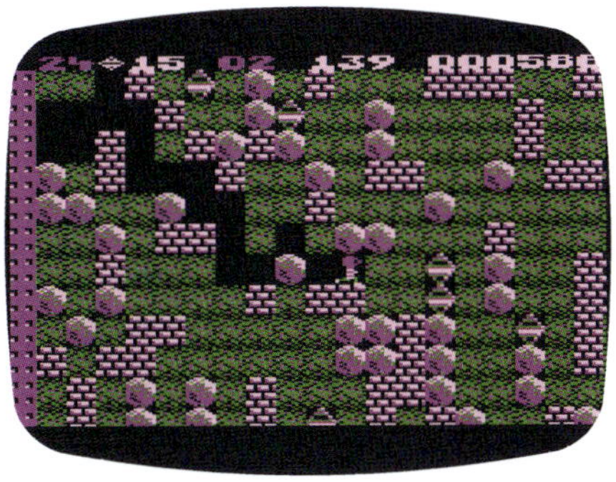

» [Atari 8-bit] Rockford takes a rest under a rock in Peter Liepa's home-coded debut, *Boulder Dash*.

» [Apple II] *Lode Runner*'s protagonist blows a hole in a game that Doug Smith started developing while at university.

1982 JANUARY
Sega harnesses the power of isometric graphics and fires its space shooter *Zaxxon* into arcades to great success.

1982 MARCH
Tod Frye's ambitious *Pac-Man* conversion munches onto the Atari 2600 and becomes a killer app for the console.

1982 APRIL
To coincide with the impressive new home computer, publisher EMAP's *Sinclair User* hits the newsstands.

1982 APRIL
The world is introduced to Pitfall Harry as Activision launches its jungle-themed platformer *Pitfall!* on the Atari 2600.

1982 APRIL
Sinclair Research's landmark computer, the ZX Spectrum, arrives in the UK and inspires scores of budding coders.

BUILT ON BEDROOM CODING

THE FIRMS THAT MADE BEDROOM CODING THEIR BUSINESS

LLAMASOFT

The trading name of surreal shoot-'em-up specialist Jeff Minter, Llamasoft alternated between self-publishing and freelancing for publishers during the Eighties, making home-baked classics like *Gridrunner* and the *Mutant Camel* series. Besides a few high-profile staff positions in the Nineties, Jeff has been a home coder ever since.

Brøderbund

Founded in 1980 by Doug and Gary Carlston, Brøderbund was set up with a view to selling the Apple II games that Doug was developing in his spare time. The company went onto publish some of the biggest US home-coded hits of the Eighties, including Dan Gorlin's *Choplifter!*, Doug Smith's *Lode Runner* and Jordan Mechner's *Karateka*.

HEWSON

Hewson had its own in-house development team, but the vast majority of its success came from working with freelance developers. Andrew Braybrook and Steve Turner were early signings, and as the Eighties unfolded bedroom coders like John Philips, Raffaele Cecco, Steve Crow, Jon Hare and Jeff Minter all graced the Hewson label.

MASTERTRONIC

Budget game pioneer Mastertronic originally sold half-decent titles for low prices, but as time went on, the quality of the firm's output markedly increased. The company didn't have its own in-house team, and instead published a wealth of indie coders, including big names like the Darling bothers, David Jones and Shaun Southern.

Code Masters

Founded by former bedroom coders David and Richard Darling, Codemasters rapidly expanded thanks to the Eighties' home coding scene. The firm secured talent like the Oliver twins – best known for their *Dizzy* series and simulator games, the latter of which became a Codemasters franchise that various indie coders contributed to.

with my parents, and I got word that someone was looking for a programmer to write games for them," David reflects. "That's how I met Albert Owen. The first game I wrote was *Bonkers*, but Ray never managed to get it sold properly, so when we started working on *Finders Keepers* he got in touch with Mastertronic, and it all went from there."

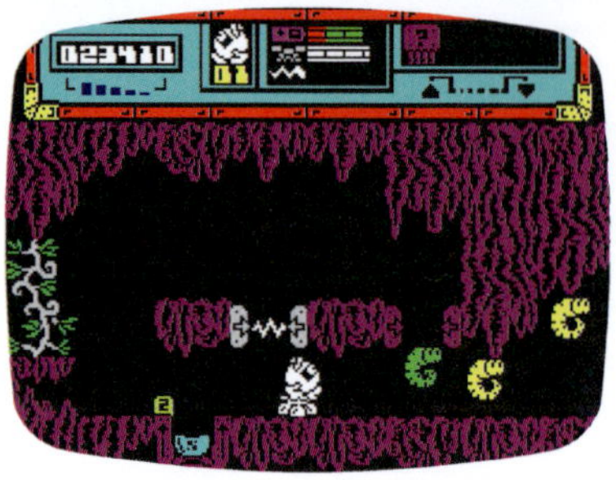

» [ZX Spectrum] A youthful Steve Crow coded all of his games from his bedroom rather than working in-house.

» [Apple II] Jordan Mechner spent years bedroom coding games before he got a publishing deal for *Karateka*.

As was common for Eighties bedroom coders, David thought nothing of working long hours, although he took advantage of his proximity to his publisher when the pressures of lone working got to him. "I would work from when I got up," David recalls, "and then when it got to evening time I'd start to get tired, and because it took ten minutes to assemble a game I got into the habit of lying down and getting a catnap. Then when it had finished I would wake myself up and carry on. So in terms of hours put in it was quite a lot, and quite intense. But it was fun, except every now and then I'd get a bit fed up working on my own, and so I'd go into the Mastertronic office where people would encourage me."

At around the same time, a teenaged Steve Crow was struggling to find himself a supportive publisher after a deal with his father's friend to release his games came to an end. "I was halfway through *Wizard's Lair*, but I couldn't get anyone to publish it," he sighs. "I was at the point where I was just going to put it on the front of *Crash* magazine. I had companies like British Telecom saying: 'Oh, we'll give you £2,000 for it,' but I was thinking I'd rather give it away than accept peanuts. Then, finally, Bubble Bus gave me an offer with a proper royalty. Bubble Bus was just in the next town over from me, and it did really well with *Wizard's Lair*."

Unlike Steve Crow and David Jones, the mid-Eighties saw David Perry leave bedroom coding behind in favour of an in-house position with a publisher, but two years later he went freelance with artist Nick Bruty. "We built benches in a bedroom at my mother's house, and the two of us worked there," David notes. "Nick was a game-changer, because not only was he amazing at art, but he also had lots of really good ideas. We found that every time we did a licensed game it would end up helping us, so we would pop in and out of doing that and then do our own things as well, and that was really fun."

As the Eighties drew to a close, John Romero took a staff job too, but he spent his spare time bedroom coding and setting up id Software. "We were working at Softdisk, and then when I went home I was programming more games, and selling those back to Softdisk," John beams. "By 1992, we were making *Wolfenstein*, literally in a bedroom, because we finally got an apartment just for the company."

The Olivers' first experience of studio development came in the early Nineties, although a year of this convinced them to give bedroom coding a second chance. "We had bought a flat in Leamington Spa, and we were driving into work everyday at Codemasters' 'portacabins'," Philip grimaces. "We thought they were *horrible*, so we decided to work at the flat. But there was no artist, so we invited an old school friend who had done an art degree to live there and do the art for us. But that started to get a bit tight, especially since we both ended up getting girlfriends! So we went and got an office."

It was the mid-Nineties before talented coder/artist Steve Crow traded bedroom development for a studio position, but before then he decided to focus on creating game art, following the trying development of *Firelord* for Hewson Consultants. "Andrew Hewson used to go around his contract people, and I remember him visiting once or twice at my house when I was working out of my bedroom," Steve recollects. "I just did graphics for Hewson after that, and all of the people who worked there were awesome. Guys like Mark Cummings, and Dominic Robinson who did *Zynaps*, were just super cool."

Like Steve, *Earthworm Jim* coder David Perry has some great memories

» [Amstrad CPC] Dizzy finds a coin in the Oliver twins' homemade hit platformer *Fantasy World Dizzy*.

» [C64] Classics like *Nebulus* and *Eliminator* were developed by John Philips while he was a bedroom developer.

1982 MAY
Two high rollers swing onto the scene as Electronic Arts and Lucasfilm Games are founded.

1982 JULY
Namco accelerates *Pole Position* into Japanese arcades and it becomes a big winner for the developer.

1982 AUGUST
A big month for hardware as the ColecoVision console and Commodore 64 home computer go on sale.

1982 AUGUST
First Star Software is formed by Richard Spitalny and its first game, the shooter *Astro Chase*, follows soon after.

1982 SEPTEMBER
Another company enters the market as Imagine Software is founded by Mark Butler and David Lawson.

> “The best part was that we could make anything we wanted. You saw that in our games; they were just an explosion of ideas”

DAVID PERRY

» The Oliver twins hard at work in their bedroom development studio, circa 1988.

> “The only place I had to code was my bedroom. Publishers were just people in their houses, they didn't have internal teams”

JOHN ROMERO

of the bedroom coding era of the Eighties, although he remembers the tech of the time less fondly. “The best part was that we could make anything we wanted,” David grins. “You saw that in our games; they were just an explosion of ideas. But the equipment back then was pretty flaky. So when my television started to act wonky I had to hit it to make it work again. Each time I would have to hit it a little bit harder, and I would end up having to hit it with a telephone book just to finish a project! ”

When asked for his thoughts, the co-creator of the *Dizzy* games, Philip Oliver, argues that Eighties bedroom coding wasn't all good, but he concedes that there were highs as well as lows. “It was a really fun time when you look back on it,” he considers, “but when you were actually doing the work it was horrible. There were a few nice bits. Taking cheques down to the local bank once a quarter was a high point. They were over £10,000 each, because our games had started to sell.”

Former Mastertronic star programmer David Jones offers an equally bittersweet assessment of the golden years of bedroom coding, tinged with regret that he wasn't able to put off taking a studio job. “Bedroom coding was about individuals who put the effort into the technical side having the opportunity to express themselves in a new medium,” David observes. “I miss the bedroom coding era, and I would have been a bedroom coder for a lot longer if things hadn't changed all around me.”

Given the final word, John Romero is unequivocally positive about the Eighties bedroom coding movement that reinvigorated the games industry, which perhaps explains his on-going commitment to bedroom development. “I *loved* the Eighties bedroom coding era,” John enthuses. “There was no internet, and you were as focused as a human could be. But what I really liked, and I'm still doing this today, was being able to experiment with stuff and take chances at home that you would never do at a company.” *

» [C64] Bedroom coders the Rowlands brothers supported the C64 long after the system's commercial prime.

BRILLIANT BEDROOM CODERS

INDUSTRY VETERANS THAT HAD HUMBLE BEGINNINGS

DAVID DARLING

After self-publishing coin-op clones in the early Eighties, David and his brother Richard began freelancing for Mastertronic, and by 1985 they owned half of the company. The brothers next went independent with Codemasters, and built it up by publishing games created by bedroom coders. David is now CEO of the app developer Kwalee.

JORDAN MECHNER

Best-known for developing Apple II hits *Karateka* and *Prince Of Persia* as a young bedroom coder, Jordan Mechner went on to design various follow-ups to his rotoscoped platformer, as well as working with Ubisoft to help reboot the series in 2003. The developer is currently contributing to a book about the making of the original *Prince Of Persia*.

ARCHER MACLEAN

Archer Maclean wasn't prolific during the Eighties, but the quality of the then-youthful coder's games more than made up for this. His debut *Dropzone* was a fresh take on the coin-op *Defender*, and *International Karate* redefined the beat-'em-up. Archer next focused on pool and snooker titles, before founding his own firm in 1997.

DAVID BRABEN

Although David Braben could have retired from games development a rich man after co-creating *Elite* with Ian Bell while the two were students at Cambridge University, he instead went on to work on the Archimedes launch title *Zarch*, and then the *Elite* sequel *Frontier*. David next set up Frontier Developments, where he is still CEO today.

GEOFF CRAMMOND

After developing a *Space Invaders* tribute and a spitfire simulator on a part-time basis, Geoff Crammond became a full-time home coder and created the BBC Micro classics *Revs* and *The Sentinel*. Geoff then produced *Stunt Car Racer* for the 16-bits, and spent the next ten years making his popular *Grand Prix* series for PCs.

1982 OCTOBER
Atari's lacklustre Atari 2600 follow-up, the 5200, launches and the NEC PC-98 makes its debut.

1982 NOVEMBER
The Vectrex, gaming's coolest vector graphics-powered console arrives, but it's lifespan will sadly be short-lived.

1982 NOVEMBER
Access Software is formed by mechanical engineer Bruce Carver and businessman Chris Jones.

1982 DECEMBER
America's infamous videogame crash starts to rear its head, and its ramifications will be felt for the following years.

1983
Budget game specialist Mastertronic and developer Ocean Software (which was originally known as Spectrum Games) both form.

JET SET WILLY

IN THE BEDROOM WITH MATTHEW SMITH

WE SPOKE (AND DRANK) WITH JET SET WILLY CREATOR MATTHEW SMITH, THE ARCHETYPAL EIGHTIES BEDROOM CODER, IN THE VERY HOUSE WHERE HE WROTE HIS MASTERPIECE

WORDS BY PAUL DRURY

Matthew Smith seems conflicted about the Eighties. "It was hell from start to finish," he says, glancing round the bedroom where he spent a fair amount of those years. "Even the music was shit. Anyway, isn't nostalgia the death of the soul?"

Yet even as he decries the decade which he is most associated with, thanks to his pair of Spectrum classics *Manic Miner* and *Jet Set Willy*, we are listening to an Echo And The Bunnymen Peel Session from 1983 and he's been reminiscing fondly about the sweet and sour sauce as we eat a Chinese bought from the same takeaway he frequented back then. Most intriguingly, when we ask him if he was impressed by the Eighties period detail in the interactive *Black Mirror* episode *Bandersnatch*, he replies, "I didn't notice it. I thought everything was still like that."

It's not clear whether he's joking, and it won't be the last time over the weekend he leaves us in doubt. We have travelled up to the family home in Liverpool to drink Guinness, talk about Miner Willy and then accompany Matthew to Manchester in the morning, where he is scheduled to appear at a Play Expo event. The plan tonight is to take a tour through Willy's mansion and for its author to comment on each of its 60 rooms, but now we feel awkward for asking him to recall a time he plainly did not enjoy. "Oh I've been sick of this shit since 1986," he says, taking a large swig of Guinness, "but go on, press play."

Thankfully, as soon as the title appears, displaying that Penrose Triangle, Matthew grins. "Ah, yeah, apparently Roger Penrose showed that to Escher and it inspired some of his paintings."

An impossible shape opening a game set in an impossible building which turned out to be impossible to complete. Rather apt, we suggest.

"It was a nod to the whole process of producing the game," he replies, his eyes flicking from screen to glass to ceiling. "If I was flaunting anything, it was I could program the impossible!"

As we revisit each room in Willy's sprawling mansion over the next few hours – you can read his recollections in a **Retro Gamer** issue 201 – he is at times witty and insightful, at others, vague or even dismissive. "Look at that," he tuts, as we arrive at the First Landing, "Three quarters black space. When I see some of the screens now, I do think… well, not, 'Why didn't I do more?' but I have bad memories remembering *why* I didn't do more."

> "If I was flaunting anything, it was I could program the impossible!"
> MATTHEW SMITH

He's referring to his experience as a director of Software Projects, the company he set up in 1983 with Alan Maton, an employee of Bug-Byte Software who had first published *Manic Miner*, and Tommy Barton, a local businessman. It's a tangled tale and the legal wrangling around who actually owns the rights to the Miner Willy games continues to this day but what is clear is that Matthew had a thoroughly miserable time through the five years it was in business.

» Matthew Smith is the coder of Spectrum classics *Manic Miner* and *Jet Set Willy*.

"Tommy was Grima Wormtongue, Alan was Saruman," remembers Matthew, in a rather cryptic JRR Tolkien reference before moving on to a Gilbert and Sullivan analogy. "Alan thought he was the Grand Poobah because he'd gone from being an employee at Bug-Byte to managing millions at Software Projects. I thought I was the Grand Poobah because I could produce the products. They kept hassling me to get the game done but I just couldn't get the equipment I needed from the company. It dragged on for eight months… and I wasn't getting paid. I didn't get anything for *Jet Set Willy*."

"But you were a director of the company, not an employee," we say, as tactfully as we can. "You should have been drawing a salary."

"Nah, I was living on fresh air, a miracle boy," he says before reconsidering. "Nah, nah, I was a mushroom boy. I didn't need fresh air. I was kept in the dark and given shit." ▶

1983 John Howard Palevich's innovative dungeon-crawler *Dandy* (later known as *Dandy Dungeon*) is released on Atari 8-bit computers.

1983 JANUARY The third model in the Apple II range, the Apple IIe, is launched great acclaim. (The 'e' stands for 'enhanced'.)

1983 MARCH Richard and Robert Garriot's Origin Systems springs to life. Meanwhile, Steve Turner establishes Graftgold.

1983 MAY The force is strong with Atari's *Star Wars* coin-op which features a full cockpit and astonishing vector graphics.

1983 MAY ZX Spectrum gamers fall hard for Ultimate's *Jetpac*. VIC-20 and BBC Micro conversions will soon follow.

PRAISE FOR WILLY

FOUR SPECIAL FANS SHARE THEIR MEMORIES OF MATTHEW'S MASTERPIECE

CHRIS CANNON

CODER AT BUG-BYTE AND SOFTWARE PROJECTS

"Matt was the archetypal bedroom coder before Software Projects. He was everything you'd expect him to be. Clever, though relatively quiet about the fact, but would enthuse about the latest breakthrough he'd made and become almost overwhelmingly full of himself when things worked out. Yet he could quickly become introverted when a 'sure thing' blew up in his face!"

MARTYN CARROLL

LAUNCH EDITOR OF RETRO GAMER

"I know *Manic Miner* is a polished piece of work, but, for me, *JSW* will always be his masterpiece, flaws and all. Exploring Willy's mansion was a revelation and I spent the longest time discovering its many secrets and bizarre inhabitants. The fact I'm still carrying a torch for the game after all these years suggests that I never really left."

RICHARD HALLAS

AUTHOR OF JSW MOD JOIN THE JET-SET!

"I created my game in 1985 when I was 16 years old using an absolutely brilliant editor written by Paul Rhodes. I wanted to recapture the spirit, humour and whimsy of the original game. My mod was nominated as one of the best at Play Expo and to meet Matthew and to hear him praise it was pretty amazing."

PAOLO SANTAGOSTINO

DIRECTOR OF WILLY: 48K ABOUT A LEGEND

"*JSW* was the first game I fell in love with. My inspiration for the film was to make a living map of the game and to tell Matthew's story. He is a legend. He pushed the limits and will never be forgotten. Meeting him was like meeting a very close friend or an old brother. He is a very kind and sweet fellow I enjoyed being with him very much."

1983 JUNE Microsoft's MSX home computer architecture is announced. The systems will prove quite popular in Japan.

1983 JUNE Arcadegoers are astonished by *Dragon's Lair*, which features gorgeous Don Bluth animation.

1983 JULY The Famicom and SG-1000 launch in Japan, kicking off a rivalry between manufacturers Nintendo and Sega.

1983 JULY Hudson Soft introduces the world to Bomberman in his self-titled debut. It will show up on a ton of different systems.

1983 AUGUST The Acorn Electron, a cut-down version of the BBC Micro with basic graphics and a green screen, launches.

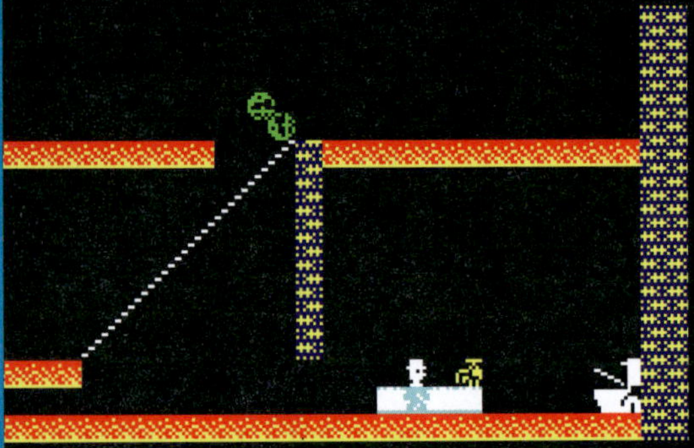

[ZX Spectrum] Where it all begins. Just 83 objects till bedtime…

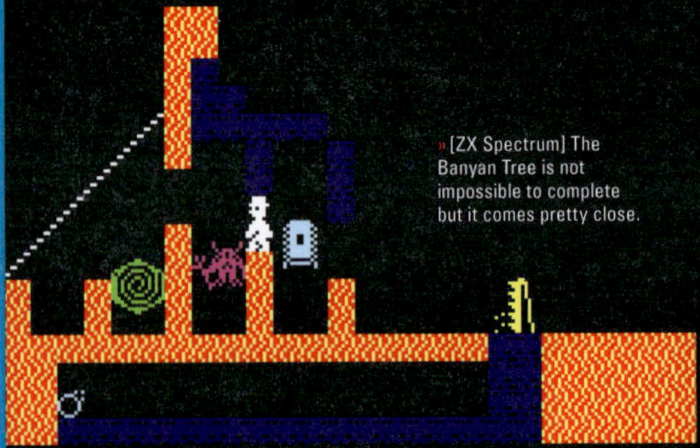

[ZX Spectrum] The Banyan Tree is not impossible to complete but it comes pretty close.

There's a knock on the door and Tim, an old friend of Matthew's, arrives, so we decamp to the kitchen. They've been mates since school, where a young Matthew, clever, shy and with a southern accent from his early years in London, could attract the attention of playground bullies. "Listen, he could handle himself," Tim assures us, "but I was two years older, so we'd walk home together and he'd be less worried. He's always been a really decent fella. A nice nature. And people took advantage of that."

"I got a reputation for being an easy mark," Matthew adds. "Let the fuckers take advantage of you and they'll all want a piece. But I'll be dead in the end and that'll stop me moaning. I can't afford to have kids so the complaining will stop when I do."

Again, it's not clear whether he's joking and we don't know how to break the long silence that follows – or even if we should. Tim steps in by reaching into his bag, bringing out two bottles and pouring us all a cocktail we were previously unfamiliar with: Absinthe and Orange Tango. It's their current drink of choice and makes a memorable evening especially hard to remember.

Yet even as Matthew continues to recall the bad times at Software Projects, at one point admonishing himself for not having the bottle to shoot his tormentors in the kneecaps, he still seems conflicted. When we ask if, in hindsight, he wishes he had just continued writing games freelance for Bug-Byte and collected royalties without the pressure of running a company, he

> "Let the fuckers take advantage of you and they'll all want a piece!"
> MATTHEW SMITH

points out what a pittance those royalties were and how hard he had to fight to get them at all. "They went belly-up soon after I left and I suppose I was partly responsible for that," he muses. "Well, I was never at Bug-Byte, they just published my games but the money they made from *Manic Miner* gave them confidence to expand. When I left, they couldn't pay the rent. They still owed me money… and I never got back the Golden Joystick I won for *Manic Miner* which they had in their foyer."

Another round of absinthe and Tango and Matthew starts talking positively about what Software Projects could have been. "I did trust Alan and Soo [Alan's wife at the time]. We didn't need Tommy. We could have got some cheap offices in Birkenhead, me just writing games, them doing the admin. The plan was to do three or four games every year until I was too rich to care. But *Jet Set Willy* took so long and I needed a holiday. And I never got one."

"He just needed a break," agrees Tim. "Some relaxing time."

"Actually, I did take six months off after *Jet Set Willy* but the company was slipping away from me while I was absent," continues Matthew. "I spent it spamming out and making theoretical reconnaissance trips. I was planning

HOW TO SPOT A MATTHEW SMITH GAME

TRICKY JUMPS
It wouldn't be a Matthew Smith platformer without some challenging leaps and many painful deaths.

STRANGE SPRITES
From snapping toilets to long-nosed monks, his games are always populated by the weird and wonderful.

SECRETS AND LIES
Matthew's games often contain secrets or give rise to myths about imagined features.

ATTENTION TO DETAIL
The way Matthew creates believable objects from just a few well-placed pixels is always impressive.

ART IMITATING LIFE
Look out for nods to Matthew's own experiences and interests – in this case a little drop of vino.

1983 SEPTEMBER
Matthew Smith's platformer *Manic Miner* is reviewed in the gaming press, and guess what? It's great!

1983 OCTOBER
Mindscape is started up by Australian businessman Roger Buoy. It will become known for the likes of *Deja Vu* and *Lego Island*.

1983 DECEMBER
Little Mac makes his arcade debut in Nintendo's *Punchout!!*. This marks the debut of Nintendo composer Koji Kondo.

1984
This is a busy year for startup software companies as Gremlin Graphics, US Gold and Psygnosis are all established.

1984 JANUARY
The first computer in Apple's long-running Macintosh series arrives along with a memorable TV advert.

to stick a camera on a trolley, take it round the roads in the Lake District, take photographs and do a racing game."

"A photorealistic racer in the mid-Eighties would have been groundbreaking. Did anything come of it," we ask?

"Er, I think I ended up going camping with my sister, getting stoned and taking some pictures of trees," Matthew replies, casually. "It was a good camera, though. I swapped it for a car."

Time for more absinthe and Tango. As we reach the end of the playthrough of *Jet Set Willy*, we ask if Matthew is surprised at the enduring interest in his Spectrum classic. "It's more that I'm disappointed," he replies, looking ruefully into his glass. "The only reason they care is that it was the last one. They wouldn't be bothered if it was the second in a series of 20."

"But they care about you Matthew," we slur, the absinthe having stimulated our soppy gland. "Tomorrow, everyone will want to shake your hand, buy you a drink and say thanks for the games you gave us."

"People confuse rich with famous," he snaps back. "I did get a sizeable cheque [£35,000] from Bug-Byte for *Manic Miner* but that was a one-off. I spent about half of it on TRS-80s and associated rubbish and £500 on a Triumph [motorbike]. I was paying other people's bills. Family. Mates. What I spent on drink and drugs was only a tiny fraction. It's not as if I had a 'Class A' habit. Though I did fancy my sister's best mate and she was good to know if you wanted to try some real cocaine on a special occasion. Oh, mother's seething again..."

Yes, Matthew's mum has wandered into the kitchen and caught the last few sentences. "I'm on steroids for my chest," she says, eyeing us all up. "Apparently one of the side effects is they make you murder people."

Another large absinthe and Tango appears in front of us and the rest of the evening is a blur.

Matthew Smith seems conflicted about his fans. The following morning we are on the train to Manchester and point out that many people will be attending the Play Expo show solely to meet him, some having travelled thousands of miles for the pleasure. "Yeah, but they're the ones that'll stab you to preserve your legacy," he says with a malevolent grin. "Anyway, they'll all be middle age balding men with a paunch."

We catch our reflection in the train window. He has a point. Yet when we arrive at the show, Matthew is all smiles, posing for endless photos, gracious with his time and happy to chat to the many hundreds of devotees who seek him out. He's even wrong about his fanbase – at one point, an over enthusiastic woman wearing an 'I love Willy' top straddles, strokes and snogs Matthew, much to his bemusement. He can even get away with casually remarking that games were better on the C64 than the Spectrum during the Q&A session, a heresy that would usually lead to being stoned to death with ZX Microdrives.

Ultimately, we think Matthew is also conflicted about *Jet Set Willy*. On stage, he repeats the painful story of its creation, his frustration at it not leading to more games nor getting paid for his efforts. "My therapist has advised me not to talk about that time," he says, deadpan, and though we're positive he *is* joking, it's not surprising that most of the audience are left in doubt.

Yet during the screening of Paolo Santagostino's wonderful film, *Willy: 48K About A Legend*, which uses in-game footage of *Jet Set Willy* to tell Matthew's tale, he is transfixed, commenting that seeing the whole mansion pieced together was just how he always imagined it in his head. When he quotes Sir Clive Sinclair's exasperated line in the TV programme *Micro Men* that all he'll be remembered for is "the man who brought you *Jet Set* fucking *Willy*", we're sure Matthew knows in his heart that he did create something truly special, something that touched so many people's lives and continues to inspire and entrance. Not a bad legacy for 'just an old Spectrum game'.

And it turns out that his Spectrum games still have some monetary value, too. Over the weekend, Matthew signs a deal with retro gaming streaming service Antstream, and bounds over to us, his wallet bulging. He explains, though, that due to the ongoing legal battle over the rights to *Jet Set Willy*, the deal only involves *Manic Miner*. "That was always my favourite of the two," he says, emphatically. "*Jet Set Willy* can fuck off and die."

Maybe he isn't conflicted after all. *

Thanks to Matthew for his hospitality and to Daniel Gromann at jswcentral.org and Martyn Carroll for all their help.

» [ZX Spectrum] How do you solve a problem like Maria?

» [ZX Spectrum] We can't imagine what was going through Matthew's head when he made this screen…

» [ZX Spectrum] Willy's night ends with his head down the loo. This never happened to Matthew. Never.

1984 FEBRUARY Newsfield Publications launch ZX Spectrum specialist magazine *Crash* with Roger Kean at the helm.

1984 MARCH *Computer And Video Games* holds its first Golden Joysticks awards, a yearly tradition which will continue to this day.

1984 APRIL Amstrad's CPC 464 enters the 8-bit arena and attempts to capture some of the market from the Speccy and C64.

1984 JUNE The backwards-compatible Atari 7800 arrives, restoring a bit of Atari console goodwill after the 5200 stinker.

1984 JUNE Technōs Japan's *Karate Champ* helps establish the format of one-on-one fighting games in the arcades.

THE RISE OF Nintendo®

FROM RELATIVE OBSCURITY AT THE BEGINNING OF THE EIGHTIES, ONE KYOTO-BASED COMPANY BECAME SO FAMOUS THAT IT BECAME A BYWORD FOR THE ENTIRE MEDIUM OF VIDEOGAMES. WE RETRACE THE STEPS OF NINTENDO'S PATH TO PROMINENCE WITH PAT CONTRI

WORDS BY NICK THORPE

If there's one company that can be said to have done everything there is to do in videogames, it's Nintendo. It has been around long enough to have had hits in the golden age of arcade games, and it has spent more than one period as the market leader in home console gaming. It has enormous success in handheld devices, and even generated hundreds of millions of dollars with mobile games in recent years. And while Nintendo has been around for well over a century, by the beginning of the Eighties it had experienced some success with its Color TV Game line and some early arcade games, but was not a dominant force in videogames. Over the course of the next ten years, the company would rise to prominence within the videogames industry.

The earliest sign of Nintendo's rise was the release of Ball in 1980. This was the first game in the Game & Watch range, a series of dedicated handheld LCD games machines that proved popular, running until the early Nineties and selling over 43 million units. However, the big success was *Donkey Kong*, an arcade game which generated hundreds of millions of dollars in sales and home format licensing for the company. The game exhibited two of Nintendo's key strengths – Shigeru Miyamoto's character designs attracted people to the games, and once they were playing, the innovative platform game design kept them hooked. But while Nintendo did well with *Donkey Kong* sequels and other games, it would stop manufacturing original arcade games as its other business took off.

Nintendo's 8-bit home console, introduced as the Family Computer in Japan in 1983, quickly took off and provided the basis for Nintendo's success over the rest of the decade. In 1985 it introduced the console in North America, rebranded as the Nintendo Entertainment System, and shrewd sales tactics got it into stores that had previously been burned by the videogames business. The company was as effective in marketing its product to players as it had been to businesses, too. One such player was Pat Contri, a video creator and author better known as Pat The NES Punk. "When I was a child, I was previously gaming on my father's IBM XT, and I experienced arcade games quite often at the mall, movie theatres and at the Jersey Shore. However, at home, nothing at the time compared quite to what the NES had to offer in terms of gameplay, graphics and cute/colourful mascot characters that appeared in their games," he remembers. "I begged and begged for a NES for the Christmas of 1987 – if I had not received it, my parents would never have had heard the end of it." Pat wasn't alone, as the console was America's best-selling toy of that Christmas according to a survey by Toy And Hobby World.

Of course, it's well-known that Nintendo and its third parties created some amazing, pioneering games for the NES, not least *Super Mario Bros.* But while most consoles rely on advancements in software alone, NES cartridges could give their host hardware a boost with extra RAM and

1984 JUNE
Alexey Pajitnov creates his iconic puzzler, *Tetris*. It will take several years before he receives due compensation.

1984 AUGUST
The *Lords Of Midnight* receives a Crash Smash and highlights Mike Singleton's mastery of the Spectrum.

1984 SEPTEMBER
Andy Gavin and Jason Rubin form JAM Software. It will later be renamed Naughty Dog and purchased by Sony.

1984 SEPTEMBER
David Braben and Ian Bell's *Elite* takes BBC Micro owners to exciting new worlds. Many ports will soon follow

1984 NOVEMBER
Alan Miller and Bob Whitehead love cofounding companies so much they leave Activision to form Accolade.

» Pat Contri is a well-known gaming figure in the US and the author of *Ultimate Nintendo: Guide To The NES Library*.

new capabilities. "The mapper chips and expandability really helped the NES live a long life, which was about ten years in North America," says Pat, who covered all of the system's software in his book *Ultimate Nintendo: Guide To The NES Library*. "While earlier 'black box' games like *Ice Climber* and *Excitebike* are fun yet simple, later NES releases like *Panic Restaurant* or *Kirby's Adventure* are so technically superior that they look like they could have been released on another console entirely. One of the features of the NES library that to me sets it apart from most other consoles is that you look at a game title and have a pretty good idea about what year it was released just based upon the look alone. It's still a crime to me that one of the most technically impressive games, Sunsoft's *Mr Gimmick*, never was released here!"

However, it wasn't just great games that kept the NES on top throughout the decade. "I believe that much of Nintendo's success in the home market was due to its pop culture and social relevance that it established through marketing and media," Pat explains. "As a child, commercials for Nintendo games were almost always on television, *Nintendo Power* was ubiquitous with children, items with Nintendo characters on them were common, and shows like the *Super Mario Bros Super Show* and *Captain N* made sure that Nintendo's brand and its characters were always in the forefront."

To its devotees, the NES became not so much a toy or a hobby, but a way of life – though this sometimes had its drawbacks, according to Pat. "I can tell you on record that Nintendo Cereal System was dreadful – I begged my mom for weeks to buy it and then couldn't even finish a single box of it."

In 1989, Nintendo released the Game Boy – a handheld console that would go on to live a long, successful life and sell millions of units – despite the perceived drawback of not featuring a colour display – thanks to its lower cost and popular games such as *Super Mario Land* and *Tetris*. To Pat, that just shows the continuation of the philosophy that brought Nintendo success earlier in the decade, and indeed in the decades to follow. "I think that the modern success of Nintendo can definitely be attributed to its earlier console foundations, as the focus has consistently been to produce fun games and not overly worry about putting out the most powerful console or the most high-tech devices," he concludes. "Games are what sell videogame consoles, and the characters and worlds that Nintendo established during the NES era will likely still be produced and sold for decades to come. Nintendo has understood branding and creating beloved characters better than all the other past and present videogame companies, and that's why I think Nintendo has firmly established itself as the 'Disney' of the videogame world." ★

FUTURE FOUNDATIONS

The key Eighties series that Nintendo would revisit for decades to come

DONKEY KONG

1981

Gaming's greatest ape might have been overshadowed by his adversary Mario, but he's had a great run of his own. While his early arcade career ended pretty quickly, he was revitalised in the mid-Nineties and has starred in classics including *Donkey Kong Country* and the bongo-driven GameCube platformer *Donkey Kong: Jungle Beat*.

PUNCH-OUT!!

1983

This boxing game was a knockout success in arcades, and the last major Nintendo series to originate there. But the series became even more of a phenomenon on the NES thanks to the backing of legendary heavyweight champion Mike Tyson, and received excellent sequels on the SNES and Wii in later years.

SUPER MARIO BROS

1985

The impact of the original *Super Mario Bros* trilogy is well-known, but what might surprise you is how well the 2D platform series has done when revived as *New Super Mario Bros*. The DS original and *New Super Mario Bros Wii* sold over 30 million copies – that's *each*, not combined.

THE LEGEND OF ZELDA

1986

After back-to-back outings in 1986 and 1987, Link and the princess of Hyrule would disappear for a little while until resurfacing on the Super Nintendo. They never stay away for long, though. The only Nintendo console not to have been blessed with a *Zelda* game is the perennially unlucky Virtual Boy.

METROID

1986

Samus Aran isn't quite a permanent fixture in the Nintendo universe, as evidenced by her skipping out on the N64 and Wii U. But when she shows up, you'd better take notice – *Super Metroid*, *Metroid Prime* and *Metroid Fusion* are considered to be amongst the greatest games on their host platforms.

1984 DECEMBER
Irem's *Kung-Fu Master* births the scrolling fighter genre and doubles as a licence for Jackie Chan's *Spartan X*.

1985
Rare, Cinemaware and Westwood Studios all form this year. Sadly only Rare will weather the later decades and stay in business today.

1985 JANUARY
Commodore's final 8-bit, the Commodore 128, launches. It is designed by Bil Heard, who also designed the Plus/4.

1985 APRIL
Zzap!64 is officially launched by Newsfield Publications as a sister mag to popular Speccy mag, *Crash*.

1985 APRIL
The 16-bit home computer Atari ST has a limited release. It becomes widely available in July, to great success.

THE HISTORY OF VIDEOGAME MAGAZINES

WORDS BY LEWIS PACKWOOD

PHOTOS SUPPLIED BY ROGER KEAN

IN WHICH RETRO GAMER STANDS ATOP THE CORPSES OF VIDEOGAME MAGAZINES PAST, BRANDISHING A LONGSWORD WHILE BELLOWING "THERE CAN BE ONLY ONE!" IN A COMPLETELY INDECIPHERABLE ACCENT

Speaking to magazine veterans for this feature, one theme comes up again and again – that back in the Eighties and early Nineties, there was a special kind of magic that was bottled by games magazines, the likes of which we'll never see again. "They have a certain tone and style to them that's very much of the period," says Julian 'Jaz' Rignall, ex-editor of *Zzap!64* and *Mean Machines*. "I mean, you know, *Mean Machines*, I don't think we could get away with saying some of the things that we used to say nowadays." Matthew Castle, who was *Official Nintendo Magazine*'s final editor when the publication closed in 2014, says that his biggest regret is that he didn't get into videogame magazines earlier, during their golden age. "I read a huge pile of old *Super Play* magazines when I joined Future, and it was just like, 'Oh, god, this is all so good. Why didn't I spend my pocket money on this instead of Boglins or whatever it was?'"

But as the Sega saying goes, to be this good takes ages, and the fusty forerunners of the mighty Eighties game mags were a bit of a dull bunch. Titles from the Seventies like *Computing Today* and *Practical Computing* catered to dedicated hobbyists, and were just as likely to feature guides on creating stock-control programs for your small business as games reviews.

Then came *Computer And Video Games*, aka *C&VG*. Launched in November 1981, it was the world's first dedicated games magazine, and arguably the 'proper start' of gaming magazines as we know them – with not a stock-control program in sight. This was quickly followed by *Computer Gaming World* later the same year, and then a trickle of magazines dedicated to the various computer formats, like *Commodore User* (1983) and *Your Spectrum* (1984), although generally these format-specific titles still had a big focus on the non-gaming side of computers.

But in 1984 *Crash* came along to flip over the publishing industry's neatly arranged tables and breathe a bit of anarchy into games journalism. Here was a magazine that was unafraid to speak its mind, and give a cheeky wink while doing it. Even the magazine's name was a wry nod to the ZX Spectrum's most egregious habit, as well as a reference to a certain controversial JG Ballard novel that Roger Kean, the mag's cofounder, was a big fan of. And *Crash*'s approach to reviewing games was revolutionary.

"The people I knew working at *C&VG* and *Sinclair User*, they were all in their late twenties, early thirties," says Roger, "professional journalists who happened to play games and wrote reviews. Whereas what we did with *Crash* was use the local schoolkids." Roger created a game review form and handed it out to pupils at the local school along with cassettes of the latest games, then the schoolkids dutifully handed in the completed forms a few days later. Essentially, the games were being reviewed by their target audience, and since these young writers had zero contact with the people who actually made or marketed the games, they had no qualms about being brutally honest. "The thing, of course, about 14-year-olds," says Roger, "is if they play a game and say it's crap, it doesn't matter what I would have said, they'd never have changed [their opinions]."

Roger also thinks that *Crash* was the first magazine to adopt a percentage score for reviews, a format that became widely used across the industry. And most importantly of all, the magazine had a rare sense of humour in the otherwise fairly dry world of computer magazines. "Games were fun, and we were on the whole having fun," says Roger, which was something that came across loud and clear in the pages of *Crash*. "I've always had a fairly irreverent sense of humour, and I didn't want the magazine to be, you know, heavy duty."

> "I'VE ALWAYS HAD A FAIRLY IRREVERENT SENSE OF HUMOUR, AND I DIDN'T WANT THE MAGAZINE TO BE, YOU KNOW, HEAVY DUTY"
> **Roger Kean**

Still, *Crash*'s irreverence occasionally got it into trouble, notably thanks to a couple of artist Oliver Frey's more racy covers. "I remember we had quite a lot of irate parents after the *Dun Darach* cover with the guy in chains," remembers Roger, "but the one that probably got us the most trouble was *Barbarian*. We did get an official letter from WH Smith saying that they had recommended we be put on the top shelf, and if we did it again, they would deselect the magazine!"

1985 MAY
Konami releases *Gradius* in Japanese arcades. For years after everyone will debate if it's an actual sequel to *Scramble*.

1985 JULY
Commodore counteracts the Atari's ST with its Amiga 1000 computer marking the beginning of the Amiga line.

1985 SEPTEMBER
Super Mario Bros launches in Japan. Amazingly, no one knows when the American launch date is to this day.

1985 OCTOBER
Future Publishing launches its first magazine, *Amstrad Action*. You can read all about its creation in issue 199.

1985 OCTOBER
Sega establishes its arcade division, Sega-AM2. The studio will be known for its run of excellent coin-op classics.

» (Clockwise from top-left) Franco Frey, Roger Kean and Oliver Frey pose for an early publicity shot.

BEST MAGAZINE GIVEAWAYS

DID YOU EVER BUY A MAGAZINE JUST FOR THE FREEBIES? (WE DEFINITELY DID…)

OFFICIAL PLAYSTATION MAGAZINE COVER DISCS

OPM's demo discs were a real boon for cash-strapped gamers with nary a full-priced game to their name. Each came with a selection of playable demos, along with trailers for new titles, and later on they'd feature full games created using specialist Net Yaroze PlayStation consoles.

THE FINAL, FINAL ISSUE OF SUPER PLAY IN RETRO GAMER 172

IT LIVES! *Super Play* was resurrected for one final issue to celebrate the release of the SNES Mini, marking surely the best magazine giveaway of all time (that sound you can hear is us tooting our own horn, *toot toot parp*). Issue 48 of *Super Play* reunited the original team of Jason Brookes, Jonathan Davies, Tony Mott and Zy Nicholson, who were joined by luminaries such as Nathan Brown (*Edge*) and Keza MacDonald (*Kotaku, The Guardian*).

THE ACTUAL GAME DISC FOR PANZER DRAGOON SAGA

Demos are all well and good, but imagine if a full-priced console game was given away on the front of a mag. Well, it happened with the May 1998 issue of *Sega Saturn Magazine*, which Sellotaped the first disc of the legendary RPG *Panzer Dragoon Saga* to the front cover. Admittedly, the proper game actually came on four discs, so really the giveaway was just a very generous demo – but still pretty amazing.

BATTY AND YOUR SINCLAIR

In 1987, *Your Sinclair* gave away a brand-new game on its cover – *Batty* from Elite, a *Breakout* clone with the added bonus of bomb-dropping aliens and a simultaneous two-player mode, along with a roster of useful power-ups.

CHRISTMAS LEMMINGS

Christmas 1991 was particularly special because it saw the Yuletide-themed *Christmas Lemmings* being given away on the front cover of *Amiga Format* – and the stunt proved so popular that the team did it all again the following year. It even led to annual retail releases of *Christmas Lemmings* (renamed *Holiday Lemmings* in the United States) in 1993 and 1994.

1985 DECEMBER
Space Harrier flies into arcades and takes gamers to the Fantasy Zone, a place they'll never want to leave.

1986 FEBRUARY
The Famicom Disk System add-on launches in Japan. Launch games include *The Legend Of Zelda* and *Castlevania*.

1986 MARCH
Sensible Software is established by Jon Hare and Chris Yates, while the Guillemot family brings Ubisoft to life.

1986 MAY
Enix releases Chunsoft's RPG *Dragon Quest* on Nintendo's Famicom to critical acclaim. Many sequels follow.

1986 JUNE
The very first issue of weekly Japanese gaming magazine, *Famitsu*, arrives. Turn to page 57 for more info.

THE AGE OF SCISSORS AND GLUE

MAKING MAGS WAS A LITTLE DIFFICULT BACK IN THE DAY...

One thing that has changed massively since the **Eighties** is the way **games magazines** are actually made. Back then, cut and paste literally meant cutting some paper and sticking it down to create a layout. "All the layout was physical" recalls **Roger Kean**, "all paper, scalpels and gum."

Still, Roger made sure that **Crash** and **Zzap!64** were kitted out with the latest Apricot computers, which meant that the writers at least had the luxury of being able to send text directly to the typesetters. That meant **Jaz Rignall** had a rude awakening when he left **Zzap!64** to work on **C&VG** at EMAP in the late Eighties. "At **C&VG** they were still doing it the old-fashioned way with typewriters. You had to use a typewriter to type up the copy, then the copy would go off to the typesetter, who would copy that document manually, and then you'd have to read the galleys. It was the way things had been done since the Fifties, so it was really old fashioned and clunky."

And getting hold of images in the days before email was often a precarious business, remembers Steve Jarratt: **"You couldn't just grab an image off the internet. I'd be sitting there on Monday morning, going 'Jesus where's the post, I've got a slide coming from America for my cover image'."**

Screenshots were no walk in the park, either, remembers Jaz. "We did that the old-fashioned way with a camera on a tripod in front of an old CRT that we would clean up so that you wouldn't get fingerprints on it. In fact, in some of the early issues of **Mean Machines**, you can see fingerprints where somebody didn't bother to clean the screen.

"Taking screenshots was a pain in the arse, because you had to hope that the game had a pause mode that didn't blank out the screen or have a huge 'pause' text right across the middle of it. If that happened, then you'd have to stop the game and try to take a picture of it as static as possible. There are some screenshots in **C&VG** that you can see things are moving and blurred."

The advent of digital cameras and screengrabbing software helped to ease the pain of taking screenshots, but even at **NGamer** in the Noughties, the process was still fraught with problems, recalls Matthew Castle. **"We had this capture machine that was big and heavy, and used to get really, really hot, so we had to stick it out of the window to get the air flow through it.** So we had this incredibly expensive PC hanging out of the window the whole time, hoping it wasn't going to smash onto the pavement below."

Nowadays, anyone can take a pin-perfect screenshot at the touch of a button, but Jaz reckons that the blurry screenshots in old magazines are actually part of the appeal of these old publications. "There's something about old-fashioned screenshots taken from a CRT, you know. The phosphorescent, glowing pixels blur together and create a very nice, aesthetic that you don't get with screen grabs these days."

» *Crash* began as a mail order catalogue before becoming a fully fledged magazine in 1984.

RATE CARD INFORMATION EFFECTIVE APRIL 1985

A NEWSFIELD PUBLICATION

CRASH ZX SPECTRUM

INSERTION RATES
Please add 15% VAT as from 1st May 1985

MONO

Eighth Page	£110
Quarter Page	£200
Half Page	£350
Full Page	£650
DPS	£1,250

Spot Colour
Publisher's Choice: +£120
Client's Choice: +£170

COLOUR

Full Page	£950
DPS	£1,850
Bleed	+10%

POSITIONS
Cover positions +20%
Other, special and guaranteed +15%

COPY DATES
Published the end of every month with following month's cover date.
Mono: 3 weeks before publication date
Colour: 4 weeks before publication date
A full schedule of copy and publication dates for 12 issues is available on request.

CANCELLATION DATES
Mono: 3 weeks prior to copy date
Colour: 6 weeks prior to copy date

COPY REQUIREMENTS

NOW 81,000 COPIES & STILL GROWING

CRASH MICRO
1–2 KING STREET
LUDLOW
SHROPSHIRE SY8 1AQ
CONTACT (0584 5851)
Client Liaison: John Edwards
Editorial: Roger Kean

Mechanical Data

DIMENSIONS	Height x Width
DPS (bleed size)	303 x 426
Full Page (bleed)	303 x 215
Full Page (type area)	263 x 180
Full Page (trim)	297 x 210
Half Page (vertical)	263 x 86
Half Page (horizontal)	130 x 180
Quarter Page (vertical)	130 x 86
Eighth Page (vertical)	130 x 45
Eighth Page (horizontal)	65 x 86

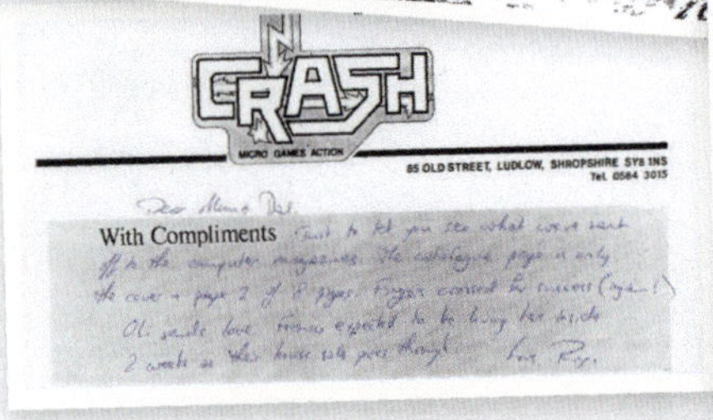
CRASH
MICRO GAMES ACTION
85 OLD STREET, LUDLOW, SHROPSHIRE SY8 1NS Tel. 0584 3015
With Compliments

» A compliments slip that Roger Kean posted to his parents in around July 1983.

"THE OFFICE WAS PRETTY CRAZY, YOU KNOW. WE'D WRITE DURING THE DAY AND PLAY DURING THE NIGHT, AND WORK AND PLAY SORT OF BLENDED TOGETHER. WE WERE HARDCORE GAMERS, SO WE COULDN'T BELIEVE THAT WE WERE GETTING THE CHANCE TO PLAY ALL THIS NEW STUFF, AND WERE BEING PAID TO WRITE ABOUT IT"
Jaz Rignall

» *Crash* moved from Roger Kean's home in Old Street after the first few issues, but here he can be seen working from home in the late Eighties, in the room where *Crash* was born.

» The members of Gargoyle Games were regular visitors to Crash's Ludlow offices: (left to right) Roger Kean, Greg Follis, Matthew Uffindell and Roy Carter.

1986 JUNE
Bethesda Softworks is formed by Christopher Weaver. The studio is named after the Maryland town it's founded in.

1986 SEPTEMBER
Sega's 8-bit console, the Master System, arrives in the US to do battle with the Nintendo Entertainment System.

1986 SEPTEMBER
Game developer Square is founded by Masafumi Miyamoto. It will become renown for its *Final Fantasy* series.

1986 SEPTEMBER
Sega's excellent driving game *Out Run* makes its arcade debut and everyone enjoys a Magical Sound Shower.

1986 OCTOBER
The Darling brothers pivot from being freelance coders to become full-fledged businessmen and found Codemasters.

Roger says the biggest incident came with issue 19, which carried a feature satirising *Sinclair User*, or 'Unclear User' as they called it. *Sinclair User*'s publisher, EMAP, took *Crash* to court, and the latter ended up paying an out-of-court settlement of around £60,000. But Roger says that the surrounding publicity helped *Crash* to have the last laugh. "We went from about 56,000 copies a month up to over 102,000 over four issues."

Crash's Commodore-focused sister magazine, *Zzap!64*, launched in 1985. Its reviews were written by full-time employees rather than schoolchildren, but, as Jaz notes, they "wanted real gamers that were very good at playing games as reviewers, rather than more traditionally trained journalists". Jaz himself won the 1983 *C&VG* Arcade Game Championship. "I played games rather than going to school," he says.

Like *Crash*, *Zzap!64* oozed personality, partly thanks to the way its journalists ended up becoming celebrities in their own right. "We had our little faces on the reviews, and putting faces on the reviewers was a really big thing back then," says Jaz. "It really helped establish us as personalities, and that was very different from a lot of magazines that were being written more anonymously."

And if readers got the impression that writing for a games magazine was some kind of dream job, then they were exactly right, says Jaz. "The office was pretty crazy, you know. We'd write during the day and play during the night, and work and play sort of blended together. We were hardcore gamers, so we couldn't believe that we were getting the chance to play all this new stuff, and were being paid to write about it."

Steve Jarratt joined *Zzap!64* as a reviewer in 1987, and he recalls his first impression was one of organised chaos. "Everybody seemed to smoke, everybody had got cans or coffee on their desks, there was clutter everywhere… it was literally floor to ceiling shelves of magazines, old Commodore 64 machines, hard drives, joypads and row upon row upon row of games. It was kind of amazing, but it was also kind of like, 'Oh my god, what have I got myself into?'"

Jaz left *Zzap!64* for *C&VG* in 1988, partly because he wanted to write about the exciting new Japanese consoles that were emerging at the time. As editor, he steered the magazine away from 8-bit computers and more towards consoles, and in 1990 he convinced the publisher, EMAP, that there was a market for a new magazine focused specifically on these new wonder boxes – what became *Mean Machines*. But EMAP took some persuading, and accordingly the first few issues were only available in limited numbers. "The first issue, we only made about 27,000 of them, but they sold out completely," recalls Jaz. "The next issue, we produced a few more and that sold out. And actually that approach was really advantageous to us, because it created extra demand. We had a lot of readers going into the newsagents asking them to reserve a copy because maybe they'd missed out the previous month. Very quickly the magazine grew to be comparable to *Computer And Video Games* magazine in terms of circulation. It was clear that the player base was very much into consoles and were excited about what was coming out."

Mean Machines was just as edgy as its title suggested, something that came across most clearly in its infamous letters page. "It was just trying to sort of bounce off the readership and make fun in the right kind of places, not be too cruel," says Jaz, before adding, "I think occasionally we were a little bit cruel. But, you know, we wanted to have fun and for the magazine to be interactive, and encourage people to write into us. We wanted the magazine to be like a community or a club that you were part of that had its own in-jokes and little insider bits of knowledge."

Mean Machines wasn't the only title to launch in this period: the late Eighties and early Nineties were something of a boom time for the UK games-magazine industry. Future Publishing put out its first title, *Amstrad Action*, in 1985, and went on to launch countless others, including the multiformat *ACE* in 1987. Paragon Publishing started up in 1991, hurling out titles like *Sega Pro* (1991), *Mega Power* (1993) and *Play* (1995), while EMAP launched the well-respected multiformat magazine *The One* in 1988 and birthed plenty more magazines throughout the Nineties, such as *PlayStation Plus* (1995) and the ill-fated *Maximum* (1995). Europress, meanwhile, held its own with publications like *Atari ST User* (1986) and *Amiga Action* (1989), and on top of that there were various videogame titles made by Dennis Publishing and Argus. In fact, to give an idea of the sheer volume of gaming publications that were adorning newsagents' shelves, at one point in the Nineties there were around half a dozen magazines dedicated to the Amiga alone.

One of the most notable of those was *Amiga Power*. Launched in 1991, it became home to many writers who had learnt their craft on the anarchic *Your Sinclair*, the magazine that evolved from the relatively humdrum *Your Spectrum*. *YS*, as it was affectionately known, devoted many of its pages to odd features like 'Peculiar Pets Corner', and *Amiga Power* followed its lead with such joyous nonsense as a massive spread on the assassination of JFK that had absolutely nothing to do with the Amiga, or even videogames in general (check out

» Matthew Uffindell and Roger Kean in 1984, with their beloved Apricot computer in the background. Jaz Rignall would have killed for one of these at *C&VG*.

» Screenshots the old-fashioned way: Matthew Uffindell photographing a game at *Crash* in late 1984.

» The *Crash* editorial team pose like mad for a PR shot: (left to right) David Western, design and photography; Roger Kean, editor; Oliver Frey, art and design; Matthew Uffindell, software reviewer; and Kevin Foster, assistant editor.

» Michael 'Skippy' Dunne, with Jeremy Spencer (editor of *Amtix*) behind, in 1986.

1986 NOVEMBER
FromSoftware is established and initially develops productivity software before shifting focus to games.

1986 DECEMBER
Japanese developer Intelligent Systems forms and kicks off a long-standing relationship with Nintendo.

1987
A big year for new game developers as Acclaim Entertainment, Bullfrog and The Bitmap Brothers all open their doors, but that's not all…

1987
…Maxis Software and DMA Design also pop up. Each one of these studios will be come renown for their excellent catalogues of games.

1987 APRIL
Commodore's Amiga 500 goes on limited release. It will become a massive success for the manufacturer.

» A *Zzap!64* editorial meeting from October 1985 featuring some outrageous posing: (left to right) Julian 'Jaz' Rignall, Gary Liddon, Gary Penn and Roger Kean. The *Sinclair User* logo was stolen from the EMAP stand at the PCW Show in Olympia.

» The Film Planning area at *Crash*'s offices in King Street, Ludlow, circa 1986, Matthew Uffindell is working with acetate and colour separations of pictures on the big light table. In the foreground is a print-down frame and a magazine flatplan.

» Franco Frey, Oliver Frey and Roger Kean outside the Newsfield admin building at 43 Gravel Hill, Ludlow, in 1987.

» The changing technology of layout and production: Roger Kean and Ian Chubb with the new all-Mac setup at King Street, Ludlow, in 1989.

▶ **Retro Gamer** issue 195 for more on how the mag was made).

But whereas there was perhaps a surplus of Amiga magazines in the early Nineties, there was also a clear deficit of Nintendo-themed titles – a gap that Future was determined to plug. That hole would be filled with the 1991 launch of *Total!*, but its genesis was rather unusual, says Steve Jarrat, who was the editor at launch. "They were aware that Nintendo was a bit litigious, so we launched it in secret. [The publishing director] Greg Ingham had a great big loft space, and so we did it up there: nobody else in Future knew we were doing it, nobody in the industry knew about it, it was just me, Andy Dyer and [art editor] Wayne Allen – just the three of us put this issue together."

Perhaps the loft-bound secrecy was unnecessary in the end, as Nintendo seemed little fazed by *Total!*'s launch, but Jaz does recall the *Big N* laying down some strict rules when *Mean Machines* split into *Mean Machines Sega* and the officially licensed *Nintendo Magazine System* in 1992. "Nintendo insisted on having the Nintendo magazine on a different floor to *Mean Machines Sega*. It was very silly, because we still all went out to lunch together and we still walked up and down the stairs to each other's offices. Maybe they didn't want that *Mean Machines* influence creeping in too much."

Officially licenced magazines like *Nintendo Magazine System* (which went through several name changes before ending up at Future Publishing as the simply named *Official Nintendo Magazine*) gained prominence throughout the Nineties and beyond. Interestingly, several publishers had concurrent 'official' and 'unofficial' magazines covering the same format, like *Sega Magazine* (1994) and *Mean Machines Sega* at EMAP, *Xbox World* (2003) and *Official Xbox Magazine* (2001) at Future, and *PSM2* (2000) and *Official UK PlayStation 2 Magazine* (2000), also at Future. The latter's original incarnation in particular – *Official UK PlayStation Magazine* (1995) – was a massive success for the publisher, with its phenomenal sales probably having a lot to do with the generous demo disc that straddled the cover each month.

Gradually, over the next two decades, 'unofficial' single-format magazines would be almost completely pushed out of the market. Matthew Castle saw both sides of the divide as editor of the unofficial *NGamer* (which evolved, via several name changes, from 1992's *Super Play*) and later on as editor of *Official Nintendo Magazine*. But when *NGamer* closed down in 2012, he was initially reticent about sailing into officially sanctioned waters. "In my head, you know, I was 'unofficial Nintendo mag for life'. We were the same company, but they were our rivals. I didn't really want to be part of it, I didn't necessarily think their world view matched up with ours – but I wanted a job."

Still, he says that although the Nintendo licence meant he was more constrained in what he could do at *Official Nintendo Magazine*, the lean Wii U years were actually somewhat of a blessing in disguise, freeing the writers to fill pages upon pages with gloriously nonsensical features thanks to the lack of new games to write about. In a way, the anarchic spirit of magazines like *YS* and *Amiga Power* flared again for an instant. "I think the last year or so of *ONM* is actually pretty strong," says Matthew. "There was some stuff where I was like, 'There's no way Nintendo is reading this magazine anymore.' There were bizarre alternative Christmas carols that were making fun of the then head of Nintendo Europe and stuff like that. There were several things we printed where I then had nightmares I was going to get fired. We did come close on a couple of occasions: I made a joke about McDonald's, which almost got me nuked because they had a Happy Meal deal with McDonald's."

"THERE WAS SOME STUFF WHERE I WAS LIKE, 'THERE'S NO WAY NINTENDO IS READING THIS MAGAZINE ANYMORE"

Matthew Castle

And so we come to the present. The past decade and a bit has seen even the most mighty magazines fall as they struggled to compete with the migration of readers online. *C&VG* closed its print version in 2004, living a half-life as an online-only publication until 2014. *Official Nintendo Magazine* bowed out in 2014 after Nintendo withdrew from print magazines. *Play* ended its print run in 2016. *GamesMaster* survived long after its namesake TV show was put out to pasture, but it eventually succumbed to the inevitable in 2018, after 25 years of publication. The multiformat *games™* from Imagine Publishing, former home of **Retro Gamer** itself, went silent at around the same time, after 16 years on sale, and then 2020 put an end to *Official Xbox Magazine*.

But there are still a few holdouts. *Official PlayStation Magazine* still carves out a space in WHSmith, and *PC Gamer* has been continually published since 1993. 2018 even saw the launch of a brand-new games magazine in the form of the indie-centric *Wireframe*, while pre-teen-focused mags like *110% Gaming* thrive on newsagents' bottom shelves. And then there's *Edge*, which has now celebrated becoming the United Kingdom's longest-running games magazine. Long may they all continue! *

1987
JUNE
The Acorn Archimedes computer is released and finds its way into schools across the United Kingdom.

1987
JULY
Irem debuts *R-Type* and Konami debuts *Metal Gear*. Both series will stick around for a very long time.

1987
AUGUST
Creative Assembly is formed. It initially finds work porting games but it will become known for its *Total War* series.

1987
OCTOBER
Future unleashes its *ACE* (*Advanced Computer Entertainment*) magazine. It will switch hands to EMAP in 1989.

1987
OCTOBER
Zany point-and-click adventure *Maniac Mansion* introduces Lucasfilm's SCUMM engine to the C64 and Apple II.

THE BIG HITTERS

A RUNDOWN OF MAGAZINES THAT HAVE DEFINED THE VIDEOGAME INDUSTRY WORLDWIDE

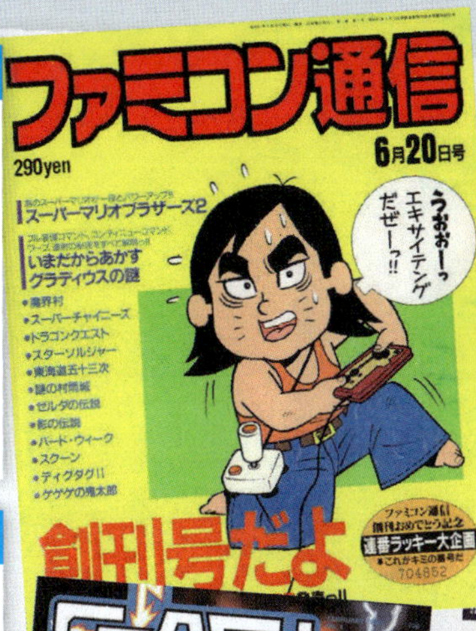

FAMITSU
(1986-PRESENT)

The Japanese magazine *Famitsu* (which is short for 'Famicom Tsushin', or 'Famicom Journal') is one of the longest running games magazines in the world, and it regularly breaks stories that are picked up by media outlets worldwide. It's most well known for its unusual reviewing system, in which four reviewers each mark a game out of ten, making a total possible score of 40.

CRASH
1984-1992

In an age when many mags still focused heavily on coding "*Crash* was certainly the first computer games magazine in which pretty much 99% of the content was dealing with games software", says cofounder Roger Kean. The magazine is famous for its beautiful painted covers by Oliver Frey, many of which are collected in the book *The Fantasy Art of Oliver Frey*.

C&VG
1981-2004

The world's first magazine devoted to videogaming had an epic 23-year run, only recently surpassed by titles like *Edge* and *PC Gamer*. The mag changed considerably over the years, notably shifting away from 8-bit computers and towards focusing on Japanese consoles under the editorship of Jaz Rignall.

MEAN MACHINES
1990-1992

Mean Machines lasted just two years before being split into *Mean Machines Sega* and *Nintendo Magazine System*, but it made a huge impact in that time, with a circulation north of 100,000. Launch editor Jaz Rignall says that in hindsight, he regrets the decision to split the mag in two: "It definitely lost something in that process."

AMIGA POWER
1991-1996

Many of the Mighty Beings of *Amiga Power* were drawn from the ranks of the similarly anarchic *Your Sinclair*, and the magazine gained a reputation for unflinching honesty and nonsensical tomfoolery, the latter reflected in ceaseless in-jokes and sprawling features that had little to do with videogames.

SUPER PLAY
1992-1996

Super Play's eminent launch editor Matt Bielby graduated from *Your Sinclair* and *Amiga Power*, and later went on to launch titles like *SFX* and *Total Film*. The magazine was famous for Wil Overton's anime-style covers, and had a heavy focus on RPGs and Japanese SNES games.

HYPER
1993-2019

This long-running multiformat games magazine gained a reputation for fierce honesty and irreverent humour. This magazine was notable as it was focused entirely on Australia, so that means Australian games coverage written by Australian writers for Australian audiences. In 2018 Future Publishing acquired the rights to the magazine and carried the torch until 2019.

ELECTRONIC GAMING MONTHLY
1989-2012

Often cited as the United States' most prestigious gaming magazine, *EGM* boasted a circulation of more than 600,000 at its peak in the Noughties. The publisher closed the magazine in 2009, but *EGM*'s founder later bought back the rights to continue producing it online.

NINTENDO POWER
1988-2012

Over in the good ol' US of A, the officially licensed *Nintendo Power* was a Big Deal. It grew out of the *Nintendo Fun Club* newsletter and had a readership of 475,000 at the time of its closure in 2012, when Nintendo decided to cease its licensing agreement. It gained a second life of a sort in 2017, with the launch of the *Nintendo Power Podcast*.

EDGE
1993-PRESENT

At a time when most gaming magazines were firmly focused on children and teenagers, *Edge* was designed to cater for the more mature gamer, with a focus on next-generation machines. The launch issue famously came in a black bag that prevented curious browsers from thumbing through its contents in the newsagents.

1987 OCTOBER
NEC releases the PC Engine, gaming's dinkiest console. It will arrive in the US in 1989 as the TurboGrafx-16.

1987 DECEMBER
Mega Man, *Dungeon Master* and *Driller* arrive. One of these titles will receive a massive string of sequels.

1988
The European Computer Trade Show opens its doors in London for the very first time. The last event will take place all the way in 2004.

1988 MAY
Core Design is set up in Derby by former Gremlin Graphics employees. It will create an iconic female hero in 1996.

1988 JULY
Nintendo fans in the United States are treated to the official magazine, *Nintendo Power*. You can read about it above.

Tetris

SO SIMPLE, EVEN I CAN PLAY IT

» VARIOUS » 1984 » ALEXEY PAJITNOV

It's hard to come up with a single defining game that sums up the Eighties, but for me, it's got to be Alexey Pajitnov's *Tetris*. Sure, I could have gone with the likes of *Elite*, *Donkey Kong*, *Manic Miner* or countless other gems, but *Tetris* feels special, *Tetris* is a survivor.

I won't bore you with my first memory of *Tetris* as I covered that in **Retro Gamer** issue 183, but it's probably worth highlighting why I think *Tetris* is such an important title. Like the very best games, *Tetris* shines thanks to its clever game mechanics that link together as satisfyingly as the walls you clear in the game. The concept of *Tetris* is easily explained and can be played by just about anyone, regardless of age or interest in videogames. Even my nan could enjoy *Tetris* on the Game Boy, and the purity of its design and simplistic-looking style has meant that many, many systems have been able to accommodate it without losing the essence of its appeal. *Tetris* has appeared on countless machines over the years, from the Electronika 60 to the ZX Spectrum, Game Boy, Amiga and numerous others, and very few of these conversions are actually poor.

Aside from seemingly endless ports, another reason why *Tetris* has ingrained itself so much into popular culture is because the game is constantly able to reinvent itself whilst staying true to the essence of what makes the game so enjoyable. Sure there have been misfires along the way (*Hatris* and *Welltris*, I'm looking at you) but for the most part, you can typically enjoy any version of *Tetris* you pick up because the base mechanics are so profoundly gratifying. *Tetris* DS fused multiple game modes with classic Nintendo characters, Sega realised that combining *Tetris* with *Puyo Puyo* was a match made in heaven, while *Tetris 99* has proven that the battle royale arena does not just belong to *Fortnite*. Hell, *Tetris* even works in VR. It's astonishing to think that over 30 years after I first encountered it Alexey's game is still managing to surprise me. *

1988 OCTOBER
Sega's mighty 16-bit console, the Mega Drive, makes its debut, stealing some thunder from *Super Mario Bros 3*.

1988 OCTOBER
Eurocom is founded in Derby with the aim to create games for the Nintendo Entertainment System.

1989 FEBRUARY
Will Wright's *SimCity* makes everyone a digital architect. It will go on to feature on an impressive number of systems.

1989 MARCH
American multiformat magazine *GamePro* launches, kicking off a print run that will last until winter 2011.

1989 APRIL
Nintendo's, Game Boy launches on Japanese shores. The company decides this handheld fad might catch on.

1989
APRIL
Satoshi Tajiri and Ken Sugimori found Game Freak. Sugimori's doodles will soon capture the world.

1989
JUNE
Peter Molyneux's innovative *Populous* makes everyone obsessed with god simulator games.

1989
SEPTEMBER
The world's first colour handheld console, the Atari Lynx, arrives. Darran plays it in Bournemouth cinemas.

1989
OCTOBER
Jordan Mechner's *Prince Of Persia* bounds on to Apple Mac computers. It's notable for its use of rotoscoping.

1989
OCTOBER
Future Publishing launches *S: The Sega Magazine*. It does well and will later become known as *Sega Power*.

MR. VIDEO GAME

THE COMPLETE HISTORY OF MARIO

To celebrate Nintendo's most popular mascot, industry legends offer up their memories of the character, and we give you the complete lowdown on the plumber's career from Popeye replacement to cultural icon

To fully appreciate why Mario is still the videogame industry's most recognised, popular and enduring character, you have to look back to the early days of videogames. Mario remains the poster child for a time where everything about them felt fresh, innovative and new, and these newfangled virtual worlds sought only to be linked to ours through the computers and consoles that projected them, and the talented visionaries who imagined them. With realism and trends now sitting where fun and creativity once ruled, today's industry is looking a much different place to one that Nintendo was helping rebuild back in the Eighties.

With every familiar-looking sandbox RPG-lite open world game that finds release, it becomes ever apparent that this industry has, in many ways, started to fold in on itself. The insane budgets required to build the games of today mean that now only a small handful of developers and publishers have the financial means to call the shots, game genres seem to be melding together, and despite now being able to utilise gazillions of colours, a lot of mainstream games are looking a little ubiquitous. Why Nintendo's Switch suddenly rocketed into success in 2017, and *Super Mario Odyssey* has scooped universal acclaim, should be obvious to anyone who enjoyed playing videogames throughout the Eighties and Nineties. Nintendo has proven, once again, that fun and creativity are king.

It's for this reason why most gamers can instantly recall the first time they ever saw Mario in action. He takes them back to an evergreen era for videogames, a time with which he has now become synonymous. For many of you reading this, we suspect that your first experience came from playing *Donkey Kong* in arcades, or on home computers and consoles. At this inaugural point in his career, Mario was known by the more literal-sounding name of Jumpman, played a bit of an antihero and worked as a carpenter instead of the heroic plumber we all know him as today. However, while Mario's personality, name and occupation would come to change quite quickly following his gaming debut in 1981, the distinct look of the character was settled on almost immediately by his creator, Shigeru Miyamoto, and has only really ever been refined, never changed, over the years.

As was the practice in the early days of game design, Mario was borne out from the technical limitations of his time. The character was given his signature flat cap owing to the fact that it would save Miyamoto the headache of animating hair, a large nose to make him look instantly more human, bright red coveralls to help him stand out against *Donkey Kong*'s dark backgrounds, and a moustache instead of a mouth for similar reasons. But Mario's creation also came about through an element of luck and good fortune – although it probably didn't seem that way to Nintendo at the time.

SUPER MARIO HIGHLIGHTS

1985 SUPER MARIO BROS

1986 SUPER MARIO BROS THE LOST LEVELS

1988 (USA) SUPER MARIO BROS 2

1988 SUPER MARIO BROS 3

1989 SUPER MARIO LAND

1990 SUPER MARIO WORLD

1992 SUPER MARIO LAND 2: 6 GOLDEN COINS

1995 SUPER MARIO WORLD 2: YOSHIS ISLAND

1996 SUPER MARIO 64

2002 SUPER MARIO SUNSHINE

2006 NEW SUPER MARIO BROS

2007 SUPER MARIO GALAXY

2011 SUPER MARIO 3D LAND

2013 SUPER MARIO 3D WORLD

2017 SUPER MARIO ODYSSEY

Professions of a Plumber

The versatile hero has appeared in a string of occupational cameos for Nintendo over the years...

CARPENTER
Donkey Kong 1981
■ Mario's first ever job was as a mallet-wielding carpenter in *Donkey Kong*. It's likely that his profession was inspired by the everyman-type scenarios on which Nintendo based many of its Game & Watch titles.

PLUMBER
Mario Bros 1983
■ After a two-year stint working as a carpenter, Mario turned his talents to plumbing – as well as the odd bit of pest extermination too – for *Mario Bros*. He kept the role for the subsequent *Super Mario Bros* series.

UMPIRE
Tennis 1984
■ Mario earned extra cash at weekends working as a tennis umpire. Later in life he decided to take up the sport himself when he realised that more money was to be had playing than interfering.

REFEREE
Punch-Out!! 1987
■ Following a successful spell as a tennis umpire, Mario caught the eye of the Nintendo Boxing Commission and was approached to work as a referee in the Famicom/NES version of *Punch-Out!!*.

DOCTOR
Dr Mario 1990
■ Making a mint working as a boxing ref, Mario left labouring to go to medical school. It took him just two years to complete his doctorate – earning him a place in *Guinness World Records*.

GOLFER
NES Open Tournament Golf 1991
■ Like most doctors, Mario found that the best way to relax after a busy day in surgery was to smash a ball into a tiny hole.

MARIO MEMORIES

Jim Bagley
ZX Spectrum coder

I first saw Mario in the local arcade halls in New Brighton roughly around 1981 when *Donkey Kong* was released. *Donkey Kong* is and always will be a classic, and a great game to boot, but I can't help but admire so many other *Mario* games. *Super Mario Bros* is another fantastic *Mario* game that even to this day I like to play – even though my nephew completed it before I did! And what favourite *Mario* list would be complete without *Mario Kart*? I loved the N64 version the most, because my nephew, niece, sister and I used to play it at the weekends with riotous laughter, especially when zapping someone on the jump in Wario Stadium. And I can't go without saying *New Super Mario Bros*. I also loved it, again, because of the original features, like being able to grow huge and sprint through the level. Out of those four, those being my favourites, if I had to choose one... I'm not sure I can! They all have a huge place in my heart. Why has Mario remained so enduring? Well because he's constantly reinventing himself, changing with the times, and because Shigeru Miyamoto is simply a genius.

John Carmack
Cofounder id Software

I have followed Mario since the *Donkey Kong* days, and id Software was pretty much launched on the merits of an internal clone of *Super Mario Bros 3*. I was away for a while after *Super Mario 64*, but the last few years with my son have brought me back into the fold – at the time of writing this, we just collected our 66th star on *Super Mario Galaxy 2* last night, and we have gone back through all the old games. Still fun after all these years. Domo arigato, Miyamoto-san!

Kevin Toms
Creator of Football Manager

I remember my first recollection of Mario being on the original Nintendo cartridge machine. Squat, cute character, red hat comes to mind. Probably I would go for *Mario Kart* on the Nintendo 64 as my *Mario* game. His lasting appeal is down to the personality he puts across: an upbeat, likeable, jolly man. Most people would get on with someone like that. So he annoys no one!

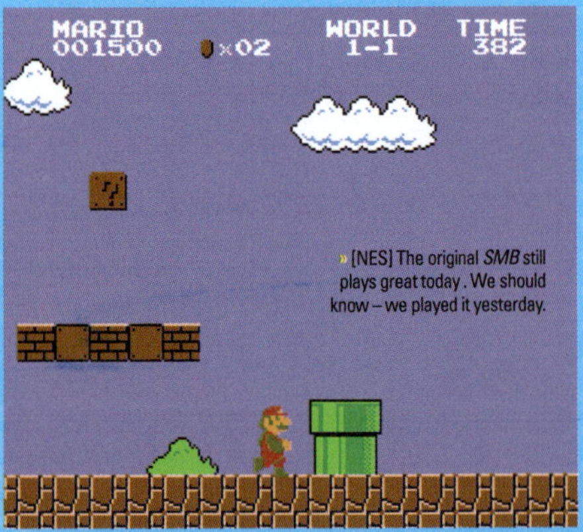

» [NES] The original *SMB* still plays great today. We should know – we played it yesterday.

[Arcade] Mario made his debut in *Donkey Kong*, where it was DK hogging the limelight for Nintendo.

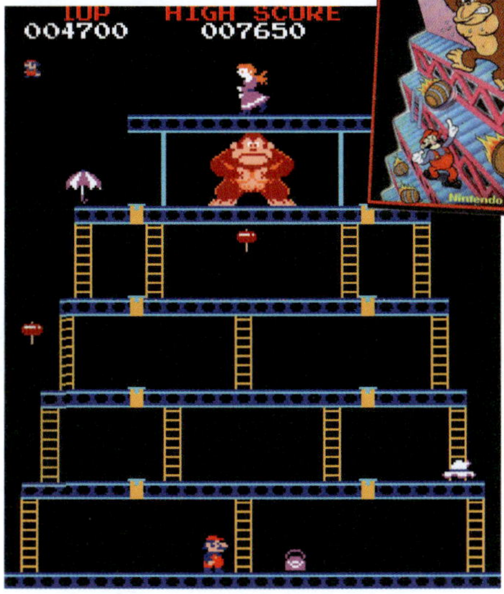

'I'LL SAVE YER, LADY!'

Before *Donkey Kong* was even considered, Shigeru Miyamoto had aims to create a new arcade game starring the characters from the popular King Features Syndicate cartoon *Popeye*. But when Nintendo failed to obtain the licence, Miyamoto was forced to come up with three central characters of his own. And, after taking pretty obvious inspiration from the 1933 stop-motion monster classic, *King Kong*, he came up with the characters Jumpman, Lady and Donkey Kong to substitute the roles of Popeye, Olive Oyl and Bluto, respectively.

When the time came for *Donkey Kong* to ship to North America, however, it was decided that Jumpman should be renamed during the localisation process. Even then, Nintendo's intention was to turn Mario into a mascot-type character by having him appear in many of Miyamoto's subsequent videogames. With this idea in mind, the first new name that Nintendo would settle on for Jumpman was 'Mr Video'. It was a name clearly derived from Nintendo's first ever gaming mascot, Mr Game & Watch.

However, in what became one of the videogame industry's most bizarre anecdotes, Jumpman's name would change once again. The tale goes that, at the time when Nintendo Of America (NOA) was trying to gain a foothold in North America, it was renting a warehouse from an Italian construction tycoon named Mario Segale. Segale was said to have looked remarkably similar to Jumpman, and when NOA's president at the time, Minoru Arakawa, realised the coincidence, Jumpman was nicknamed Mario and the name stuck. What makes the story all the more ironic is the fact that Mario Segale's business was construction, an industry that played a prominent role in the look of *Donkey Kong*'s stages. It can not be neither confirmed nor denied whether Mario Segale once owned a giant gorilla that he would occasionally mistreat, though it's easy to guess that it was highly unlikely.

With the hero character renamed, Lady rechristened Pauline, and the localisation process complete, Nintendo pushed *Donkey Kong* out onto the US market, where it became a huge, runaway success. And with the millions of dollars it earned, the company was able to better fund development of its first true videogame console, the Famicom. But it was Donkey Kong, not Mario, who was gaining the most celebrity for Nintendo. Despite the fact that the big angry ape was assigned the role of big dumb antagonist in *Donkey Kong*, his domineering presence and cartoon qualities made him a clear standout character in the game. And it is perhaps for this reason why Mario was then made to play villain in the game's 1982 sequel, *Donkey Kong Jr.*

That said, Nintendo, obviously not wanting to turn its moustached hero character into an out-and-out baddie, did give Mario his very own game in the same year, plonking him back in the saddle of hero and gifting him a green coverall-wearing brother called Luigi into the bargain. The game in question, *Mario Bros*, was a single-screen action platformer that looked and played similar to the earlier Williams arcade game *Joust*. It saw Mario and his brother battle through 'phases' of enemy attacks inside a New York sewer, and was the first game to ever depict the brothers as plumbers – it's believed that this was done simply to explain the game's culvert setting. However, with its premise finding the pair trying to prevent an infestation of insect and reptilian pests escaping into the city, the brothers are clearly acting more like exterminators in the game. Nevertheless, as well as portraying the brothers as plumbers, *Mario Bros* also introduced a few common enemy types too, such as Shellcreepers – a precursor to Koopa Troopas – and the spike-shelled foes, the Spinies. It also established the idea of having the brothers collect coins through bonus rounds, as well as the concept of brick-punching and unconscious enemy kicking, all of which would become staples of the *Mario* series.

Mario Bros received a lukewarm arcade reception, certainly nothing in the same league as *Donkey Kong*, but it later proved to be a popular release for the Nintendo Entertainment System console in North America. Two variants of the game were also developed by Hudson Soft, under licence from Nintendo. Released exclusively on Japanese home computers, the games featured all-new original stages and gameplay mechanics. The first, *Mario Bros Special*, was an interesting update of the original game that saw players having to fight their way to exit points at the top of each stage, while the second title, *Punch Ball Mario Bros*, was a quirky dodgeball-inspired iteration that saw the brothers punching balls at their subterranean foes and hitting switches. Hudson Soft also later released its own version of *Super Mario Bros*. Titled *Super Mario Bros Special*, this unfairly punishing home computer version featured all-new levels, hair-pulling level design and maddening flick-screen scrolling. In fact, the dodgy scrolling hurts the experience so much that it shows just how important a factor scrolling actually played in *Super Mario Bros*' ultimate success.

But we're jumping ahead of ourselves a little bit here, as Mario hadn't quite gone 'super' just yet. In fact, while it's debatable that Shigeru Miyamoto dabbled with the idea of giving Mario enhanced powers in the *Mario Bros* arcade game by finally giving him the ability to survive a large fall – he wasn't capable of bending his knees in *Donkey Kong* – it wasn't really until the release of *Super Mario Bros* in 1985 that the legendary game designer gave his creation actual super powers. Before reaching this watershed moment, however, the character could be seen busily living up to his 'Mr Video' duties. The multipurpose butterball could be seen popping up in a bonus stage in the NES game *Pinball* that same year, guest appearing as an unshaven umpire in *Tennis* (1984), and influencing the look of *Golf*'s (1984) moustachioed golfer Ossan, a character often mistaken for Mario, owing to his stark resemblance to Nintendo's mascot.

[NES] Who can forget this trick in World 1-2? Who was it that said cheating doesn't pay? Someone who'd never played *Super Mario Bros*, clearly.

MARIO MEMORIES

Eugene Jarvis
Arcade legend

My first recollection of Mario was in *Donkey Kong*. The character was ridiculous. Why am I a carpenter trying to rescue a princess from King Kong? *Super Mario Bros* is the greatest videogame of all time. It is etched in my brain like a phosphorescent cattle brand. Mario is the video star. He has been flogged and baked into the collective memory of humanity for over 30 years. When the last cockroach is dead he will dance on the grave.

Jamie Woodhouse
Creator of Qwak!

I'm fairly sure my first experience of Mario was *Mario Bros* on the NES; I remember it not scrolling, just a static screen, with lots of turtles that go into pipes in the bottom corners of the screen, then coming out of pipes in the top corners. Characters were all simple, yet fun-looking, with a cutesy round feel to them. I think my all-time favourite *Mario* game is probably *Super Mario Land* on the Game Boy: simple, fun gameplay, not too complicated graphically, and of course, it was portable! I think maybe Mario's appeal is down to the personality of the character; I mean, he's not really a violent kind of dude, is he? And he's only there in the first place because he's trying to sort out the big bad boss or rescue his girlfriend – or was that the other game, the one with the big monkey? So I guess, maybe because he's not too violent, and he's there for a good reason, people maybe relate to that. Also, it can't hurt having the Nintendo marketing department on your side!

MARIO MEMORIES

Jon Hare
Cofounder Sensible Software

First time I saw Mario was *Donkey Kong* in the arcades in about 1980. I didn't focus on the character much, to be honest – nothing that special. I thought the monkey was the best thing in the game. My all-time favourite *Mario* game has to be *Mario Golf* on the N64. It just has the most perfectly tuned learning curve ever. I spent a whole year trying to win every trophy and kept missing the final one by just one shot. Next best titles would be *Mario 64* and *Mario Kart*. I think Mario endures because he is a really good everyman character, funny but not too irritating, and he has an army of fellow characters that add a lot to him. Miyamoto is the only game designer that I look up to.

» [Famicom] If you think this game looks a lot like *SMB2*, that's because 95% of it is.

MARIO MEMORIES

Scott Miller
Founder of Apogee Software

I first remember Mario playing *Donkey Kong*, of course! When I first discovered this game in an arcade I knew it had something special about it, interesting characters, unique gameplay, variety, and it was a deeply polished game. From the get-go I knew it was the start of a new era, but no one could have guessed the staying power of this squatty plumber!

Alex Trowers
Designer of classic Bullfrog games

I suppose the first time I saw Mario in action was in *Super Mario Bros*, but that's only because the Mario in *Donkey Kong* was called Jumpman. I found *SMB* a bit 'meh' – despite the knocking-things-over-from-underneath mechanic and a two-player option, the whole thing felt a little repetitive. I loved *Donkey Kong* in the arcades, though, and the ColecoVision version, which was the scene of some epic high-score battles between my brother, my mum and I. I can also remember a version of *Super Mario 3* on an old Nintendo Play Choice 10 machine in a local kebab shop. That was entertaining. Suddenly, Mario could do all manner of interesting things and that was quite appealing. My favourite *Mario* game is a toss-up between *Super Mario World* on the Super Famicom and *Super Mario 64* on the N64. Some guys from Imagineer brought a Super Famicom over around the time of the Japanese launch and lent it to us. It had two games: *F-Zero* and *Super Mario World*. We played them both pretty religiously, to the extent that we managed to overheat and blow up the console.

Super Mario World was one of the first games I completed in Japanese despite there being a whole ton of stuff that Mario could do. I couldn't read any of the hints, meaning I missed the one about being able to throw shells up in the air. This meant that to complete the final boss, I had to get the cape on an earlier level and make it through the last castle without getting hit. Once at the boss stage, I had to wait on one side of the screen for him to drop a Koopa before running along, jumping, hitting the thing and grabbing the shell all in one go before using the momentum to fly up to the top of the screen and dropping the shell on him from above. I remember thinking it was a bit tricky at the time but I put it down to just being the end of the game.

John Romero
Cofounder of id Software

The first time I saw Mario in action, I was at an arcade in Roseville, California, called Supercade. It was a weekend in 1981 and my friend Robert was with me. At this time in 1981, new games were showing up every week. The arcades were the most exciting places in the world. And in this particular arcade, this particular weekend, was a new game called *Donkey Kong*. We went up to the game, dropped in our quarters, and lost ourselves for several hours. When the smoke cleared, we had found a new favourite game and a favourite carpenter named Jumpman, who would be renamed in four years to the familiar name: Mario. We loved Mario's pixelated figure, his cute animations and cuter sound effects. His job was to rescue the princess and put out fire with a mallet. We loved the ridiculousness of it, and it fit in perfectly with the extreme abstractness of games of that time. For me, *Super Mario 3* was the pinnacle. It was just so epic. That game pushed the original NES to the extreme. The cartridge was packed to the limit with data – the game was huge at the time. And it took a while to play through. I was playing it in my Gamer's Edge office next to John Carmack as he coded.

SUPER MARIO... FINALLY

Super Mario Bros was, in many respects, the natural next step for the main series to take. It took the popular 'rescue the lady in distress' premise of *Donkey Kong*, applied it to the theme and two-player mode – albeit not simultaneous this time – introduced in *Mario Bros*, and then stretched the gameplay into a revolutionary side-scrolling platform game. Set in the fantasy fungal world of the Mushroom Kingdom, the 'Super' prefix came from the brothers' peculiar reaction to ingesting magic mushrooms, which took the form of power-ups in the game. Eating a mushroom would cause Mario and Luigi to grow in size, this growth spurt essentially acting like a shield but at the cost of making the heroes easier to hit. And while in this state the eating of a Fire Flower power-up would make the plumbers truly super-powered, dressing them in lustrous white overalls and giving them the ability to lob fireballs around the environment.

Speaking in 1991's *Mario Mania Player's Guide*, Miyamoto revealed how the brothers' iconic growth spurt ability came about: "We developed programming techniques that allowed us to create a larger character than we originally thought possible. At first, we planned to make the game so that the player was always 'big' Mario, but eventually, we came up with the idea for the power-up mushroom to make Mario 'Super'."

Super Mario Bros was praised for its innovative gameplay, great visuals, catchy music, super-smooth scrolling, and wealth of secrets to discover – the most notable of which saw Mario actually breaking out of his own videogame in World 1-2 – a truly mind-bending concept at the time, made even more impressive by the fact that doing so rewarded the player with the opportunity to warp to later levels in the game.

Selling over 40 million copies, *Super Mario Bros*' popularity can be largely attributed to the success of the Famicom/NES, and thus for also playing a key role in helping to resurrect the console industry in North America following its crash in 1983. In fact, *Super Mario Bros* currently stands as the sixth best-selling videogame of all time, topped only by the likes of massive modern hits like *Grand Theft Auto V* and *Minecraft*, demonstrating the sheer impact that this single game had on the games industry.

But *Super Mario Bros* wasn't the only *Mario* title released in 1985. The little-known NES game *Wrecking Crew* saw Mario continue in the tradition of his earlier arcade-style games. Rearmed with his trusty carpenter's hammer, and accompanied by Luigi, the game was a fun mix of smash-'em-up and puzzle game. Capping the brothers' ability to jump, *Wrecking Crew* saw Mario and Luigi race around, smashing bricks and pillars in an advantageous order so as to clear each stage of everything destructible. It even came with a level designer. But while a neat concept, it fell into obscurity in the shadow of *Super Mario Bros*.

Sequel sequel panic

Now if there's one thing that Nintendo was seen to struggle with during the 8-bit era, it was sequels. While *Donkey Kong Jr* was an enjoyable enough successor, it really wasn't a patch on the tight, engaging and insanely addictive gameplay of *Donkey Kong*. And while *Zelda II: The Adventure Of Link* had its good moments, to this day it's still deemed by many fans to be one of the weakest entries in the series. The *Super Mario Bros* series is no different and follows this peculiar pattern.

Owing to *Super Mario Bros*' success, Nintendo was understandably keen to capitalise on the game's popularity and so quickly pushed out an expert version exclusively for the Famicom Disk System to satiate demand. Released in 1986 as *Super Mario Bros 2* in Japan, it was a single-player game only, with players given the choice of picking between a 'Mario game' or 'Luigi game', and the brothers were given different attributes: Mario had better traction; Luigi a higher jump. On top of this, the difficulty level was also increased, and the game made more challenging through the inclusion of poisonous mushrooms and more aggressive enemies. But when the game came to ship to North America, NOA stressed its concerns that the game wasn't different enough to be deemed a true sequel, and would be too challenging for western gamers. Consequently, Nintendo was forced to do some rapid troubleshooting, and this led it to re-skin another platform game by Miyamoto and his team titled *Yume Kojo: Doki Doki Panic*.

Released for the Famicom Disk System in Japan, *Doki Doki* garnered modest sales, likely owing to its Disk System exclusivity, and so Nintendo had the brainwave of switching the game's four heroes with Mario, Luigi, Toad and Princess Toadstool (Peach) and repackaging it as *Super Mario Bros 2* in the west. Without the aid of the internet back then, a very large proportion of the planet would be none the wiser of this cheeky game swap. Of course, we later got the chance to test our skills on the Japanese sequel when it was remade as *Super Mario Bros: The Lost Levels* for the 1993 *Super Mario All-Stars* compilation pack on the Super Nintendo.

To tie everything together, *Doki*'s story was altered to explain away all the crazy leftovers – something about Mario entering a dream world called Subcon to defeat an evil frog overlord to free some enslaved fairy kids – and the game switch also explains why many of the enemies in the game never reappeared in subsequent *Mario* games, and Mario and pals' peculiar new attack method, which ditches head-stomping to see them instead pick up objects and enemies and toss them at other enemies.

> **"Mario played a key role in resurrecting the American industry"**

Released in the US in 1988, the re-skinned *Doki Doki* version of *Super Mario Bros 2* became a hot seller for the NES, becoming the third-bestselling game on the console, trading more copies than *The Legend Of Zelda*. And owing to its success, this version was later released in Japan in 1992 under the name *Super Mario USA*.

Hollywood comes-a knockin'

Towards the end of the Eighties, *Mario*-mania was starting to take effect, and its momentum was to be fuelled even further with the release of a game that many fans still consider to be the best game in the series. Taking two years to create, *Super Mario Bros 3* introduced more staples to the *Mario* series than any sequel before or since. It introduced elements such as an overworld map, complete with patrolling enemies that whisked the player to battle screens; enjoyable diversions by way of photo-fit minigames; multiple routes through the game's eight massive worlds; new power-ups in the form of abstract costumes for the brothers; an inventory that allowed you to carry over items obtained in one stage into another, and more secrets than you could shake a Warp Whistle at.

To help create awareness and excitement for the release of the game in the US, *Super Mario Bros 3* was memorably first unveiled to Americans in the 1989 feature film *The Wizard*. Released into theatres a few months prior to the game's North American release, the movie's plot culminated

[NES] If we had to pick the best game in the series, we'd have to hand it to *Super Mario Bros 3*. Way ahead of its time, it's *Mario* gaming at its very best.

FROM CARPENTER TO SPACEMAN

HOW MARIO HAS EVOLVED OVER THE GENERATIONS

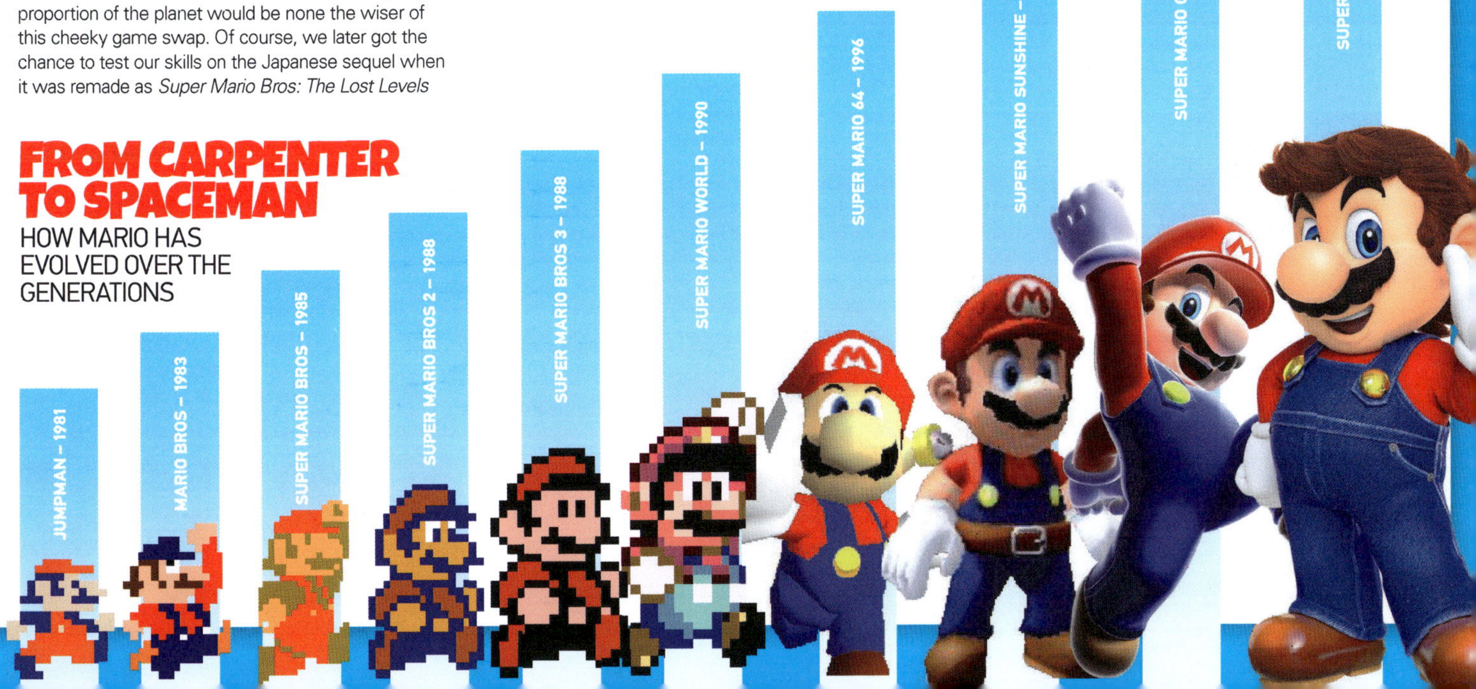

[SNES] The colourful *Super Mario World* stuck close to the *SMB3* template.

MARIO MEMORIES

Gary Bracey Software Manager Ocean Software

I spent quite some time in the early Eighties playing in the arcades, and so my first actual introduction to Mario was *Donkey Kong*. I recall he was the first 'human' character I had seen in games, as all others were cartoon or abstract like *Space Invaders* and *Pac-Man*. My next major encounter was when Ocean obtained the rights to convert the first *Mario Bros* platformer, which was an okay game. However, when I discovered *Super Mario Bros* on the NES, I was completely blown away and spent many, many weeks playing it to completion... and then playing it again! It's one of the few franchises that has never suffered from compromise. Nintendo recognises this and *Zelda* to be its bar-setting titles, and also its console-shifting games. If they released a sub-par version then not only would the whole perception of the franchise suffer, but it would probably impact sales of the hardware. As for the character itself, he is as synonymous with Nintendo as Mickey Mouse is to Disney, yet a lot more contemporary. Over the years, they have managed to develop his personality to keep pace with the advances in console technology, so from the original few pixels there is now a 'fleshed out' character with personality and charisma. From my own perspective, Mario is a reason alone to purchase any new Nintendo console, and I can think of no greater compliment to pay.

Trip Hawkins Founder of Electronic Arts

Naturally, my first time seeing Mario was *Donkey Kong* in an arcade in Silicon Valley, many years ago. Miyamoto-san is the best game designer in the history of the industry, and Mario's appeal is ubiquitous.

in a Nintendo videogame tournament that ended with the finalists competing on a mysterious 'new game', which is revealed to be *Super Mario Bros 3*. Probably at the request of Nintendo, the game is hilariously unveiled in the film as if it were the single most brilliant objet d'art in the history of mankind. Although in hindsight we should let Nintendo off a little, as it actually comes pretty darn close.

But that wasn't all in the way of *Mario* marketing that year, as 1989 also spawned an animated/live action television show: *The Super Mario Bros Super Show*. The programme was an odd format that comprised a short ten-minute cartoon bookended by a peculiar live-action sitcom, in which Luigi was played by actor Danny Wells and Mario by former professional WWF wrestler Captain Lou Albano. Filmed in front of a probably perplexed studio audience, the show saw the pair conversing with drop-in celebrity guests from inside their *Bottom*-style dilapidated New York apartment, and in some episodes dress up in women's clothes to portray female versions of Mario and Luigi named Marianne and Luigeena. And if you think that sounds like a bizarre idea for a *Mario Bros* television show, during the holiday season of 1989 and 1990, Southern Californians witnessed *King Koopa's Kool Kartoons*, a live-action Krusty The Clown-type kids' telly show in which a guy dressed as Bowser presented cartoons to a room full of children, fondly referred to in the show as 'Koopa Troopas'.

1989 also marks the release of the Game Boy and saw Mario lose the pounds for his first proper portable adventure, *Super Mario Land*. A launch title for the Game Boy in Japan and North America, *Super Mario Land* was overseen by the *Donkey Kong* codesigner and *Metroid* and *Kid Icarus* producer, Gunpei Yokoi, and his solo involvement in the game resulted in a unique *Mario* title for the handheld. Putting his own stamp on the series, head-stomping Koopa Troopas now turned them into ticking time bombs, while striking some enemies in the game transformed them into a pile of decomposing bones. And elements of Yokoi's earlier work also found their way subtly into the game, such as a subterranean-style stage reminiscent of *Metroid* (Level 3-4) and the game ending with a side-scrolling shooter stage that saw Mario piloting a plane – a similar closing stage also occurred in *Kid Icarus*. Likely owing to Mario's popularity and the Game Boy's high installed base, *Super Mario Land* became a hugely successful *Mario* title, going on to sell more than 14 million units. It also spawned two sequels: *Super Mario Land 2: 6 Golden Coins*, notable for introducing Mario's doppelgänger Wario to the series, and *Wario Land: Super Mario Land 3*, in which the demented-looking villain took centre stage as a controllable character, in another first for the series.

The arrival of the fourth generation of consoles was an exciting time. Both the arcade and console markets were thriving, the NES had successfully brought gaming back home in North America, and Sega was officially first off the mark to make inroads into this new 16-bit era of gaming with the Mega Drive. With Mario now a household name, gamers were anticipating the release of Nintendo's next instalment, especially as it was to be launched alongside its newfangled 16-bit games console.

Released in 1990, *Super Mario World* stuck close to the *Super Mario Bros 3* template. Miyamoto and his team set about using the extra technical power of the Super Nintendo to create an enhanced, but not necessarily more innovative, version of the NES classic. Gone were the enjoyable minigames and inventory, and Mario received a new makeover as well as an array of new power-ups, including a yellow cape that afforded him the power of temporary flight, and a lovable green dinosaur companion in the form of Yoshi – a character whose grabbing tongue was possibly inspired by Nintendo's popular Ultra Hand grabbing toy, and whose name could have derived as a portmanteau of Nintendo's then-president, Hiroshi Yamauchi. This is all pure speculation, of course.

Following the release of *Super Mario Bros*, it was Miyamoto's intention to give Mario a dinosaur steed – an idea said to have been inspired by *Excitebike*. In answering a question about how he and his team approached *Mario* sequels in the *Mario Mania Player's Guide*, Miyamoto explained the delay in Yoshi's debut: "Once the game is released, we start thinking it may not be such a bad idea to add another title to the series. We usually have lots of ideas that we haven't been able to implement yet. A good example is Yoshi. We wanted to have Mario ride a dinosaur ever since we finished the original *Super Mario Bros*, but it was impossible technically. We were finally able to get Yoshi off the drawing boards with the Super NES."

Nintendo then followed up *Super Mario World* with *Super Mario Kart*. It became the best-selling racing game on the system, and one of Mario's most successful spin-off series. Mario was now showing himself as a cultural icon, and the versatile face of Nintendo. In fact, his popularity had swelled so much that it was almost a given that the character would pique the interest of film studios wanting to cash in on his celebrity. And so Mario and Luigi did the inevitable, heading to the big screen for a live-action retelling of their videogame antics for the 1993 movie *Super Mario Bros*, plonking actors Bob Hoskins, John Leguizamo and Dennis Hopper in the roles of Mario, Luigi and Bowser respectively. However, for all its promise and hype, the movie, which decides to throw out the colourful *Mario Bros* universe to place the brothers inside some kind of rubbish version of *Total Recall*, tanked at the box office and was branded an unmitigated big-budget failure, and Mario has never made a return to Tinseltown since.

Mario's next big Super Nintendo release came in the form of *Super Mario World 2: Yoshi's Island*. In the game, Mario and Luigi were depicted as babies, with the player now fully assuming the role of a Yoshi and tasked with completing a colourful relay race to get Mario safely to his parents. Of course, given the infant ages of the brothers in the game, *SMW2* is deemed a prequel to the entire *Mario* series. Its story is thus pure retcon, as the game's ending shows the brothers delivered to their parents, who are seen living inside a house in the Mushroom Kingdom. That said, when you remember that before this point we were all accepting of the fact that Mario was the story of a gorilla-abusing carpenter-turned-plumber/pest exterminator who gets whisked away to a mushroom land through a pipe and must then rescue their princess from a giant turtle king, we guess such changes can be forgiven.

Released in 1996, Mario's final Super Nintendo outing saw him throw his cap into another new genre,

"SMB3 WAS UNVEILED LIKE THE MOST BRILLIANT OBJET D'ART IN HISTORY. IT'S ACTUALLY CLOSE"

Yoshi took centre stage in the sequel to *Mario World*, *Yoshi's Island*.

MARIO MEMORIES

Philip and Andrew Oliver
Cofounders Blitz Software

PO: We first saw Mario appear in the *Donkey Kong* arcade game in 1981. A few years later, in 1988, we went to the Consumer Electronics Show (CES) in Las Vegas and were stunned by the magnitude of the games industry and the size of Nintendo's presence. And at the heart of it all was Mario. At that time, *Super Mario Bros* was at its height on the NES – I think they'd sold in the region of 20 million copies, which was incredible.

AO: I remember seeing *Mario Bros* on a Japanese imported NES in about 1986. I remember it looking clean, slick and very playable. And best of all, it was instantly easily accessible. The first time I saw Mario as a character was in the arcade game *Donkey Kong*. Back then he didn't strike me as a brilliant character, but he always starred in brilliant games.

PO: All the Mario games are great. I guess we played the original a fair bit, but it was *Super Mario 64* that proved to the world that character games work better in 3D. Andrew will definitely go for *Mario Kart*, as it's his all-time favourite game! It's up there near the top with me, too.

AO: Mario represents games of brilliant gameplay. He's also had a lot of work done on his 'personality', as the graphical powers of machines have been updated. Each revision has been very skilfully managed and has served to embellish and deepen Mario's qualities – they've been careful never to change his persona fundamentally, so the Mario today is essentially the same guy as the Mario of the Eighties.

Steve Lycett
Sumo Digital

Boringly, I'll have to plump for *Super Mario World* as my favourite *Mario* game. I got a SNES for my 18th birthday, and lost weeks of my life hunting down all the hidden exits, completing Star Road and then rinsing it twice for the second credits sequence. An amazing game that's clearly ageing better than I am! I think his appeal simply boils down to quality. Bar the odd exception, if it's got 'Mario' in the title you know you'll be getting something that's been built with love, care and attention to detail, and will provide you with hours of fun. I'll happily buy a *Mario* title without reading a single review. Nintendo will always deliver the goods!

The late Ralph Baer 'The father of videogaming'

To me, Mario is a living presence. I still have the original NES and the *Duck Hunt*/*Mario* cart that goes with it. Over the decades I have demonstrated interacting physically with the *Duck Hunt* game in the manner of today's Wii games. As has been so often the case, I was 20 years too early with those concepts. Meanwhile, who can resist playing the original *Mario* game when that old TV set is turned on in my demo area and I'm not bringing down those ducks by lobbing something physical at them?

HONOURABLE MENTIONS

Here are some of the more unusual Mario games, which aren't part of the Super Mario canon

MARIO CLASH
VIRTUAL BOY
■ This red-looking 3D redux of the original *Mario Bros* coin-op was the first of two *Mario* games released for the Virtual Boy, the other being *Mario Tennis*. It's also the first ever 3D *Mario* game, if you discount *Super Mario Kart*.

ALLEYWAY
GAME BOY
■ Although not really a *Mario* game per se, this decent *Breakout* clone saw Mario piloting the game's bat. You couldn't actually tell this from the in-game graphics, mind, but he's there on the front of the box art, sporting some natty overalls.

MARIO PAINT
SUPER NINTENDO
■ One of the few games to use the Super Nintendo's mouse peripheral, which came as a pack-in with the game, this artistic spin-off allowed budding artists to create drawings, stamps and animations and then set them to sounds using a music generator.

HOTEL MARIO
PHILLIPS CD-I
■ Often cited as being the worst *Mario* game ever. This CD-i puzzle title was a waste product from the messy Super Nintendo CD saga and tasked players with rescuing Princess Toadstool by closing a whole bunch of doors, for reasons never explained.

ALL NIGHT NIPPON SUPER MARIO BROS
FAMICOM DISK SYSTEM
■ This game would be considered one of the most bizarre *Mario* clones to find release, were it not released by Nintendo. This *Super Mario Bros*/*Lost Levels* fusion featured DJs from a popular Japanese radio show.

MARIO EDUCATION GAMES
NES, SNES, PC
■ The plumber also appeared in a series of educational games. These included the geography-themed *Mario Is Missing!*, the typing trainer, *Mario Teaches Typing*; and *Mario's Time Machine*, a thinly veiled history lesson.

SUPER MARIO EXCITEBIKE
SUPER NINTENDO (SATELLAVIEW)
■ Mario and friends appeared in this little-known *Excitebike* title, which meshed together *Mario Kart* with motocross. Released in four parts, it was only available through the Satellaview service.

A FRIENDLY RIVALRY… EVENTUALLY

No feature on Mario would be complete without at least mentioning the epic 16-bit videogame war that Mario played a major part in. During the height of the 16-bit generation, school playgrounds around the globe were divided. One side bound together by a love for a dinosaur-riding Italian plumber named Mario; the other in support for a skittish, edgy and nippy blue hedgehog called Sonic. These two company mascots could scarcely be more different, but together their rivalry spearheaded one of the most exciting periods in gaming ever. With each console generation that passed, their competition softened, until Sega eventually bailed out of the hardware market altogether in 2001. What happened next, no school kid back in 1993 could ever have predicted: Sega started releasing *Sonic* games on Nintendo consoles, starting with *Sonic Adventure 2 Battle* on Nintendo's GameCube. And then two videogame mascots got to finally settle their differences publicly when they appeared together in the game *Mario & Sonic At The Olympic Games* in 2007, followed by the long-awaited chance to beat the crap out of each other in 2008's *Super Smash Bros Brawl*.

MARIO MEMORIES

Martyn Brown Team 17 Founder

Obviously, like many people, I first saw Mario in *Donkey Kong*, but he really played second fiddle to DK. It's amazing to think that Nintendo took the Mario character and threw him into the *Super Mario* world, as it was an anonymous character before then. I wasn't super sure what to make of the first true *Mario* game in terms of character, other than it being brilliantly playable – I was too busy with the Amiga around that time anyway. I think my favourite *Mario* game has to be *Super Mario 64*, the first 3D offering, because it was so incredibly well-considered for its time. I've enjoyed the past games, but they get a bit too hardcore for me. Mario's remained so enduring because he's so charming and a lot of fun. The games are generally so well-balanced to play that it's difficult to get too frustrated and therefore swear at him, although I'm sure it's been done a few times – even by me.

David Braben Co-creator of Elite

I think my first experience of Mario was in a pub, with the original *Donkey Kong*. To be honest I didn't particularly register the character, more the way the game was played, which seemed a little bizarre at the time! *Mario 64* on the Nintendo 64 was the first *Mario* game I really enjoyed playing, as it was, for me at least, less annoying than the previous outings. Later games are great too, but *Mario 64* sticks in my mind the strongest, as for its time it was a great trailblazer. Interestingly, in the days of *Donkey Kong* and *Super Mario Bros* the character image was pretty indistinct and heavily pixelated. Later games featured him as an image, and I think that is when he started to be identified, but *Mario 64* was the first game, I think, that really made a character out of him, for example, when he spoke on the title screen of the game. If anything, especially in the USA, I think he has become the icon of Nintendo. Other factors – like the fact that he seems to run like a toddler does – makes him pretty endearing. He is a pretty nonthreatening character.

[Wii] Mario returned top form following two superb *Galaxy* Wii titles that are literally out of this world.

this time the RPG with the Square-developed *Super Mario RPG: Legend Of The Seven Stars*. The game was a mixture of isometric platform RPG and turn-based battles, and the game's visuals utilised the snazzy ACM graphics techniques seen in *Donkey Kong Country*. But coming late in the Super Nintendo's life, and only released in the US and Japan, it was largely missed by many on its release.

MARIO REACHES 64

Another new console saw another groundbreaking entry in the *Mario* series come, this time in the form of *Super Mario 64* for the N64. Always innovating, Nintendo once again sought to revolutionise the platform genre, and in doing so proved undoubtedly that the creative, fun, engaging and abundant gameplay of previous *Mario* adventures could adapt to a true 3D polygon world unscathed. The N64's analogue controls also worked overtime to further enhance the experience. With a wealth of new acrobatic moves at Mario's disposal, *Mario 64* turned him from portly jumpy plumber into a gaming Baryshnikov. Finally, through a series of open-ended levels – all connected by a castle-shaped hub – that unfurled with each revisit, it offered players the chance to really immerse themselves in the colourful and enchanting world of the Mushroom Kingdom. It was truly the gaming equivalent of chasing the rabbit down to Wonderland, and with the inclusion of Mips the rabbit in the game, who spouted dialogue very similar to Lewis Carroll's tardy White Rabbit, this notion was clearly not lost on Miyamoto and his EAD team.

Following the release of *Mario 64*, Mario himself then broke into even more game genres with the first entry in the Hudson-developed *Mario Party* series. And the N64 era also saw Mario return to his NES sporting roots in *Mario Golf* and *Mario Tennis*, before appearing in the first *Super Smash Bros* and making his final 'so long' for the console with *Paper Mario*.

Owing to the early release of *Mario 64* on the N64, it comes as a surprise to many that a sequel was never released on the system. Well, in actual fact, for a time a *Mario 64* sequel was in development, albeit for the 64DD. In 1997 Miyamoto revealed at E3 that work had started on the game. However, following the disastrous launch of the add-on in Japan, and its subsequent poor domestic sales, Nintendo promptly stopped support for the hardware and the game was scrapped.

During Nintendo's Space World event in 2000, the company showcased the power of its brand-new console, the GameCube, with a *Mario* tech demo dubbed *Super Mario 128*. The short demonstration showed a large 2D Mario splintering into 128 smaller versions that ran across the surface of a globe. It showcased, for the first time, the 'sphere-walking' tech that was to be later utilised for *Super Mario Galaxy*.

The following year, however, and at the same show, *Super Mario Sunshine* was unveiled to the crowds, and while it shared little likeness to *Super Mario 128*, it was formally announced as the official sequel to *Mario 64*. Apart from a story that saw Mario partaking in a spot of community service after the squeaky plumber is forced to clean up the mess left by a muck-spraying imposter, *Sunshine* stuck very close to *Mario 64*'s template.

Set in the sun-drenched Isle Delfino, *Sunshine* kept the hub structure of *Mario 64*, and progression still relied on the collection of Shine Sprites. As well as the 3D return of Yoshi, the most novel feature in *Sunshine* came in the form of an odd rucksack armament called FLUDD (Flash Liquidizing Ultra Dousing Device) that Mario could use not only as a cleaning weapon but also as a way to help get around the stages. Clever aiming of the FLUDD's spray nozzles could launch Mario up into the air and even afford him a handy spray-powered speed boost. However, the device quickly became a bone of contention with many fans when they soon discovered that it hindered the responsive control of Mario, and made retrieving stars almost feel like Mario-endorsed GCSE physics exercises.

MARIO MEMORIES

Ste Pickford
Legendary 8-bit coder

Definitely *Donkey Kong* in Stockport Arcade, or maybe on holiday in Blackpool or Southport. Of course, I never knew that was actually Mario at the time. I could never get past the second screen, but I must have spent dozens of 10p pieces trying. The first real introduction I had to Mario was at Rare. We had a meeting there in about 1988, and they showed us *Super Mario Bros* on a NES. We must have just screwed our faces up because of how ugly it looked. We were heavily into developing Amiga and Atari ST games at the time, and we had sort of graduated from blocky four-colour graphics to higher res 16-colour graphics with large, non-repeating bitmaps. The Stampers told us to ignore the fact that it didn't look that good, and insisted that we play it because it was better than any Amiga game. We laughed, but I think they lent us a NES with a couple of games, and sure enough, *Super Mario Bros* was brilliant. The irony is that the simple, functional graphics of *SMB* have dated much better than the overworked Amiga graphics of the same period. Without a doubt, my favourite *Mario* game is *Super Mario Bros 3*. We were developing NES games ourselves when it was released and we were just blown away by how much better this game was than anything we were working on at the time. It was at that point that I first began to appreciate what a great designer Mr Miyamoto was, and what a great developer Nintendo is. They were streets ahead of everyone else in the world at that time. That game introduced so many new ideas, and had so much imagination – every new level was surprising and delightful. I don't think that level of consistent invention in one game has been matched by any game since, until *Super Mario Galaxy*, but *Super Mario Bros 3* wins for me because of the big impression it made on me when I was younger.

MARIO MEMORIES

Greg Omi
Atari Lynx progammer

I first saw Mario in *Donkey Kong*, but the first time I really recognised Mario was in *Super Mario Bros* for the [NES]. I was working at Epyx at the time and the testers were playing it. That year, I bought NES consoles for all of my nieces and nephews.

Mario Kart 64 is probably my favourite *Mario* game because it led us to make *Crash Team Racing*, which I consider to be the most fun game I've ever worked on. I loved the slide mechanics and the random power-ups to rubber-band the gameplay, helping out the players in the back. I love Wario Stadium, with the unintentional shortcut at the beginning of the track where you could jump over the wall twice to get a really low lap time.

Mario came to represent Nintendo as a mascot because of the success of *Super Mario Bros*. This led Nintendo to market based on Mario, which increased the character's popularity.

Popularity is a power function, so once you have brand recognition, you have inertia to give you a leg up on the competition. That's why everyone makes sequels, why movie companies try to make blockbuster movies, and why indies and original material have a hard time breaking through.

Just look at social gaming: *FarmVille*, which I [used to] work on, was twice as popular as the next most popular game; there are a bunch of games around second place, followed by the 'long tail' of games after that. There can only be one super popular game at a time, and at some point *FarmVille*'s popularity will fade and another game will rise to fill its spot. *World Of Warcraft* is another example of this.

» [N64] *Mario 64* was a landmark game for the Nintendo mascot, and it set a high benchmark for future 3D games to try to meet.

With *Mario Sunshine* failing to capture or stir up the same level of popularity as previous big-budget *Mario* titles, and it becoming increasing likely that the GameCube would become Nintendo's most unsuccessful console to date, outwardly it seemed that the once-infallible videogame giant was finally losing its grip on the market it formerly dominated, and Mario seemed to echo this sense of dispassion, appearing in a series of decent but uninspired sports sequels – *Mario Power Tennis*, *Mario Superstar Baseball* and *Mario Golf Toadstool Tour* – following a good but equally uninspired *Mario Kart* sequel with *Mario Kart: Double Dash!!*. But just as it seemed Nintendo was becoming crestfallen by its fall from greatness, the Wii happened and changed its fortunes in a way that nobody could have predicted.

» [Switch] *Super Mario Odyssey* lets you take control of the plumber's foes by using his brand-new 'Capture' ability.

A SPACE ODYSSEY

Both *Mario Galaxy* and *Mario Galaxy 2* stand as nigh-on flawless examples of expert game design, and rank among the best games in the *Mario* series. By making inspired and sensible use of the Wii's motion-sensor controls, Nintendo was able to recapture the keen sense of fun, exploration and enjoyment that dazzled gamers in *Mario 64*. Making use of the sphere-walking technology first demoed in *Super Mario 128*, Miyamoto and his team shot for the stars by opting to set the games in outer space, with levels taking the form of galaxies, all filled with individual planets and worlds to explore. Like *Mario 64* before it, the controls were also wonderfully implemented. Players could steer Mario in comfortable fashion, but also aid him using the Wii Remote, which, through an on-screen reticule, could be used to suck up 'Star Bits' and launch Mario between planets. The *Galaxy* games also saw a return of the costume-style power-ups of old, including a bee costume that gave Mario the power of flight, a spring suit to heighten his jump, and the first 3D iteration of the Fire Flower.

Complementing these two interstellar adventures was another *Paper Mario* game, and a real return to the character's Famicom roots in the four-player platformer *New Super Mario Bros*, a game that brought simultaneous multiplayer back to the series for the first time since the original *Mario Bros*.

"THIS INDUSTRY WOULD BE A FAR GLUMMER PLACE WITHOUT MARIO"

Mario's adventures continued on Nintendo's next hardware releases with *New Super Mario Bros 2* and *Super Mario 3D Land* for Nintendo 3DS and the excellent *Super Mario 3D World* on Wii U. The Wii U got another surprise in the form of the brilliant *Super Mario Maker*, which allowed players to create their own levels and share them online. It was later released on 3DS. The eighth *Mario Kart* also made its debut on Wii U and introduced *F-Zero*-styled anti-gravity sections.

And then came the Switch in March 2017. Nintendo's most current games machine showcases a hybrid design that lets it straddle home console and handheld roles. The system launched with a brilliant *Zelda* title, *Breath Of The Wild*, but the heroic plumber didn't surface in a new adventure until October that year. It would turn out that *Super Mario Odyssey* was worth the wait. Enabling Mario to take control (or 'Capture', get it?) creatures by flinging his hat at them, the Nintendo icon's newest outing continues the series' runaway success, selling 9.07 million units by the end of 2017 alone.

Mario's long-term success is nothing short of a magnificent achievement. Always entertaining and almost always innovating, love him or not, you cannot deny that this industry would certainly be a far glummer place without him. *

THE 1990s

A DECADE OF GREAT INNOVATION AND SEISMIC SHIFTS

There was a distinctive shift during the Nineties that continues to this day. Consoles finally took over from home computers as the systems of choice for many gamers, while Japanese developers (who had largely been confined to the arcades) began to lead the charge for many genres, from platformers and shoot-'em-ups, to survival horror and fighting games to name just a few they excelled in.

8-bit micros still bravely battled on, but many gamers were focused on 16-bit systems like the Amiga and Atari ST, which were far more capable of embracing the move to 3D games. Still, it was becoming clear that consoles were finding it far easier to deliver the 3D-focused, arcade-like experiences that gamers craved during this period. It wasn't all bad for computers, though, as PC titles like *Command & Conquer* and *Doom* proved, but change was coming, and as big businesses continued to replace the cottage industry that had kicked things off for most of the Seventies and Eighties, the expectations of gamers shifted accordingly.

GAMES OF THE DECADE

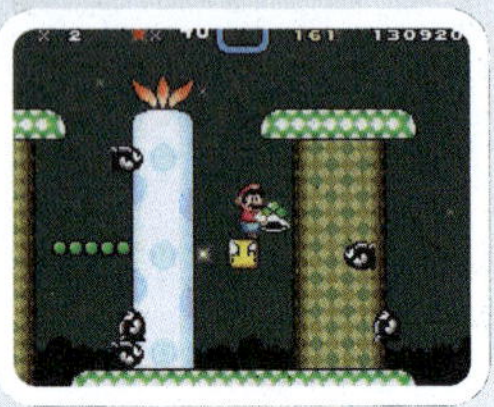

1990
SUPER MARIO WORLD

We're always hesitant to suggest that a game is perfect, but it's hard to see how Mario's first 16-bit adventure doesn't deserve such a lofty accolade. It remains as satisfying to play today as it did in 1990 thanks to its exceptional level design, balanced play mechanics and challenging structure.

1991
STREET FIGHTER II: THE WORLD WARRIOR

Capcom's brawler was always going to make the cut. After all, it massively improved on its ropey predecessor, introduced gamers to the joys of combos, let you play as a host of iconic characters and created a template that countless developers copied (with varying degrees of success).

1992
SONIC THE HEDGEHOG 2

Sega's supercharged sequel appeared to be everywhere in 1992, largely thanks to an aggressive $10 million marketing campaign that not only saw Sega's sequel receiving a global UK/US launch, but also the invention of a brand-new day, namely 'Sonic 2sday'. It's also the best *Sonic* game [Hey! - Nick].

1993
DOOM

id Software's shooter was a huge deal on release, shaking up the concept of what PC games were capable of and laying blueprints for the first-person shooter genre in the process. *Doom* helped establish competitive multiplayer, delivered cutting-edge tech, played like a dream and spawned countless clones.

1994
SENSIBLE WORLD OF SOCCER

Before *FIFA* came along and rewrote the rules of football, *SWOS* was considered the definitive football videogame (and some will still happily die on that hill). While it wasn't the most accurate representation of the sport, it offered an intense competitive experience that few sports games of the time could match.

1990
Codemasters reveals the Game Genie this year, originally for use on the NES. A fierce court battle will ensue, but the Codies will win it.

1990 MARCH
Nintendo starts the Nintendo World Championships. Its custom cartridge will eventually sell for thousands.

1990 APRIL
SNK releases the Neo-Geo MVS in arcades and the AES in homes. Both pieces of hardware have identical cutting-edge tech.

1990 APRIL
Williams' *Smash TV* hits arcades. The shooter heavily channels futuristic films like *Running Man* and *RoboCop*.

1990 APRIL
THQ is founded by Jack Friedman in Agoura Hills. The company name is an abbreviation of 'toy headquarters'.

THE NINETIES...

AS TOLD BY GREGG MAYLES

RARE'S DESIGNER LOOKS BACK AT THE DECADE THAT DEFINED THE STUDIO AS A SERIOUS PLAYER AND OFFERED EXCITING NEW PROSPECTS FOR DEVELOPERS

If the Eighties had been a time of experimenting and staking a claim on the still-blossoming videogame market, then the following decade really saw the games industry begin to grow up. "The Nineties felt like the decade when gaming became mainstream," begins Gregg when we ask him about the era where Rare rose to dominance, "where it shook off some of its introverted 'hobbyist' image and transformed itself into a recreation that a much broader audience enjoyed. It even started to become an aspirational industry to work in, rather than a, 'You do what!?'"

While the games industry certainly felt like it had become more established during this period, elements of it still felt fresh and exciting for those working within it and the gamers that enjoyed their games. "It was probably the most innovative period," admits Gregg. "Games moving from 2D into 3D was by far the biggest change, but it also heralded the establishment of many game genres – most notably first-person shooters. Handheld gaming became widespread thanks to the Game Boy, and Nintendo also established the blueprint for which most controllers would follow. By the end of the Nineties, the Dreamcast hinted at the massive phenomenon that online gaming was to become."

Of course, one of the biggest shake-ups of the decade was the introduction of Sony's PlayStation, something that isn't lost on Gregg. "For the early part of the Nineties, nothing seemed to suggest that Nintendo and Sega wouldn't continue their somewhat polite rivalry, with the Super Nintendo and the Mega Drive both being capable machines with great games," Gregg continues. "Then the big brash newcomer crashed onto the scene! Sony's PlayStation, full of CD swagger and 3D cool, really shook things up and set the industry on a path that it is still largely on today. Nintendo responded to this challenge with the N64, but sadly it was the beginning of the end for Sega as a hardware creator."

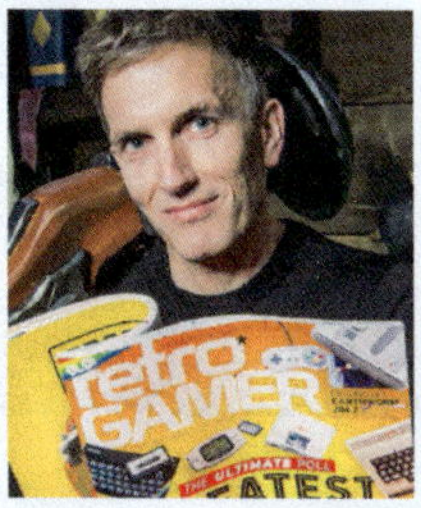

The Nineties wasn't just a time when new console rivals emerged, it was also a period of some truly phenomenal games and ones that were truly genre-refining, too. "In terms of games, *Super Mario 64* absolutely defined the decade for me," highlights Gregg. "The sense of freedom was magical, Mario running gleefully around the grounds and into the castle was symbolic of the direction it took the industry towards. Whilst not the first first-person shooter, *Doom* established a genre that is still dominant 25 years later, and I clearly remember one late night working on *Donkey Kong Country* trying to download the initial single-level demo and being wowed by its accomplishment."

And then, of course, there's that critical move to 3D, a painful transition that was first hinted at during the Eighties, but solidified during the Nineties as developers harnessed its exciting capabilities and possibilities for games, both in the home and in arcades. "On more a personal level, myself and Rare found the transition from 2D to 3D liberating," Gregg concludes. "Challenging in many new ways, but so exciting! We were amongst the first to use 3D models in our games, but once we went fully 3D there was no looking back. It finally felt like you were *in* a game, rather than *looking at* a game."

1995 COMMAND & CONQUER

Westwood's excellent real-time strategy opus is very much like *Doom* – it wasn't the first game of its type, but it was the one that ultimately shaped the genre it found itself in. Also like *Doom*, *Command & Conquer*'s success led to many copycats and it spawned a successful series of sequels and spin-offs.

1996 TOMB RAIDER

Core Design's game is not only important for redefining adventure games, but for also creating an iconic character that transcended videogames – one Lara Croft. It's notable as well for offering an incredible sense of scale and exploration of its world and tombs, something that the newer games simply haven't bettered.

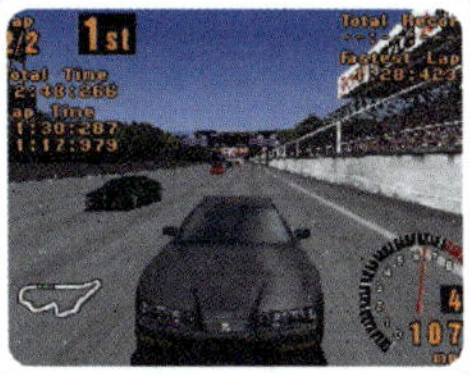

1997 GRAN TURISMO

It's easy to pick Polyphony Digital's racer apart today, but it's also easy to forget just what it brought to the table back in 1997. *Gran Turismo* offered incredible visuals, a wealth of tweakable options, two huge game modes and an exceptional number of licensed cars. We call it the flight sim of racing games.

1998 METAL GEAR SOLID

An amazing year of videogames meant this wasn't an easy pick, but Hideo Kojima's epic just sneaks into the lead. *Metal Gear Solid* arguably laid the groundwork for videogames being heavily influenced by movies and it also created the blueprints for the multitude of stealth games that followed.

1999 SHENMUE

Granted it was released right at the end of the year, but there was still nothing quite like Yu Suzuki's Dreamcast game in the 11 months that preceded it. It might not have matched every gamer's expectations, but that was always going to happen considering the sheer scale of developer, Yu Suzuki's ambitions.

1990 AUGUST Atari Games' *Pit-Fighter* hits arcades. The one-on-one brawler becomes a big success thanks to its digitised visuals.

1990 SEPTEMBER Amstrad releases its GX4000. Despite looking like a Snowspeeder, it will fail to gain traction and became a flop.

1990 OCTOBER The Game Gear, Sega's handheld, launches in Japan. Available games include *Columns*, *Pengo* and *Super Monaco GP*.

1990 OCTOBER *The Secret Of Monkey Island* sets sail from LucasArts and immediately charms gamers the world over.

1990 NOVEMBER The Super Famicom launches in Japan. Available games include *F-Zero* and the pack-in, *Super Mario World*.

REVENGE OF THE CONSOLES

The Nineties was a remarkable decade, in which games went from 2D visuals and chiptunes to complex 3D graphics and rich CD-quality audio. The videogame market shifted towards consoles during the Nineties, as the world was first captivated by the 16-bit console war, and subsequently enthralled by the 3D capabilities of the PlayStation. The power of consoles increasingly began to rival that of arcade machines, ultimately leading to convergence at the end of the decade. The market for diverse home computers also faded away, replaced by the dominance of the PCs that had grown out of the old IBM compatible machines.

1

NINTENDO STEPS UP ITS GAME!

1 SNES

Nintendo, 1990

It took its time in creating a successor to the NES, but Nintendo's patient approach ensured it had a powerhouse on its hands – the SNES could handle more colours than the competition, and advanced scaling and rotation effects. Of course, the game library is legendary too, starting with two classics in *Super Mario World* and *F-Zero* and accumulating many more from there. The console quickly overtook the PC Engine in Japan, but faced a fierce war with the Mega Drive internationally. Despite the competition, it was the best-selling machine of its generation with 49.1 million units sold worldwide.

2 NEO-GEO AES

SNK, 1990

The first home console from SNK offered true arcade quality, as it used exactly the same hardware as its arcade games. The price was prohibitive and relatively few players bought consoles, but the long life of the arcade hardware and hardcore nature of Neo-Geo collectors kept the system alive until 2004.

3 GAME GEAR

Sega, 1990

This entry into the handheld market shared the Atari Lynx's primary problem – poor battery life due to a backlit colour display. However, the Game Gear was easy to develop for thanks to its Master System-based hardware, and games like *Sonic The Hedgehog* ensured it sold reasonably. With relatively few great exclusives, its popularity has dwindled over time.

4 AMIGA 1200

Commodore, 1992

The final entry-level Amiga from Commodore was the last gasp of the old home computer market, which was giving way to the PC/Mac duopoly. Though the AGA chipset was an improvement, it didn't offer a compelling reason to choose the Amiga over other computers, and Commodore was bankrupt two years later.

5 SATURN

Sega, 1994

The Saturn was an undeniably powerful piece of kit, but it was certainly not a friendly one – developers struggled to make the most of its dual CPUs and video processors. The complexity of the hardware also made it expensive, with a launch price of £400 – which was undercut by Sony and its PlayStation. Despite hosting great conversions like *Sega Rally* and *Virtua Fighter 2*, the Saturn failed to gain a foothold in the west. The system fared better in Japan, and became a favourite amongst import gamers and 2D aficionados. Just 9.2 million Saturn consoles were sold worldwide, making it an undisputed commercial failure.

BEST AMIGA COMPUTER EVER!

4

THREE WHOLE HOURS OF BATTERY LIFE!

3

5

OUT OF THIS WORLD GRAPHICS!

1990 DECEMBER
Nec launches its TurboExpress handheld in Japan. The miniature PC Engine is able to use all existing HuCard games.

1991 FEBRUARY
id Software is founded by Adrian Carmack, John Romero, Tom Hall and John Carmack. It'll go on to have a hit or two...

1991 FEBRUARY
Allen Adham, Frank Pearce and Michael Morhaime form Silicon & Synapse. It will be later renamed Blizzard Entertainment.

1991 FEBRUARY
DMA Design releases *Lemmings* on home computers to acclaim. The puzzler is soon ported to various systems.

1991 MARCH
Capcom's arcade hit *Street Fighter II: The World Warrior* appears. It will go on to change the fighting genre.

6 PLAYSTATION

Sony, 1994

It might not have had a renowned in-house development team, but what Sony did bring to the market was brand recognition, wads of marketing cash and a friendlier approach to third-party developers. The machine was easy to work with, leading to visually superior 3D games compared with the competition, and it was priced affordably. Consumer expectations changed over its lifetime, with arcade experiences like *Ridge Racer* giving way to content rich games like *Gran Turismo*. Though early units frequently suffered CD-ROM drive failures, the system was a success, becoming the first ever console to sell over 100 million units.

7 NINTENDO 64

Nintendo, 1996

The N64 was designed by the 3D hardware specialists at Silicon Graphics Inc, and with it Nintendo made huge leaps in 3D game design – games like *Super Mario 64* and *The Legend Of Zelda: The Ocarina Of Time* are rightly regarded as all-time classics. However, Nintendo's decision to stick with ROM cartridges meant high prices and low storage capacity, causing many players and developers to choose the PlayStation. While it was a strong competitor to Sony's console in North America, the Nintendo 64 lagged far behind it in other regions and finished its life with 32.9 million units sold.

8 DREAMCAST

Sega, 1998

At long last, Sega delivered some great hardware – it was considerably easier to work with than the Saturn had been and more affordable for consumers, though its internet capabilities were perhaps a step ahead of the market. However, Sega's past mistakes had alienated key developers including Electronic Arts, and while the system had a great line-up of games, few of them matched the market's growing taste for longer, more cinematic experiences. Hindered by marketing blunders and anticipation of the PlayStation 2, the Dreamcast failed to turn a profit and Sega left the hardware market to become a third-party publisher.

9 GAME BOY COLOR

Nintendo, 1998

Having finally managed to get acceptable battery life from a handheld with colour display, Nintendo elected to upgrade its ageing Game Boy. The system was very popular, particularly due to the *Pokémon* games, but was also short-lived – its successor, the Game Boy Advance, was released two-and-a-half years later.

OTHER SYSTEMS FROM THE NINETIES

GX4000 • Amstrad, 1990

Amstrad's attempt to energise its dated home computer hardware in console form was met with an overwhelming rejection from consumers.

Jaguar • Atari Corp, 1993

This cheap and relatively capable machine was Atari's last roll of the dice. Unfortunately, it had too few killer games and a later CD add-on didn't help.

3DO • 3DO Company, 1993

3DO's various manufacturers couldn't lose money on hardware as they made no money on software, and high prices scuppered the system.

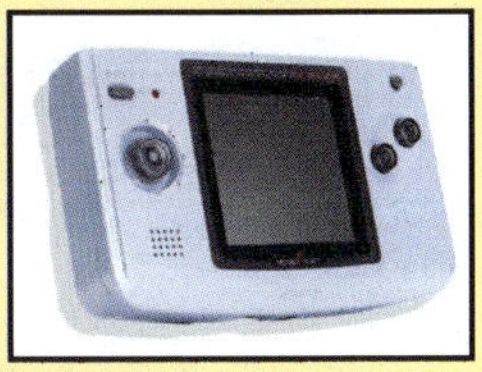

Neo-Geo Pocket Color • SNK, 1999

This Game Boy Color competitor had great games, specs and battery life, but SNK's financial woes helped bury it.

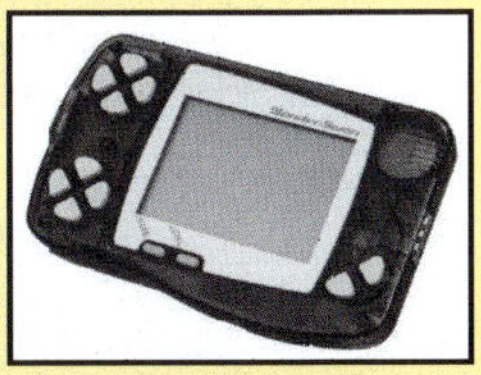

WonderSwan • Bandai, 1999

Bandai's wealth and licensing muscle allowed this handheld to gain a reasonable Japanese audience, but the monochrome display dated it.

1991 MAY
Amiga Power hits the shelves. The magazine's distinctive voice and hard-hitting approach goes down well.

1991 JUNE
Sonic The Hedgehog is released as a rival to *Super Mario Bros.* It will become the Mega Drive's best-selling videogame.

1991 AUGUST
Super Mario Kart launches on the SNES. The Mode 7 racer proves the versatility of *Mario*. Several sequels will follow.

1991 SEPTEMBER
EA founder Trip Hawkins forms The 3DO Company in Redwood City, California, with the aim to make a new console.

1991 SEPTEMBER
Namco's shooter *Starblade* wows arcadegoers with its cutting-edge 3D visuals and its superb cinematic presentation.

THE RISE OF THE *WORLD WIDE WEB*

Words by John Szczepaniak

IT PERMEATES EVERY ASPECT OF EVERYONE'S LIFE – FACILITATING, MONITORING, SOMETIMES EVEN CONTROLLING YOUR ACTIONS. BUT THE BIRTH AND RISE OF THE WEB, AS WE KNOW IT TODAY, IS HAZILY REMEMBERED. WE TRAVEL BACK TO THE NINETIES TO SEE IT GO ONLINE

» Sir Timothy Berners-Lee invented the World Wide Web, emphasising visuals, interaction, and hyperlinks. (Image courtesy of CERN).

» Like a lot of publishers, Working Designs had a website. What's unusual is Victor Ireland was known to talk directly with fans on forums.

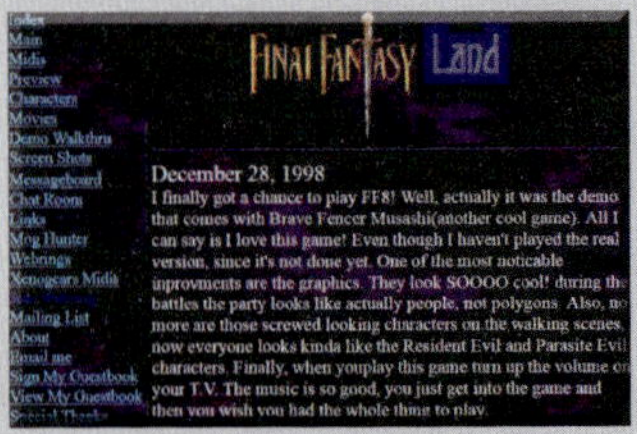

» Matt Pannella, "age unknown" according to his About Me section, encapsulating much of the early web in his Final Fantasy Land site from 1998.

Remember in 1983's WarGames, when Matthew Broderick uses a computer to dial his school's network to change grades? It's a good representation of the early internet as conceived in the mid-Seventies: computers interconnected to others in a network over phone lines, sharing data and displaying text – somewhat dull and also quite different from the World Wide Web. The internet is computers joined by cables; the web is an abstract virtual world of images and sounds built by people. The mistake is so common the web's creator, Sir Timothy Berners-Lee, dedicates a section online (w3.org) explaining the difference. It was December 1990 when Sir Berners-Lee, together with a team at CERN, launched the first web browser and gave the internet form, and also humanity a new method of expression.

Media reaction was eclectic, drunk on the web's potential. Hollywood produced a glut of techno-paranoia films; the BBC's Tomorrow's World ran documentaries; beginner's 'cyberspace' books were published. All struggled with the nomenclature and imagery to describe the web. Over time, games magazines led the way, naturally, many with dedicated sections. Games World had its Cyberville, while Computer And Video Games had CVG World to document the online world. Even Manga Mania had its CyberDrome column, written by award-winning British sci-fi author Jon Courtenay Grimwood.

With many UK magazines starting columns, it seems almost like there was a push from above to indoctrinate the public. But Jon doesn't think so, "The web at the start was pretty niche, and thinking about it in cultural terms even more so. If there was a push, it was subtle enough not to be noticeable. I don't think anyone up the food chain thought, 'We must cover this.' It was a ground swell of geeky people thinking: 'I'm going to write about this!' It was the aftermath of cyberpunk and we all happily assumed games, computers and reality would ultimately mesh. My columns reflected what interested me, influenced by games, reading New Scientist, whatever I was researching for my stories. I'm not sure how I got the gig. Maybe simply emailing and suggesting it. That was still possible then; I got gigs at the Guardian and Independent doing just that."

Little did magazines realise their latest opium was also their executioner. As websites matured, taking on further roles – albeit faster and free – print media endured an agonising exsanguination. Tips mags folded first, thanks almost single-handedly to GameFAQs. Created by Jeff 'CJayC' Veasey, its popularity and growth is one of the web's greatest success stories. Aiming to provide advice for every game in existence, its importance can't be overstated. Long-time GameFAQs moderator and staff member Jack Hebb describes his conversion away from print: "I was impressed how much info there was. I'd search for cheats, tricks, GameShark codes, and after many AOL searches repeatedly pointed to GFAQs, I decided it was *the* go-to source. Rarely has there been anything I couldn't find. Given how reliable it was, and easier than digging though Nintendo Power magazines, I was hooked."

» Hypnospace Outlaw (PC) is a game which plays on nostalgia, trying to replicate the feel of old pre-millennium websites.

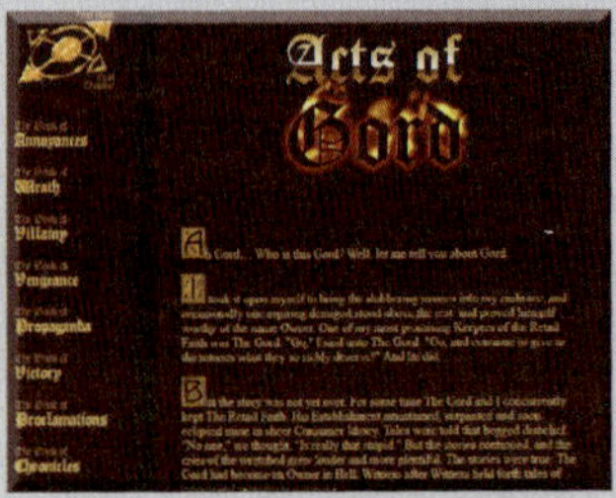

» Many old websites have died – in fact, the whole of GeoCities is gone. But Acts Of Gord, satirising the struggles of a games store, is still very much alive!

» Launched in 2001, and running on web browsers via Java, RuneScape was a landmark free-to-play MMORPG having over 200 million user accounts.

1991 OCTOBER Johnson Voorsanger Productions debuts *ToeJam & Earl* on the Mega Drive. It proves to be very, very funky.

1991 NOVEMBER Eric Chahi releases *Another World*. It's a big success for Delphine Software and will receive numerous ports.

1991 NOVEMBER Nintendo releases *The Legend Of Zelda: A Link To The Past* for the Super Famicom to critical and commercial success.

1991 DECEMBER Sega's Mega-CD add-on for the Mega Drive launches in Japan. *Heavy Nova* and *Sol-Feace* are its first titles.

1992 JANUARY *GamesMaster* is the first TV show about videogames in the UK. It's hosted by Dominik Diamond and stars Patrick Moore.

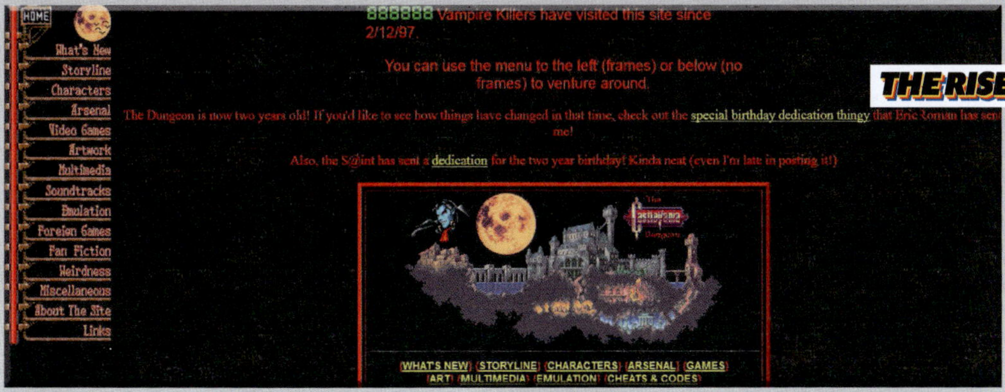

» Kurt Kalata, founder of Hardcore Gaming 101, started on GeoCities in the mid-Nineties with The Castlevania Dungeon.

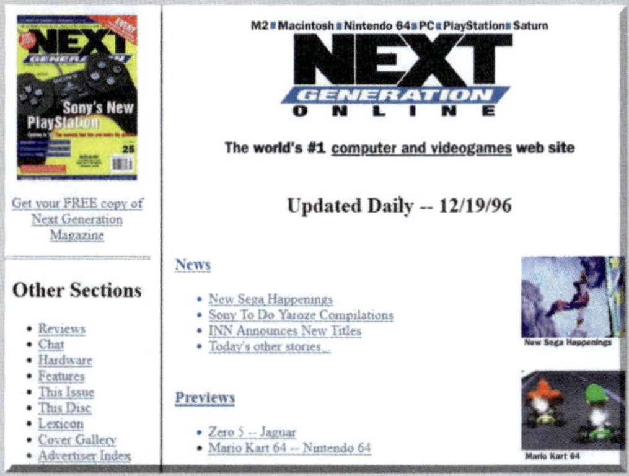

» The Next Generation website circa 1996, somewhat dry and sterile compared to other games websites of the era.

» Magazines like GameFAN embraced the web as early as 1996, but prioritised its print product.

The web was also the new frontier for the technoliterate. The inception of console emulation is intrinsic with the web. Zophar's Domain was an early hub for collaborators. Site founder Brad Levicoff explains, "I wanted something interactive, forums where people could request and provide help. I wanted to take advantage of things emulators were capable of – new concepts like save states and movie recordings via capturing controller input. I looked around, but there wasn't a site that had everything – news, emulators, save files, forums, etc. Archaic Ruins and Node99 were the closest, but weren't constantly updating. So I said: 'Why not make one?'"

Zophar's Domain rode the zeitgeist as emulation evolved. Brad puts it succinctly, "It was an exciting era, the genesis of the web as we know it, and a giant mess at the same time. Web design was hit-or-miss, graphics and music files would cause your 28.8Kbps dial-up modem to take ten minutes to load a page, and all sorts of broken links took you to places you never intended. But as time went on gaming sites improved. Sega tried to be the forefront – remember The Sega Channel? How about the Dreamcast's build-in modem, or Shenmue pass disc? It all seemed so futuristic..."

Given the last 30 years, a sense of nostalgia has risen. Forums have topics discussing GeoCities sites long deleted, many creators just kids at the time. Art imitates life and in March 2019 Hypnospace Outlaw was released, a game inside a satirical reimagining of the web. Its creator Jay Tholen explains, "The early web occupies a strange chunk of my memory. I recall more of the media hubbub and bizarre CGI ads of people 'surfing information superhighways'. Not knowing the boundaries of possibility made the old web feel like an adventure. People online back then started with a blank slate; so much personality could be relayed through how one might structure their site. Pages were often garish and hard to navigate, but I'd rather that over the sterility of social media. Hypnospace is both a celebration of the freedom inherent in a new medium and a critical look at the world of investors and whiz-kid startups."

It's important to acknowledge that for those who discovered the web in its formative days, each person's experience differs. These are highlights. We invite you to the forum on forum.retrogamer.net to share: how did you discover the web?

» Introducing Cyberspace (1991), later republished as Cyberspace For Beginners (1995), is pretty much how every book/magazine/article portrayed the web.

» The mid-Nineties saw most games magazines running sections dedicated to the weird and wonderful on the web.

TANGLED WEB

PRE-MILLENNIUM INTERNET MILESTONES

FREE WEB HOSTING

Animated gifs, autoplay MIDI music, poorly compressed images, affiliate webrings, plus a whole lot of unbridled passion and creativity. Whether Angelfire, Tripod, GeoCities, Homestead or any other hosting solution, this is probably how most remember the early web. Youngsters hand-coding shrines to everything, long before Blogger or YouTube.

GAMEFAQS • 1995

Staff mod Jack Hebb: "Through the Nineties everyone had a web page, a cheesy MySpace profile or AOL page, and GFAQs wasn't much different, but it grew and kept up with those accessing it. Most one-man sites outdated fast, or lacked structure to keep information organised. GFAQs grew from an occasional helper to an essential part of any game."

EBAY • 1995

Would *Panzer Dragoon Saga* still reach eye-watering prices were it not for online auction websites? It's difficult to say, but the ability to find and buy any game ever made, no matter how rare or old, changed the hobby forever and defined what people were willing to pay for things for decades to follow.

ZOPHAR'S DOMAIN

Site founder Brad Levicoff: "If not for emulator programmers and emulation websites we wouldn't have any of this stuff today. Consider the NES and SNES Mini – both are emulator-based, by Nintendo, over 20 years after companies like Nintendo went after emulator websites. How times change! I'm incredibly proud of what we accomplished."

BROWSER GAMES • 1996

Today with social media and 'free-to-play' it's easy to forget the days of browser games. Flash, Java, Shockwave, and other plug-ins, all promising free play online. Admittedly, most were ugly and clunky, but it set things rolling. Admit it, you created a *RuneScape* account after it launched in 2001 – we all did.

1992 MAY
id Software releases *Wolfenstein 3D*, a homage to *Castle Wolfenstein*, with cutting-edge graphics and a robotic Hitler.

1992 JULY
Madeline Canepa, David Morris and Judy Lang form Crystal Dynamics. Its HQ is based in Redwood City, California.

1992 AUGUST
Sega unleashes *Virtua Racing* in Japanese arcades. It improves on earlier 3D racers such as *Hard Drivin'*.

1992 OCTOBER
Mortal Kombat launches in arcades and *Night Trap* hits the Mega-CD. Both games will find themselves upsetting censors.

1992 OCTOBER
Commodore releases the Amiga 1200. A UK pack called Desktop Dynamite included two games, *Dennis* and *Oscar*.

A NEW DIMENSION: 3D GAMES TAKE OVER

» [PC] Unlike its predecessor, *Doom*, *Quake* uses real polygons, and does so for most of the game's objects.

THE NINETIES WAS THE DECADE THAT SAW 2D GAMES FINALLY GIVE WAY TO THE DOMINANCE OF 3D EXTRAVAGANZAS, AS TECH PROGRESS MADE FAST, DETAILED 3D AVAILABLE TO ALL. WE LOOK BACK AT ONE OF GAMING'S BIGGEST TECHNOLOGICAL LEAPS

WORDS BY NICK THORPE

ALEX TROWERS

Working at Bullfrog in the Nineties, Alex was a designer for games such as *Magic Carpet*, *Hi-Octane* and *Dungeon Keeper 2*.

IAN ANDREW

Together with brother Chris Andrew, Ian designed pioneering 3D games in the Eighties and early Nineties using the Freescape engine.

SHINICHI OGASAWARA

As a game designer at Sega AM3, Ogasawara worked on 3D games including *Gunblade NY*, *The Lost World* and *Jambo!*.

Plenty of graphical fads gained popularity in the Nineties, but have virtually disappeared today. We quickly learned that FMV was a poor basis for a game, and it's rarely used today. When was the last time you saw digitised sprites, or prerendered 3D ones for that matter? But today, many console games use 3D polygonal graphics – and that's been true ever since that turning point when 2D sprites fell out of favour, in the latter half of the Nineties.

For almost as long as we've had videogames, people have been attempting to represent 3D spaces in them. Early developments began in the Seventies – on the mainframes, *Maze War* was a precursor to first-person shooters and *Spasim* used wireframe models of spaceships, while arcade players got a first-person driving experience in *Night Driver*. 3D games developed further in the Eighties, with the arcades leading the way. *Battlezone* used a vector display to represent 3D tank battles in 1980, and the technologically important (if commercially unsuccessful) *I, Robot* used filled polygon graphics in 1983. By the end of the decade, Japanese developers were introducing the first arcade boards designed specifically for polygonal graphics, Namco's System 21 and Taito's Air System.

In the home, games like *Elite* and *Starglider* had used wireframe 3D graphics, but filled 3D was very rare – and Ian Andrew, formerly of Incentive Software, can explain why. "As a games designer and publisher in the Eighties, we faced the choice of going over to the new consoles or staying with the 8-bit home computers. I didn't like the idea of losing control of what and when we published to a console-maker, so I instead planned to do something different on the home computers." The result was the Freescape engine, which allowed players to navigate 3D environments from a first-person perspective.

"We spent over a year developing the Freescape game engine, my brother Chris being behind the coding and program design," Ian recalls. "One experienced programmer told me it could not be done." This motivated Ian and Chris to get it finished, but the task came with plenty of difficulties. "Organising the depth of the 3D objects in a scene was the biggest challenge. As pixel-based z-buffering was hugely processor-intensive, we had to find a way around this problem. We came up with 'box buffering'. It was an innovative solution that speeded up the accepted slower way hugely." Even with optimisation, using machine code to speed up the process, *Driller* – the first Freescape game – had very limited performance. "I designed the game around the fact that the framerate would be about a frame a second on the 8-bit machines," Ian explains. This was a monumental achievement at the time, but also one which highlights the reason why 3D games

1992 OCTOBER
Super Play magazine arrives. Its Wil Overton-designed covers and focus on anime and imports make it a big success.

1992 NOVEMBER
Sonic The Hedgehog 2 hits the Mega Drive. It introduces the world to Tails and releases on 'Sonic 2s Day'.

1993 JANUARY
Future launches *GamesMaster* magazine to complement the TV series. It covers all aspects of videogames.

1993 FEBRUARY
Star Wars: X-Wing flies onto computers. The space sim goes down extremely well with fans, leading to several sequels.

1993 FEBRUARY
The FM Towns Marty is released in Japan. Gamers around the world drool over its amazing arcade conversions.

» [Arcade] Enemy animations in *Gunblade NY* were designed on an arcade stick and buttons due to a lack of standard 3D tools.

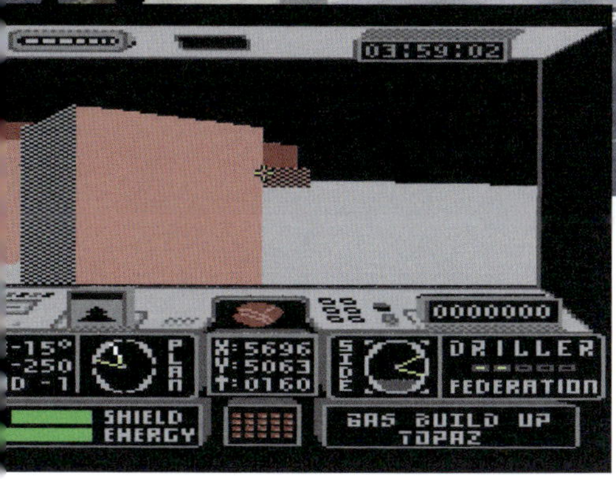

» [Arcade] Sega's Model 2 technology was extremely impressive and was utilised for games like *Top Skater*.

weren't so widespread – the level of performance severely restricts the types of games you can make.

Even with the advent of 16-bit computers in the mid-Eighties, 3D games on home systems tended to look abstract and suffer restrictions on speed and complexity, as compared to their 2D counterparts. As a result, advancements were primarily made in the arcade, where the high cost of dedicated 3D hardware could be justified. Sega had held leadership in pseudo-3D sprite-scaling games during the Eighties, but Namco and Taito had introduced true polygonal 3D games at the end of the decade. The first major advance of the Nineties came in 1992 when Sega introduced the Model 1, a powerful polygon-pushing board. Having spent the Eighties working on the 'Super Scaler' games, Yu Suzuki and the AM2 team had made the leap to full 3D to provide a flagship game in the form of *Virtua Racing*.

However, 2D games were as much a target as rival 3D games, according to Shinichi Ogasawara, a game designer who spent the Nineties at Sega's AM3 division. "I personally think Sega needed to beat the *Street Fighter* series in Japanese arcades. However Sega knew that it was a very tough mission, as they featured excellent game design and graphics." Initially, Sega attempted to use its 2D sprite-scaling technology to create a 3D game design. "*Dark Edge* was one of the counter games against *Street Fighter*, with a sense of 3D, but it was not successful. The last strategy for Sega was bringing new technology." Using the Model 1 board, AM2 created the hit fighting game *Virtua Fighter*. "3D looked very different and was a new experience for the players, and allows for different game designs from 2D games," Ogasawara adds.

This technology opened up a huge performance gap with the existing 16-bit home consoles. Though the Mega Drive had displayed simple polygonal graphics in games like *LHX Attack Chopper*, there was no way it could pull off a convincing rendition of *Virtua Racing* or *Virtua Fighter*. Ironically, it was Sega's bitter rival that would show the way forward, as Nintendo released the 3D shoot-'em-up *Star Fox* in 1993 – each cartridge contained a Super FX chip codesigned by Argonaut, included to accelerate the processing of 3D graphics. A year later, Sega released a Mega Drive version of *Virtua Racing* featuring the similarly functional Sega Virtua Processor. However, even these advances wouldn't be enough for those consoles to keep up.

A technological arms race was on in the arcades. Namco soon outperformed Sega's Model 1 with the System 22 and *Ridge Racer* in 1993, which introduced texture mapping. Sega quickly fired back with *Daytona USA* on the Model 2 board, which incorporated texture mapping technology from ▶

3D GAMES TAKE OVER

TRICKS OF THE TRADE

SOME OF THE KEY TECHNIQUES THAT IMPROVED 3D GAMES OVER THE COURSE OF THE DECADE

TEXTURE MAPPING

The application of 2D images to a polygonal model to provide additional detail. Early systems had severe size and colour restrictions on textures. Applying multiple textures on a single object can generate certain effects, such as environmental reflections.

LIGHTING

The modification of the colouring applied to polygons, based on the proximity of defined sources of light in the scene. In this shot, lighting is applied per vertex (that's one side of a polygon), but today per-pixel lighting effects are more common.

GOURAUD SHADING

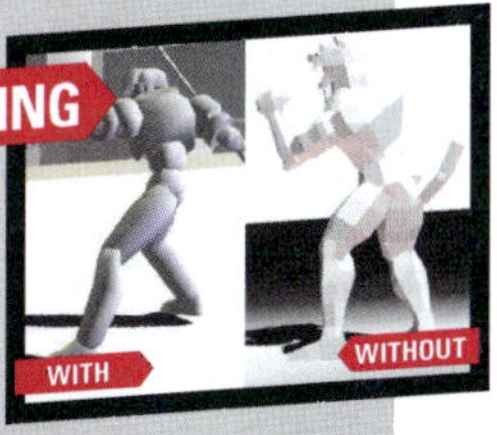

A technique for colouring polygons, designed to give the appearance of smooth curved surfaces. In these untextured shots, *Battle Arena Toshinden 2*'s models benefit from Gouraud shading and *Tekken 2*'s jagged-looking models don't.

MOTION CAPTURE

This is the practice of gathering animation data from real actors, with the goal of providing more realistic movements. Various technologies exist – in this case, marks on a suit are tracked by a camera to provide points of reference.

MIPMAPPING

If textures are drawn at full size everywhere they appear, they can use more resources than necessary and create a shimmering effect in the distance. Mipmapping mitigates this by using lower resolution copies of the texture further from the camera.

1993 APRIL
Trilobyte releases the atmospheric *The 7th Guest*, making gamers who had invested in an expensive CD drive happy.

1993 JULY
SNK shakes up the fighting scene with *Samurai Shodown*, a weapons-based brawler that is set in feudal Japan.

1993 AUGUST
Daytona USA goes on limited release in Japan. Sega AM2's racer remains a familiar sight in arcades today.

1993 SEPTEMBER
Graphic adventure *Myst* is a gigantic hit for Cyan and becomes the best-selling PC game of all time (until *The Sims*).

1993 SEPTEMBER
Ryan Brant forms Take-Two Interactive in New York City. It will go on to own big names like *GTA* and *BioShock*.

EVOLUTIONARY GALLERY

TAKE A LOOK AT HOW 3D REPRESENTATIONS OF DIFFERENT GENRES DEVELOPED OVER THE NINETIES

RACING GAMES

RACE DRIVIN'

1990: The track in Atari's *Race Drivin'* utilises filled polygons with no shading applied. The scenery is sparse, with the 2D background providing the majority of the track's theme.

RIDGE RACER

1993: Namco's *Ridge Racer* introduces fully texture-mapped tracks, with significantly more trackside detail. Cars use Gouraud shading, giving them a smoother look than in other games.

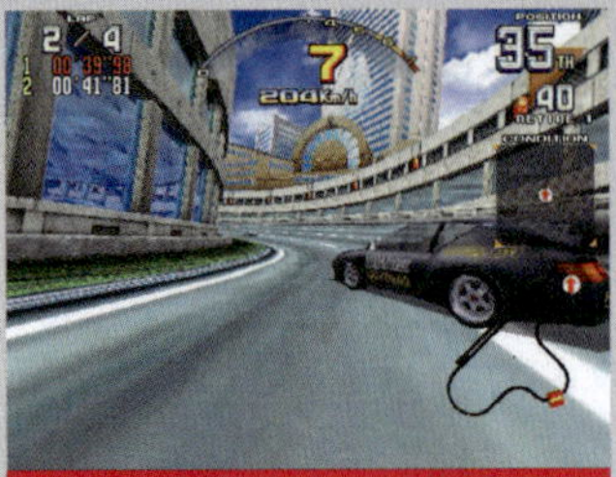

SCUD RACE

1996: As well as more detailed 3D models and filtered textures, Sega's *Scud Race* shows extra details on the cars, including reflections, transparent windows and visible drivers.

F355 CHALLENGE

1999: *F355 Challenge* pushes further towards realism with greater model and texture detail. Some cabinets feature a triple-monitor configuration, for an ultrawide display.

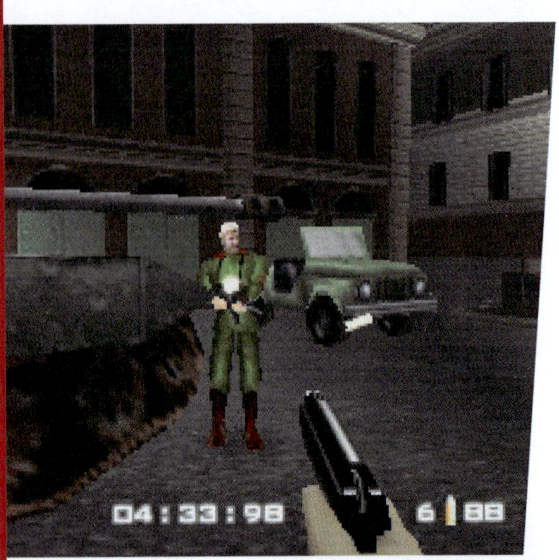

» [N64] The N64 excelled at producing 3D worlds that looked much smoother and more solid than those on PlayStation and Saturn.

military contractor GE Aerospace, with texture filtering for a smoother look. Other companies started to introduce their own new or updated 3D technology, including Midway, Konami and Taito. The new generation of consoles dawned in earnest at the end of 1994, and they were able to keep up with the explosion in 3D game output. While the Saturn stumbled initially with unfortunate conversions of *Daytona USA* and *Virtua Fighter*, the system ultimately proved capable of competent conversions of Model 2 games like *Sega Rally*. However, the PlayStation was easier to get good results from, and a great version of *Ridge Racer* allowed it to establish an early lead. Both systems did share some common issues, though – neither offered perspective correction for textured polygons, leading to a signature 'wobbly' look, and neither had a hardware z-buffer, leading to instances where overlapping objects would visibly fight for priority.

The final part of the puzzle allowing for game designers to shift priorities to 3D was the computer market – and in the mid-Nineties, it began to shift away from raw CPU power for 3D rendering, thanks to the introduction of dedicated 3D accelerator cards. Early models such as the 3DFX Voodoo and PowerVR didn't include 2D acceleration like modern GPUs, but did perform sufficiently well to gain favour amongst players. ATI's Rage series started to gain favour beginning from the Rage II, too. Popular early games offering support for 3D accelerators included id Software's first-person shooter *Quake* and Activision's *MechWarrior 2*. Another was Bullfrog's *Magic Carpet Plus*, although like many games of that era it couldn't rely entirely on polygons. "Only the landscape was made that way – everything else was still sprites," notes Alex Trowers, a level designer on the game. This was a common approach when faced with limited hardware – though the reverse approach, displaying 3D images over 2D backgrounds created from 3D renders, was also popular.

» [SNES] *Star Fox* was only possible on the SNES thanks to the SuperFX coprocessor contained in its cartridge.

However, even those fortunate enough to work with cutting-edge hardware didn't have the technological access you might expect. "3D games in the Nineties mainly used handmade animations," says Ogasawara, who created the animations for *Gunblade NY* using arcade controls. "There were no tools for art designers. We could find good motion designers, but nobody wants to animate with a joystick and buttons!" The AM3 team did attempt to use motion capture, but Ogasawara doesn't remember them meeting much success. "I remember one programmer wearing a black suit and ping pong balls for *Manx TT*. It made me laugh so much. [Tetsuya] Mizuguchi was the producer so he wanted to use it, but I can't remember if it was used for the actual game. For *Top Skater*, it was just testing. At that time, the team decided to select handmade animation as realistic motion was not suitable for their game concept. It's the best hand-animated arcade game – it should be a legacy game of animation history."

3D presented designers with new opportunities for open environments, but this gave rise to new

1993 OCTOBER
The 3DO Interactive Multiplayer is released. Despite its innovations, a high price does it no favours.

1993 OCTOBER
Future Publishing launches *Edge* magazine and it becomes a firm favourite with readers and developers alike.

1993 OCTOBER
Virtua Fighter arrives in arcades and is the first fighting game to feature polygonal graphics. Namco takes notes.

1993 NOVEMBER
Atari releases the Jaguar in North America. Launch games include *Cybermorph* and *Trevor McFur In The Crescent Galaxy*.

1993 DECEMBER
id Software's *Doom* hits MS-DOS. It spawns countless copycats and lays the groundwork for first-person shooters.

FIGHTING GAMES

4D SPORTS BOXING

1991: In Distinctive Software's home computer game *4D Sports Boxing*, character models are very simple. You can view a simple 3D ring or detailed 2D background, but not both.

VIRTUA FIGHTER

1993: Sega's *Virtua Fighter* has significantly more complex character models, showing a degree of light-based shading, and it simultaneously displays a 2D background and a 3D ring.

FIGHTING VIPERS

1995: *Fighting Vipers* utilises texture-mapped character models and 3D background elements. Though the ring remains flat and square, it is now surrounded by walls.

DEAD OR ALIVE 2

1999: In *Dead Or Alive 2*, Tecmo offers very detailed character models with clothing movement. The irregularly shaped 3D stages feature uneven floor surfaces, walls and cliffs.

difficulties, particularly when it came to directing the player and guiding their actions. "You could just fly to wherever you wanted to go, and that's just no fun – it wasn't as if slopes or hills would present a problem. It's a real pain to try and curate an experience for something like that," remembers Alex. "We introduced walls that you couldn't fly over, despite being able to gain enough altitude. That allowed us to funnel the player where we wanted them to be, although for the most part, the player was completely free to attempt the level how they wanted." It was even more of a problem in arcade games, where immediacy is paramount. "You probably know that there are few aerial combat arcade games. The main reason is that searching for enemies needs special control and analysis of the map where the player is at the same time," says Ogasawara, who notes that Namco found an elegant solution. "At that time, *Air Combat* did very well. The phases are 'select' and 'chase'. Instead of searching for enemies, selecting them is an easier task, and in the chase it's clear what players should do."

In 1996, the introduction of the N64 brought many arcade market innovations into the home, thanks to hardware designer Silicon Graphics Inc. The system featured hardware transform, clipping and lighting, and perspective correction made worlds look so much more solid than on rival systems. Antialiasing and texture filtering ensured that objects looked as good as possible at any distance, too. In the arcade, Sega introduced Model 3 and Namco introduced System 23, pushing special effects further including particles, motion blur and clothing movement and reducing the need for 2D shortcuts. But as the decade went on, the progress being made by the specialist 3D graphics hardware manufacturers of the PC market began to overtake the advances being made in the arcade market, and those manufacturers attempted to break into the console market.

The result was a great convergence in graphical power. Sega chose NEC's PowerVR 2 as the graphics hardware for the Dreamcast, and then chose the Dreamcast-based NAOMI board as a successor to Model 3, bringing arcade and console hardware near to parity and allowing for virtually identical conversions. Microsoft and Nintendo were also developing new consoles, which would eventually form the basis for arcade hardware too, and they followed suit by partnering with Nvidia and ATI. "The link between STV and Saturn, Naomi and Dreamcast, Chihiro and Xbox was very attractive for the arcade developing staff," says Ogasawara. "I think the biggest hit was *Crazy Taxi*. [It is] still one of Sega's legacy games, but without that arcade/consumer compatibility, *Crazy Taxi* would just be a hidden arcade great today."

» [PC] Despite advances such as texture mapping, *Magic Carpet* uses 2D sprites for objects and characters.

» [Dreamcast] *Soulcalibur* looked better on Sega's home console than on Namco's arcade hardware, proving the convergence in quality.

Unfortunately, the rapid technological progress had massive repercussions for developers. "There'd usually be some things you could bring over from previous projects, but you had to keep pace with the technology which meant that engines had to be rewritten every couple of years," says Alex. "I mean, some studios tried to keep reusing the same old stuff years down the line, but they'd inevitably run into a lot of problems and would simply fall off the curve." Projects also became longer and required more staff. "At about the time when I joined, there were eight of us. It'd take us about a year to make a game on the Amiga and ST along with a data disc as well. Then about the time the PC and 3D began taking off, team sizes would be 20 or so people and it would take us two years to make a game. By the time I left, as *Dungeon Keeper 2* was finishing, the team must have been 40-odd for the same timescale." However, Alex feels that graphical advances weren't solely to blame. "Some of that is down to the 3D nature, but a lot of it is down to the fact that the games just became so content-heavy and that took a lot of time to make."

But while the rise of 3D undoubtedly resulted in some industry upheaval during the Nineties, there's no denying that it was hugely exciting for players, enabling game designs and visual realism that had never been possible before. While 3D graphics have naturally developed since the end of the Nineties, there hasn't been any comparable advance in technology since which has fundamentally changed the kinds of games we could make in 3D. Long live the humble polygon. *

1993 DECEMBER
PC Gamer is launched and initially includes a 3.5-inch floppy disc. The magazine will go on to celebrate over 300 issues.

1994 APRIL
Jeff Minter creates *Tempest 2000* for Atari's Jaguar. The psychedelic shooter supercharges the original design.

1994 JUNE
The Super Game Boy is released and allows SNES owners to play their Game Boy cartridges on the 16-bit console.

1994 AUGUST
The King Of Fighters 94 launches in arcades. It features teams from several SNK franchises, including *Fatal Fury*.

1994 SEPTEMBER
Looking Glass releases its first-person RPG *System Shock*, introducing the gaming world to the evil AI SHODAN.

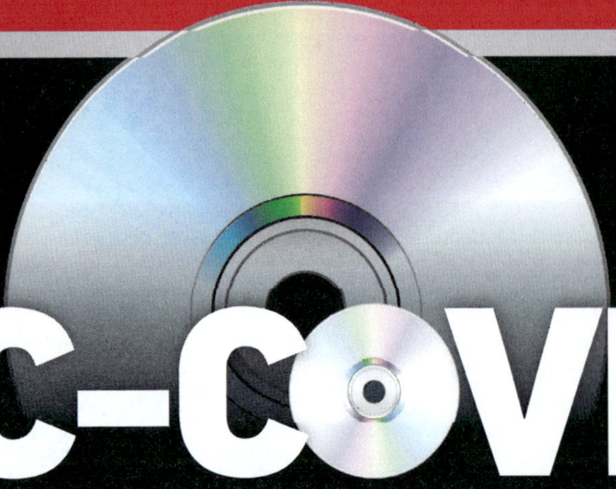

DISC-COVERY

THE IMPORTANCE OF CD-ROM

FEW FORMATS MADE SUCH AN IMPACT ON GAMING AS THE CD-ROM, NOT ONLY ALLOWING GREATER AMOUNTS OF STORAGE SPACE AND A MEDIUM THAT PROVED CHEAPER FOR CONSOLES BUT ALSO PROMPTING DEVELOPERS TO CONSIDER FRESH WAYS OF MAKING VIDEOGAMES

WORDS BY DAVID CROOKES

GRAEME DEVINE

» *The 7th Guest*, which Graeme programmed, highlighted the huge potential of CD-ROM.

LODEWIJK COEN

» A Former Digital Pictures' graphics artist, Lodewijk worked on *Night Trap*.

NICK BURCOMBE

» *WipEout* benefitted massively by being on CD-ROM and Nick helped create it.

CD or not CD? That was the burning question for game devs and console manufacturers, particularly during the Nineties. They'd already used cassettes, disks and cartridges. They'd even tried a few experimental media such as VHS and vinyl. But as the need for a cheap, large storage medium became ever more pressing, they turned to a format that had been around since 1965 – the invention of James Russell who worked in the Pacific Northwest National Laboratory of Battelle Memorial Institute in Richland.

It would be a while before CDs became widely adopted for gaming. The first step came in 1984 when Sony and Philips licensed the technology and announced the CD-ROM format. They wrote the 'Yellow Book' which laid down the standard for CD-ROM, following on from the 'Red Book' that had successfully established the audio CD. It covered the disc specification, the optical stylus parameters, modulation and error correction, and the control and display system as well as the CD's digital data structure. A 12cm disc would have the capacity to store 650 million bytes – a considerable advantage over the floppy disk.

Initially, CD-ROM was used for reference software such as Microsoft Bookshelf in 1987 but, the following year, an add-on CD-ROM attachment was introduced for the TurboGrafx-16/PC Engine. The drive could transfer data at 150 kilobytes a second – the single-speed standard – and it led to the first CD-ROM console games, *Fighting Street* and *Monster Lair*. Come 1989, however, and Activision took Cyan's adventure game, *The Manhole* – initially produced by Rand and Robyn Miller for the Apple Macintosh on floppy disks – and released it on CD-ROM for the Mac. That became the first computer CD-ROM title.

The year was also notable for the first computer to include a CD-ROM drive: Fujitsu's FM Towns. In December 1991, Philips launched the CD-i having set a standard for CD-interactive discs in the 'Green Book' of 1987, placing an emphasis on audiovisual applications. The 3DO Company was also formed, creating a set of specs for a console that boasted CD-ROM which was licensed to third parties. Commodore, meanwhile, released the CDTV.

Psygnosis was among a handful of developers to seize the opportunities presented by CD-ROM. "Psygnosis was absolutely at the forefront of the CD-ROM revolution," says Nick Burcombe, who was a lead designer at the company. "We had games such as *Microcosm* on the FM Towns and on the follow-up FM Towns Marty. We also produced *Scavenger 4* (named *Novastorm* in the US) for both PC CD-ROM and the Sega CD add-on for the Mega Drive. The CD-ROM format was essential for the survival of the industry and it had to win because the cartridge stakes were too high."

Certainly, CD-ROMs were less expensive to make than cartridges so greater risks could be taken. "In the early days, it was partly about speed and partly about the standards that were followed," says Bernie Luskin, the then-president and CEO of Philips Interactive Media and Philips Education And Reference Publishing. "We were free to experiment with new techniques and standards, and so CD-ROM began with alphanumeric capability, developed graphics and eventually video that combined audio and video capability."

The way developers approached games began to change and it heralded an era of full-motion video as well as digitised sound and images. Digital Pictures, which began creating games such as *Night Trap* for the VHS-based NEMO system, for instance, converted its titles to the Sega CD. "There was a big leap forward from classic pixel graphics to 'real interactive movies'," says former graphics artist Lodewijk Coen. "We could have real actors and voices and the challenge was to make switching between data on the CD seamless and instant."

Console manufacturers largely preferred the format – Nintendo aside. In came the Amiga CD32 in 1993 with the Sega Saturn and Sony's PlayStation not long behind. The PC also embraced CD-ROM and it became popular among gamers thanks to titles such as *Myst* and *The 7th Guest*.

"When we looked at CD-ROM, we didn't see dictionaries and encyclopedias," says Trilobyte founder Graeme Devine. "We saw it as a huge storage device for lots of images, possibly in video format, that could be used to tell stories and play games in a new way. Floppy disk installs had gotten silly and the market seemed to be calling for something new."

Developers sought to fill the CD-ROMs. Some would pack them with music as seen in the CD-ROM versions of games such as *The Secret Of Monkey Island* with its high-quality soundtrack streamed from the disc. Others would add more levels. FMV and CGI cutscenes became popular, padding out games with narrative and stunning visuals. Levels could be prerendered and voices digitised.

"I remember Sierra sent a copy of *Phantasmagoria* to every single employee of Trilobyte in 1995, and graphically rich RPG games and MMOs started to ship on CD-ROM," Graeme says. "Whereas before we would have cut graphics and cut scenes because there would be no way that would fit on the floppy disks, that all changed. And, because of that, the makeup of videogame teams changed: more art meant more artists, more levels meant more level designers, more characters meant more animators and so on."

By the time the fifth generation of consoles arrived, CD-ROM was firmly standard, although Nintendo decided to stick with cartridges. The PlayStation was the biggest success and games sold for less than cart-based rivals thanks to the ease of manufacturing. "CD-ROM was a huge sea change for storage," concludes Graeme. "Basically, everything became possible." *

1994 NOVEMBER
Rare releases *Donkey Kong Country* for the SNES. It attracts attention thanks to its prerendered graphics.

1994 NOVEMBER
Sega launches its 32-bit Saturn in Japan. Key games include *Virtua Fighter*, *Myst*, *Tama* and *WanChai Connection*.

1994 DECEMBER
Sony soon counters Sega's plans with the Japanese PlayStation launch. Its launch titles include *Ridge Racer* and *Tama*.

1994 DECEMBER
Namco's *Tekken* arrives and proves to be a solid alternative to the likes of *Virtua Fighter*, thanks to a focus on combos.

1995 FEBRUARY
Star Wars: Dark Forces proves that you can be called a *Doom* clone and still make plenty of genre innovations as well.

» [PC] *MegaRace* had 20 minutes worth of FMV featuring a fictional game host called Lance Boyle.

» [PC] *The Beast Within: A Gabriel Knight Mystery* boasted impressive-looking FMV sequences.

» [Mega-CD] *Sewer Shark* was the first game to use FMV as a key part of its gameplay.

» [PC] CD-ROM allowed *MegaRace* to make use of prerendered 3D graphics.

» [PC] Some games such as *Indiana Jones And The Fate of Atlantis* added full voice acting on the CD-ROM version.

MAKING USE OF THE STORAGE

HOW CDS BENEFITTED OLDER GAMES, TOO

In 1989, Codemasters bundled 30 of its 8-bit titles within *The CD Games Pack* for the Spectrum and Commodore 64, asking users to connect a standard CD player via the joystick port in order to load the goodies it contained. In this case, an audio CD rather than a CD-ROM was used, but it meant 8-bit fans could dabble with the format.

"CDs were a great solution to tackling the massive piracy problem the games industry faced since anyone could copy cassettes and floppy disks," says Philip Oliver, who played a key role in the development. "Their higher capacity also meant being able to save more data, although the limiting factor was the 8-bit computer memory capacity."

WHO NEEDS CARTS?

THE GAMES THAT WERE ONLY POSSIBLE ON CD-ROM

MYST

Myst was a key driver of the CD-ROM format and, for a time, the best-selling PC game. Slow drive read speeds were a constraint that needed to be overcome but, aside from music, the storage capacity allowed for 2,500 rich and detailed scenes and 66 minutes of QuickTime Animation.

NIGHT TRAP

Given its reliance on full-motion video, CD-ROM was certainly the way to go for *Night Trap* – in fact, it couldn't be ported to Nintendo consoles because they lacked a CD-ROM drive. Despite lacking great gameplay, its visual realism drew criticism amid claims it was promoting violence and sexual aggression.

THE 7TH GUEST

This classic adventure game was only released on CD-ROM and it made good use of the format by packing it with live-action video clips and astounding hi-res, 256-colour, prerendered animation running at more than ten frames per second. The 'GROOVIE' game engine allowed for continuing data streaming.

WIPEOUT

WipEout featured an electronica soundtrack as well as music by established artists such as The Chemical Brothers and Orbital. The CD-ROM format meant the tunes could be streamed straight from the disc with the developers making use of the storage space for up to 12 tracks – a good album's worth.

FINAL FANTASY VII

Known for its abundance of 3D graphics and FMV, the developers of *Final Fantasy VII* chose the PlayStation over the Nintendo 64 mainly because of the increased storage capabilities offered by CD-ROM. The game placed 3D characters over 2D prerendered backgrounds and had large interactive areas.

1995 MARCH
Panzer Dragoon arrives on Saturn and shows that the 32-bit console is perfectly capable of creating great 3D games.

1995 MAY
The first Electronic Entertainment Expo (E3) opens for business at the Los Angeles Convention Center.

1995 JULY
Nintendo's 32-bit Virtual Boy launches in Japan. Available games include *Mario's Tennis*, *Red Alarm* and *Galactic Pinball*.

1995 AUGUST
Remedy Entertainment is founded in Espoo. Its cofounders include Markus Maki, Sami Nopanen and John Kavaleff.

1995 SEPTEMBER
Westwood Studios takes everything it learned from *Dune* and creates the hit RTS *Command & Conquer*. It's a big hit.

SONY'S GAME-CHANGER

Few consoles have had as strong an impact on the videogame industry as the *PlayStation*, which has enjoyed over 25 years in the world of gaming. *Retro Gamer* looks at how it ignored conventions, proved to be Sony's saviour and created one of gaming's most important brands

Words by David Crookes

» Colin Anderson is one of the musicians that harnessed the PlayStation's audio power.

» Michael Troughton is one of the coders that worked on *Destruction Derby*.

» Benjamin Heckendorn is a console modder that once owned the super-rare 'SNES Station'.

On its very first day of sale in Japan on 3 December 1994, Sony sold 100,000 PlayStation consoles. When the console was finally released in the United States the following September, it shifted the same amount again but what made jaws truly drop is that the PlayStation went on to become the first console in history to surpass 100 million sales just six months short of its tenth anniversary.

By that time, the PlayStation brand had firmly established itself in Europe, Australia and other parts of the world, too. It had also blown the Nintendo 64's 33 million sales out of the water and decimated Sega which could only muster fewer than ten million units for the Saturn. That latter figure was a particular triumph for Steve Race, president of Sony Computer Entertainment of America. At E3 in Los Angeles in 1995 after Sega announced its console would cost $399, Steve walked to the podium, uttered "$299" and left with cheers ringing in his ears.

If anything, Steve's quip had been a stroke of marketing genius and Sony certainly proved rather adept at carving out a market for its fledgling console in an industry long dominated by Nintendo and Sega. Sega itself had battled against Nintendo to smash the near-monopoly it once held, and Sony took them both on with arguably greater success. "We had a very clear idea and plan on the hardware and platform in terms of appeal and aspirational positioning," Steve tells us. The company played a blinder.

For most of its years, however, Sony – founded in 1946 – was not known for being interested in videogaming. It had achieved great success with the Walkman throughout the Eighties and its 8mm Handycam camcorder was very popular. But Sony's negative approach to games was such that engineer Ken Kuturagi ended up secretly developing the SPC700 sound chip for Nintendo which used it in the SNES. When Sony finally awoke to gaming's possibility, it initially sought to do so in partnership with Nintendo – a decision that caused it to be stung (check out the SNES Station boxout over the page) but ultimately gave it a golden route to success.

And boy, did Sony desperately need it. After all, it had not long struggled to convince consumers of the merits of Betamax over VHS; the company's reputation for televisions also appeared to be fading, and it was still reeling from the fallout over singer George Michael's protracted attempts to free himself from a contact with the corporation which did it no favours at all. There was much disquiet, too, over the purchase of Columbia Studios which had left it with a £1.98 billion loss. Ken Kuturagi was allowed to go ahead and create a Sony console rival and the 'Father Of PlayStation' proved something of a saviour for the electronics manufacturer.

The first battle was to set it apart from its rivals. "The problem was that Sony's products were geared for a 16-year-old's dad or uncle and we had no cache with our key demographic profile," Steve Race explains. Cue strange television adverts containing game footage that got tongues wagging, if only for the confusing tagline '[E]NOS Lives'. It would transpire that E meant 'ready' and NOS referred to the US launch date of the 9 September. "We were flying the Jolly Roger relative to the games industry and corporate Sony," Steve explains. "And if you look at the first box, there was no Sony logo on the package, either."

Not that everything went entirely smoothly, particularly between Sony's Japan and US divisions. Sony in Japan had been working with third parties such as Namco – which created an arcade-perfect port of *Ridge Racer* – and insisted all of the resulting games would be released in the US. America, meanwhile, wanted to change the console's name.

"I felt it was downmarket and skewed too young – what 16-year-old 'plays'?" Steve quizzes. "But turns out we could have called it 'dog poop' and it would have sold. As for third parties, we went out and hired

"We were flying the Jolly Roger relative to the games industry and corporate Sony"
STEVE RACE

» **Crash Bandicoot** Sega had Sonic. Nintendo had Mario. And Sony had a character called Crash Bandicoot but while it didn't become an official mascot for the PlayStation, the initial exclusive kickstarted a run of games that eventually appeared on the likes of the Xbox, Game Boy Advance, GameCube and across subsequent console generations.

1995 OCTOBER The Sega Nomad is released exclusively in NA. It's a portable version of the Genesis and can connect to a TV.

1995 NOVEMBER Team17's *Worms*, a brilliant strategy game that takes multiplayer mayhem to frantic new heights, is released.

1996 Fighting game tournament the Evolution Championship Series launches as Battle Of The Bay. It will be renamed as EVO in 2002.

1996 FEBRUARY *Pocket Monsters Red & Green* are released in Japan. You might actually know them as *Pokémon Red & Blue*.

1996 MARCH *Resident Evil* redefines survival horror with its prerendered backdrops, cheesy voice acting and effective jump scares.

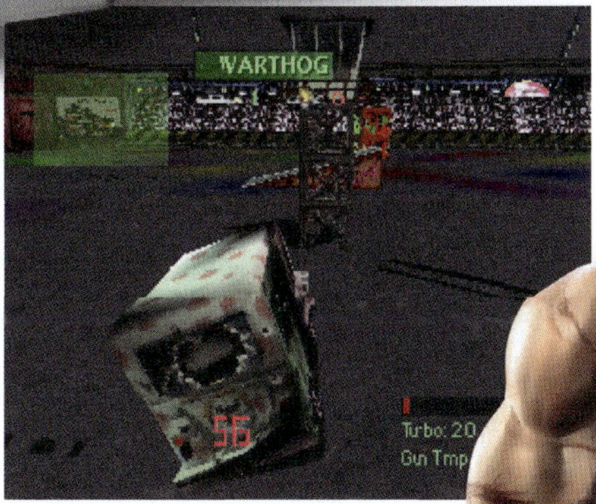

» [PlayStation] As one of the longest-running PlayStation-exclusive franchises, *Twisted Metal* has seen millions of players tearing around in modded vehicles while lobbing weapons at their opponents.

» [PlayStation] Not all games were aimed at adults. *Croc* was one of many child-friendly games.

KILLER APPS

Five exclusive games that defined the system

PaRappa The Rapper

1 Masaya Matsuura's quirky rhythm game kicked and punched its way into the minds of gamers in 1996 before spawning a spin-off – *Um Jammer Lammy* – and a sequel *PaRappa The Rapper 2*. More than that, the button-tapper set the tone for scores of other popular games based on music.

Gran Turismo

2 The collective *Gran Turismo* series – which has never driven away from the PlayStation since it debuted in 1997 – is a massive Sony-exclusive franchise, with more than 80.4 million units sold over its 20-plus years of life. It's known for its superb graphics, accurate driving physics and huge number of licensed vehicles.

Ridge Racer

3 Motoring over to the PlayStation from the arcades, *Ridge Racer* was a launch title that truly helped to sell the console. With impressive 3D cars, drifting mechanics, glossy presentation and a blistering soundtrack, it showed that Sony's console was able to replicate coin-op play – there was even a mini version of *Galaxian* to play.

ISS Pro Evolution

4 This exclusive kicked *FIFA* off the pitch, and it was promptly heralded as the best football game ever made when it was released. As a faithful and intelligent simulation of soccer, matches could be punishing but it set the genre on a new course of realism that scored highly with players.

Tekken 3

5 *Tekken* had already impressed when it was released on the PlayStation in 1995 but this second sequel introduced a new cast, sold 8 million copies and firmly established itself as one of the console's – and gaming's – greatest ever fighters, capping off an amazingly accomplished trio of games.

1996 JUNE
The N64 arrives in Japan. Launch games include pack-in *Super Mario 64*, *Pilotwings 64* and *Saikyo Habu Shogi*.

1996 JUNE
Quake reinvents the first-person shooter and offers real-time 3D rendering as well as stacks of multiplayer options.

1996 JULY
Nintendo releases the Game Boy Pocket in Japan. Unlike the original Game Boy, the console runs off just two AA batteries.

1996 AUGUST
This month saw two big gaming events launch, Japan's Tokyo Games Show and QuakeCon. Both are still going today.

1996 SEPTEMBER
Naughty Dog's *Crash Bandicoot* hits the PlayStation. It scores well and Crash becomes an unofficial mascot.

» **Metal Gear Solid** Hideo Kojima's stealth game can actually be traced back to *Metal Gear* on the MSX2 computer, but the *Solid* series which emerged in 1998 will forever be closely aligned with PlayStation.

"Nintendo was appealing to a very young audience and we were appealing to that kid's older brother"
STEVE RACE

experienced professionals with strong reputations as key management and we put those reputations on the line, convincing the CEOs of companies such as Activision and EA to come over. There were no special concessions like Sega gave on royalties so we could tell everyone it was a level playing field."

Those publishers were also interested in Sony's use of CD-ROM as opposed to cartridges. The PlayStation teams would point out that CDs could be produced at a lower cost and without the long waiting lines associated with cart production. It also helped that the Saturn wasn't Sega's finest machine – "It plain sucked," says Steve Race. "Nintendo was technologically behind, too," he continues. It was time for Sony to hammer home the point in all of the territories it was targeting.

In Europe, this meant spending £20 million ahead of the 32-bit console's first Christmas and Sony did so very cannily. It placed adverts, not solely in the specialist gaming and computing press, but in more than 40 fashion, music and style magazines including *The Face*, *Ikon*, and *Dazed & Confused*. Since Sony Computer Entertainment wanted young adults to engage in gaming, it also firmly pushed the industry away from the bedroom image of old by consciously placing PlayStation consoles in the wild – notably at nightclubs, celebrity parties and music festivals – where 'cool people' would play and influence others to do so the same.

"Nintendo was appealing to a very young audience and we were appealing to that kid's older brother," Steve says. "Young kids always want to emulate older kids and somehow that was lost on Nintendo, so we were in fact able to poach their key demographic by just being PlayStation. It was a huge marketing mistake by Nintendo which was also far too insular (something like 75% of all software sales for the Nintendo platform was made by Nintendo). We were the prettiest girl at the dance and available. Oh and Sega was a lost cause."

» **Resident Evil** Originally developed on the PlayStation, gamers were introduced to Chris Redfield and Jill Valentine in a groundbreaking survival horror that made up in scares what it lacked in acting prowess. Played from a third-person perspective and blessing the eyes with prerendered backgrounds, it would define this popular genre.

SNES Station

Before the PlayStation, Sony intended to work with Nintendo

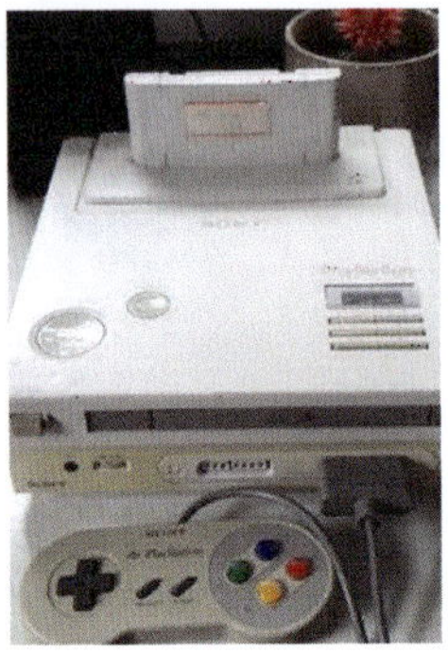

Before Sony developed what we know today as the PlayStation, it worked with Nintendo in order to develop a CD-ROM add-on for the SNES. It also sought to supplement that with a Sony-branded console based on the SNES that could play 'Super Discs' as well as cartridges.

The device didn't make it past the prototype stage. Nintendo felt the terms of the agreement went against its interests and it struck a deal with Philips instead. The move prompted Sony to go it alone but just what was that prototype like?

Console modder Benjamin Heckendorn got his hands on one. "As a prototype, it was pretty far along," he tells us. "There were a few bodge wires on the PCB to fix mistakes but that wasn't uncommon for the era. The case tooling was very good and the power buttons had a very 'Sony-esque' complex mechanism. The cartridge slot was also a separate piece of plastic – since the Japanese/US SNES carts are different shapes, they clearly planned to just swap out the piece."

Even so, he says the system "would have been a dog". "It was basically just a SNES with CD-ROM storage attached," he continues. "A game cart was also needed to work because it contained the boot BIOS along with 8K of battery backup save RAM and 512K of game load RAM. This is where game data from the CD-ROM would have been copied to and then executed to play games. But the cart did not contain any coprocessor or expansion chips so it would have severely limited what games were capable of."

As if to underline those credentials, Sony got itself a roster of instantly recognisable games, the gameplay of which would be easily guessed from a simple glance. So while it had launched the PlayStation with a limited number of games – the UK, for instance, had *Battle Arena Toshinden, Kileak: The Blood, NBA Jam: Tournament Edition, Rapid Reload, Ridge Racer, Street Fighter: The Movie* and *WipEout* – it was enough to convince the gaming world of PlayStation's intentions. More than that, Sony would not shy away from licensing games that would have had Nintendo flinching.

This was a platform, after all, which had titles as violent as *Grand Theft Auto* or frightening as *Silent Hill*. Developers also dearly wanted to get involved. Colin Anderson, musician and producer at Rockstar, said the PlayStation let him eschew chiptunes for a CD soundtrack. "The PlayStation cemented CD soundtracks as the standard throughout the industry pretty quickly after it launched," he tells us. "*GTA* probably wouldn't have established the CD soundtrack as a centrepiece of the game if the

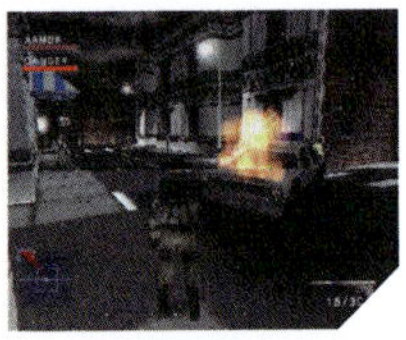

» **Syphon Filter** Making its debut late into the original PlayStation's life, *Syphon Filter* was often in danger of never seeing the light of day. But its mix of third-person stealth shooting and a good number of puzzles (think *Metal Gear Solid* and *Tomb Raider*) caught the imaginations of players and led to a further five titles.

1996 OCTOBER
Core Design's *Tomb Raider* launches. It becomes an instant hit thanks to its explorative gameplay and its lead, Lara Croft.

1996 NOVEMBER
Everyone goes mad for Bandai's Tamagotchi, a small digital pet that you have to keep alive for as long as possible.

1997 JANUARY
Final Fantasy VII breaks limits when it's released on PlayStation. Nintendo probably regrets sticking with cartridges...

1997 MARCH
Castlevania: Symphony Of The Night reinvents the series, adding *Metroid*-like aspects and light RPG mechanics.

1997 JUNE
Bullfrog's *Dungeon Keeper* arrives on PC and immediately stands out thanks to its focus on dungeon building.

» The PlayStation legacy continues on, and today we have just seen the launch of the PlayStation 5.

PlayStation hadn't made chip music more or less obsolete when it did."

Graphics artists and programmers were impressed, too. "Although 3D had taken off on the PC with games such as *Doom* and *Wolfenstein*, PlayStation brought full 3D gaming to the masses for the first time," says Michael Troughton, one of the programmers of *Destruction Derby*. "From a development point of view, if you wanted to create a 3D computer game, you had to write your own polygon rasterisation and 3D maths code which was difficult and time consuming, but the PlayStation opened that up with its custom graphics processor and geometry engine in hardware."

Developers were finding themselves creating games on the PlayStation and porting them across to other platforms which worked in Sony's favour. "The PlayStation ended up with the better quality games and the Saturn versions of titles would suffer quite badly in translation," says Michael. "Sega's console, for example, was unable to simulate the translucent sprites used for smoke and other effects." Gamers spotted this and flocked to Sony's machine.

"The PlayStation cemented CD soundtracks as the standard throughout the industry pretty quickly after it launched"

COLIN ANDERSON

Sony Computer Entertainment also created its own development studios and acquired others such as Psygnosis which produced the futuristic racing game *WipEout*. It published an eclectic range of games including Naughty Dog's *Crash Bandicoot*, Revolution Software's *Broken Sword: The Shadow Of The Templars* and *Twisted Metal*. *Final Fantasy VII* was taken under its wing – the game was originally earmarked for a Nintendo release but developer Squaresoft needed the space available on CD-ROMs and jumped ship.

In this sense, though, Sony was sticking with convention. "Never in the history of videogames has a console developer been void in making first-party games," says Steve Race. But it also consolidated Sony's position and allowed it to steer the types of games it wanted on its platform. "We'd have been fools to build a highway and not put our car on it."

The money made from "highway toll charges" – the licensing fee charged to third-party software companies – proved vital. "Frankly, we lost money on each console sold for the first couple of years," Steve explains. "The cost of each disc was pennies and packaged was under a dollar so if, as a developer, Sony could amortize the development cost, the incremental profit was 90 per cent."

That said, piracy was rife. Blank discs were cheap and gamers found a way to burn games on to them. Even so, it likely helped: at the very least a pirate would have to buy a PlayStation and it would continue to spread the word about the console. Since developers were knocking them out at a rate of knots, there were plenty of games to get stuck into. Impressive polygon visuals, mature content and games that could last as long as 100 hours providing talking points. A homebrew scene would even flourish thanks to special Net Yaroze development units further setting it apart. Meanwhile, a Platinum range of games was launched in January 1997 and allowed titles that achieved sales of more than 400,000 worldwide after a year to be sold at a lower price.

The magazines played their part as well, particularly the official ones. The *Official UK PlayStation Magazine*, for instance, came with a popular demo disc – a first for console magazines – and it undoubtedly helped the publication to a staggering circulation that topped out at 453,571 – making it the world's bestselling videogame magazine. Having a taster of games each month, in turn, boosted game sales and allowed players to experience a far wider range of titles than they would otherwise have been exposed to in the shops. It also granted a distribution outlet for Net Yaroze games. PlayStation was pushing boundaries.

All of these things, together with ongoing clever marketing such as the TV ad, *Double Life*, in 1999 gave the PlayStation the finest of starts. It was a console that kept on giving thanks to its power, allowing titles such as *Tomb Raider* to shine and the likes of *PaRappa The Rapper* to define new genres. There were excellent tools and documentation for developers and CD-ROMs allowing for larger games. Most of all, there was a concerted effort to look players in the eye and grant them respect, something which put PlayStation on the industry map and has kept it there. *

» **Oddworld** "Follow me," implores the game's main character, Abe, and so many gamers did, with Lorne Lanning directing a debut that harked back to the 2D platformers of old while infusing it with a fresh next-generational twist. The franchise eventually spread its wings: the third game switched mid-development from PS2 to the Xbox.

» **Silent Hill** Survival horror was taken to fresh and frightening heights with *Silent Hill* and the PlayStation ramped up the tension but not for the reasons you'd expect. Instead, the game's fog, snow and a dark foreboding atmosphere masked the console's graphical limitations but it helped to attract a legion of fans.

1997 AUGUST
Tiger Electronics launches the Game.com in North America. Available launch games include *Batman & Robin* and *Indy 500*.

1997 DECEMBER
Gran Turismo shakes up the racing sim with its realistic-looking visuals and its gigantic number of licensed cars.

1998 JANUARY
Capcom's *Resident Evil 2* appears and introduces gamers to Leon S Kennedy. A remake will follow in January 2019.

1998 MARCH
Blizzard Entertainment releases the RTS *StarCraft*. It will become popular with the esports scene and be remade in 2017.

1998 SEPTEMBER
Hideo Kojima's stealth hit, *Metal Gear Solid*, arrives on PlayStation. Players feel like they're in an interactive movie.

1998 OCTOBER
The Game Boy Color launches in Japan. SNK counters with the monochrome Neo-Geo Pocket. Oops.

1998 NOVEMBER
It's a fantastic month as *Half-Life*, *The Legend Of Zelda: Ocarina Of Time* and *Tomb Raider III* are all released.

1998 NOVEMBER
Sega's last console, the Dreamcast, launches in Japan. Games include *Virtua Fighter 3tb* and *Pen Pen Trilcelon*.

1999 JANUARY
Konami's *Silent Hill* terrifies gamers, dropping you in the shoes of Harry Mason who is searching for his daughter.

1999 MARCH
Bandai's WonderSwan launches to combat the success of the Game Boy and SNK releases the Neo-Geo Pocket Color.

Super Mario 64

A NEW DIMENSION IN GAMES

» RETROREVIVAL

» N64 » 1996 » NINTENDO

When you've spoken to as many videogame developers as we have, you start to get a taste for their likes and dislikes – especially when it comes to other games. When we polled our readers on the greatest games of all time, way back in issue 150, *Super Mario World* came out on top. But if we were to ask developers exclusively, I strongly suspect that *Super Mario 64* might be the game that got the nod instead. More than any other game, the Nintendo 64 launch title seems to be one that draws universal admiration from those who know the games business best.

The reason why developers love it so much is that, having worked in the industry at the time, they recognise what a monumental achievement it was. The Nineties marked one of gaming's most important transitions, as the dominance of 2D games gave way to an era where 3D designs became the standard expectation of players. It was a turbulent time for all game developers – some struggled but eventually made the transition, while others fell by the wayside. Very few managed to seamlessly embrace the new technology, but Nintendo was unarguably one of the developers that did so.

There was an incredible elegance to *Super Mario 64*. Rather than simply trying to shoehorn the old obstacle course style of 2D *Mario* games into 3D, Nintendo's team designed 3D spaces with no defined end point, and incorporated a variety of objectives into each – puzzle-solving, racing, battles and more. But that was just a part of the game's genius. Mario was a joy to control, punctuating every twisting leap with a "wahoo!" and cartoonishly falling on his face as he failed to climb a steep slope. And then there was the technical side of the game, where Nintendo demonstrated mastery of 3D cameras and graphics that still evaded its contemporaries. *Super Mario 64* would have been a masterpiece at any point in its generation, but the fact that it came at the launch of the console, providing a polished experience when everyone else was still experimenting? It's proof, were it ever needed, of Nintendo's greatness. *

1999 JUNE
Driver proves itself to be a thrilling cars and crime caper... providing you can get out of the car park tutorial, of course.

1999 AUGUST
Looking Glass Studios and Irrational Games join forces to create the space horror epic *System Shock 2*.

1999 SEPTEMBER
Neversoft releases *Tony Hawk's Pro Skater*. It helps popularise the extreme sports genre and will receive many sequels.

1999 NOVEMBER
Medal Of Honor, overseen by director Steven Spielberg, hits PlayStation. Mre WWII games will follow in its wake.

1999 DECEMBER
Shenmue is released on Dreamcast. Yu Suzuki's ambitious title delivers an authentic slice of Yokosuka to explore.

THE STORY OF SONIC THE HEDGEHOG

With Sonic celebrating his 30th birthday in June 2021, let's look back at the impact of the original Mega Drive platform games with Sonic Team head and Mega Drive development veteran, Takashi Iizuka

Words By Nick Thorpe

There aren't many games that could be described as revolutionary, and far fewer series – yet the quartet of *Sonic The Hedgehog* platform games on the Mega Drive can justifiably be described as such.

At the highest level, the *Sonic* games had a wide impact that both drove and reflected the changes the videogame market was undergoing in the Nineties. The original game intensified the rivalry between Sega and Nintendo, bringing the two companies to an even footing for the first time, as well as providing an early example of celebrity involvement in game development. The sequel signified the growing globalisation of the videogame market – the game was the result of collaboration between Japanese and American developers, and a full global launch was managed within a week. For *Sonic 3* and *Sonic & Knuckles*, the concept of an expansion pack was pioneered on consoles. However, first and foremost they were platformers featuring fantastic game design and amazing technical achievements.

One of the people who best understands the importance of *Sonic*'s 16-bit era is Takashi Iizuka, a Sonic Team veteran who now heads up development of the series. "While I was seeking employment at Sega, I bought *Sonic The Hedgehog* to understand the job and products of the company, and that was my first encounter with *Sonic*," he recalls. "At that time, I only had Super Nintendo, so I was impressed by the vivid screen and speedy gameplay of *Sonic*, and I remember thinking that I wanted to make a game like this if I got hired by Sega."

The simple fact that Iizuka only had a Super Nintendo highlights one of the key reasons that Sega needed *Sonic*. After being slow to jump into the 16-bit generation of consoles, Nintendo had arrived – and while Sega had a sales headstart, Nintendo had a more powerful machine. Sega needed to differentiate itself from the competition, and to its credit it was already doing so. The Mega Drive was already catering to older audiences with complex RPGs and sports simulations. What's more, Sega was aggressively advertising against Nintendo.

To advance Sega's agenda of distinguishing its offering from the competition, *Sonic* needed to achieve three things. Firstly, the game and character had to fit into the plan to appeal to a slightly older demographic than the preteen audience associated with Nintendo's machines. Naoto Ohshima's initial designs of Sonic gave him sharp teeth, a human girlfriend and cast him as the vocalist of a rock band. While these harder-edged attributes would ultimately fall away, Sonic's attitude remained – he was impulsive, impatient and cool. "In the Nineties, Mickey Mouse, Pooh, all those animal-themed ▶

» We're glad a lot of these early concept bosses were dropped. Why on earth is Dr. Robotnik a bee?

THE MOD SCENE

The Sonic community has been producing interesting mods for the Mega Drive games for years – here are five of our favourites

SONIC THE HEDGEHOG MEGAMIX

■ This ambitious team project is a complete overhaul of the original *Sonic The Hedgehog* game, featuring new visuals, music, bosses and gameplay mechanics, as well as a range of additional characters. What's most impressive is that the entire thing has been ported to Mega-CD, allowing anyone with a blank CD-R to play it on actual Sega hardware.

SONIC 1: THE NEXT LEVEL

■ If you want to see how far a Mega Drive can be pushed technically, take a good look at this short, but incredible, effort. The animation in *Sonic 1: The Next Level* is superb, the sampled music is amazingly clear, and some of the special visual effects call to mind Treasure's programming prowess – especially the climactic final boss fight.

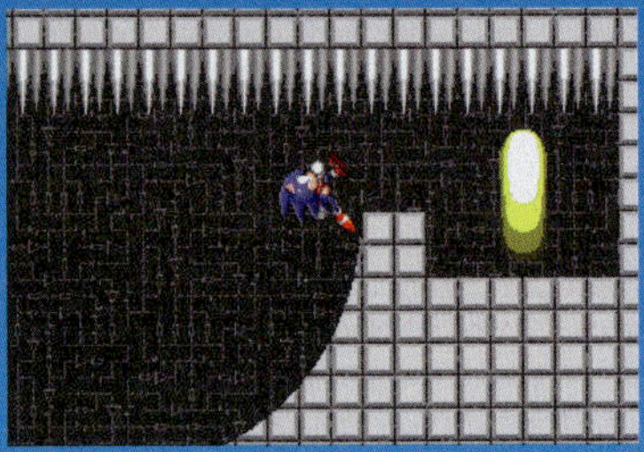

SONIC VR

■ Do you consider yourself an expert on everything *Sonic*? Beating this fiendish mod without cheating will prove it. This 'virtual reality training' game gives you a variety a short challenges which test your speed, problem-solving skills and mastery of *Sonic*'s physics. Highlights include challenges such as 'The Pain Train' and 'Roadkill Factory'.

SONIC CLASSIC HEROES

■ Remember the core mechanic of 2003's *Sonic Heroes*, where you controlled teams of three characters instead of individual characters? This impressive technical mod adds that function to the first two *Sonic The Hedgehog* games, allowing you to switch between Sonic, Tails and Knuckles on the fly in order to use their unique abilities, based around speed, flight and power respectively.

BIG'S FISHING DERBY

■ This might just be the craziest mod that we have ever seen – not only does it do away with the Blue Blur (in favour of everyone's favourite big purple cat), it chucks the entire platform gameplay concept out of the window and replaces it with a fun arcade-style fishing game. When you've finished it, try *Big's Big Fishing Adventure 3* for more fun.

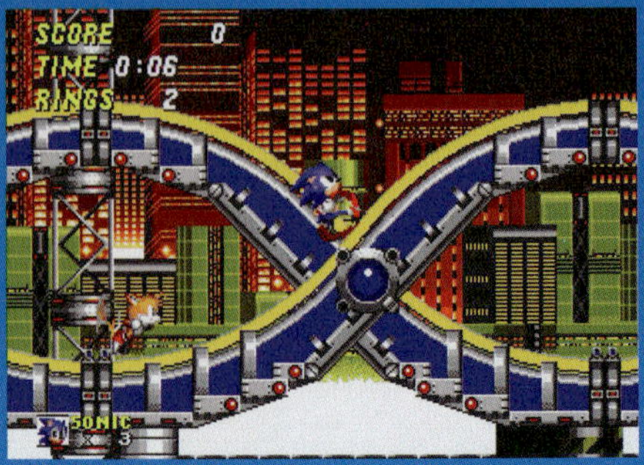

» [Mega Drive] *Sonic 2*'s Chemical Plant Zone provided a fine opportunity for Sonic to show off his extra speed.

▶ characters were all friendly and cute, and that was the matter of course," remarks Iizuka. "So seeing Sonic being speedy and edgy in that time, made me feel that he is a character whom has the exact same identity of the company Sega itself. Maybe everyone felt that way at the time too."

The second thing that Sega's new game needed to do was provide a strong demonstration of the Mega Drive's capabilities. The machine had been out for a couple of years, and was a known quantity, but there was no 'killer app' that new consumers could associate with the console. "I think the first *Sonic The Hedgehog*, which was born in Mega Drive, was the title that drastically expanded the possibility of the Mega Drive hardware," says Iizuka. "Although the spec of the Mega Drive hardware was lower than Super Nintendo, the graphics were as good as the Super Nintendo games." This was the joint work of the experienced graphic artist Rieko Kodama, whose previous work included *Phantasy Star* and the *Alex Kidd* games, and relative newcomer Jina Ishiwatari, who would go on to help define the look of the *Sonic* series. "It also achieved screen rotation, which was never done in the previous Mega Drive games," Iizuka continues. This was the responsibility of programmer Yuji Naka, who had cut his teeth on high-profile arcade conversions for the Master System. As well as this technical feat, he was responsible for *Sonic*'s advanced physics and the efficiency that allowed Hirokazu Yasuhara's stage designs to be brought to life.

» [Mega Drive] Sonic's speed was more of a reward than a requirement – the original game often slowed things down.

» Once upon a time, Sonic was going to have a girlfriend and this is what she was going to look like.

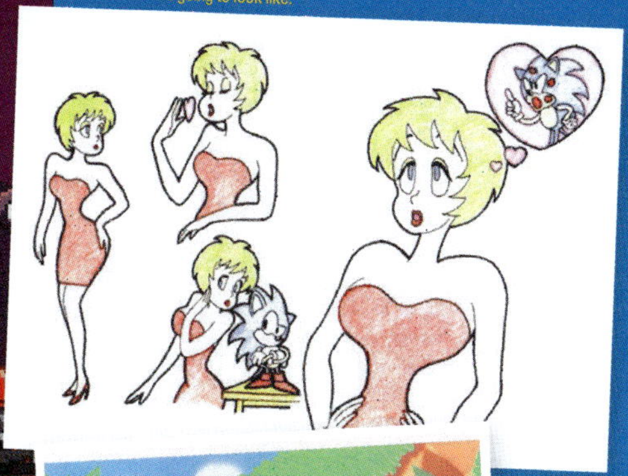

» We're big fans of the original *Sonic The Hedgehog* art. It still manages to look fantastic.

"I think Sonic was a title which contributed on improving the quality of future Mega Drive-released titles"
Takashi Iizuka

For the audio, an oft-noted weak point of the Mega Drive hardware, Sega did something incredibly bold and sought celebrity involvement. While Dreams Come True might not be a household name in the west, in Japan the pop band was making huge waves – it had already produced a platinum debut album and was gaining momentum, hiring the bassist and composer for the band, Masato Nakamura was a coup for Sega. The company had licensed music before with games like *Michael Jackson's Moonwalker*, but this was a bigger deal – here was a legitimate star from the wider world of entertainment taking an active role in game creation.

"I think *Sonic* was a title which contributed on improving the quality of future Mega Drive titles," says Iizuka. We can't argue – it's hard to keep track of how many coders have cited the game as a bar against which they measured their own work.

The last thing *Sonic* had to do, and arguably the most important, was crack the American market. Sega was already doing good business in Europe, and the Mega Drive was never going to usurp the SNES in Japan. North America was up for grabs – *Sonic* would be going head to head with *Super Mario World*, and Sega Of America seized the opportunity. A promo tour invited players to try both *Super Mario World* and *Sonic The Hedgehog*, and advertising aggressively compared the two. Tom Kalinske made the call to bundle the game with the console, a move which would boost Mega Drive sales considerably.

It was that success in North America that led to another unusual move – the creation of a truly international game development team. *Sonic The Hedgehog 2* was developed at Sega Technical Institute in the USA, with a variety of Japanese staffers making their way across the Pacific to collaborate with local talent. The arrangement was put together by Mark Cerny, who had previously spent time working at Sega in Japan.

Sonic The Hedgehog 2 was a straight evolution of the original game's concepts. It had more stages, it was more varied and it was faster – but the latter wasn't always a sure thing. Sonic's speed was always something that needed to be used with caution, and in the early stages of the game the team considered making it even riskier by allowing Sonic to be stunned by running into walls at top speed. In the end, they went the other way. Sonic's running speed

RING COLLECTOR

Peter Robinson is the admin of the Sonic Collections Page on Facebook, and owns some incredible Sonic merchandise

What was your first encounter with *Sonic*?
I was eight or nine years old and I begged my mum and dad for a NES one Christmas, but my best friend was getting a Master System, so I got one as well with *Sonic 2*. That's where it all began.

What was the first piece of *Sonic* merchandise you picked up?
Very first was a plush that a friend gave me at school, which I still have. It was Fleetway's *Sonic The Comic* where I really got into the character of Sonic.

What is it about *Sonic* in particular that drew you to collecting?
I used to collect everything from Nintendo to Xbox and had so much that one day, I thought I'd just like to concentrate on one particular character. Sonic has always been my favourite videogame character, even when the games have dipped quality-wise. I guess it's because it's the first game I played, what I grew up playing and in the Nineties there wasn't much around that was cooler than the blue fella.

How many *Sonic The Hedgehog* items do you currently own?
I've never sat and tried to count it all, to be honest. I know Guinness World Records needs 3,000 individual items to consider an entry, I'm fairly sure I'm not far off that including everything – it's just getting the time and patience to go through it all!

Are there any items or curios in your collection that you'd consider particularly unusual or noteworthy?
I've got a few different prototype items, like the ReSaurus action figures and funky bobble heads which I've never seen before, then there's original artwork I own. The fruit machine [inset below] is always a favourite of people who see it too.

Are there any items you're still after but haven't found yet?
One thing I want, and I've always said once I had it I would be happy, is one of the six-foot statues like the one that was at Alton Towers. I've seen a few pop up on eBay but never managed to get one… yet!

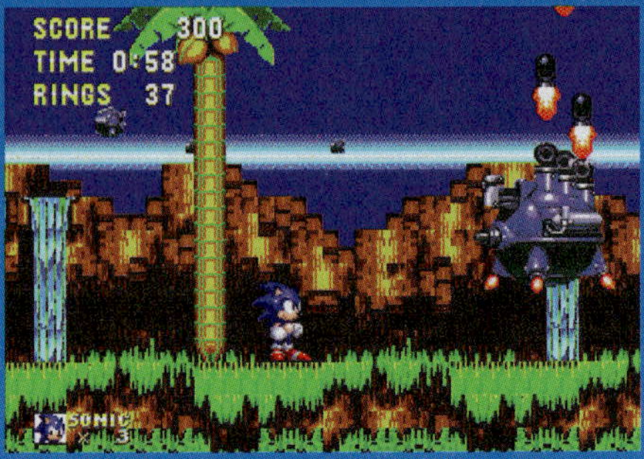

» [Mega Drive] Not everyone was a fan of *Sonic 3*'s distinctive-looking art style. Personally, we quite liked it.

cap was listed, and Sonic gained a new move in the form of the Spin Dash – a variation on Sonic's trademark spin attack that could be launched from a standing start, providing instant momentum and a new way to attack enemies.

However, the biggest new addition was a little fox by the name of Miles Prower. "In *Sonic 2*, Tails was added as a player character, and along with the two-player versus mode, you were able to play in '1.5 player' gameplay, allowing two players to play at the same time in the normal mode, too," Iizuka notes, and it's an addition that he feels brought a lot to the series. "Titles which you can say, 'Want to play together?' when your friend comes to your place, will be played for a long time, so, personally, I think multiplayer is a meaningful feature. So not only in *Sonic 2*, but also in *Sonic Adventure 2*, *Sonic Heroes*, etc, we added multiplayer features several times in the *Sonic* series."

***Sonic The Hedgehog 2* was a tough game to develop, with revisions being made right up until the production deadline.** However, it was a resounding critical success – in fact, many players still consider the game to be the finest entry in the series. Why does Iizuka think the game is held in such high esteem to this day? "Game design, level design, graphics – in all aspects, I think that *Sonic 2* exceeded the previous title and had a high perfection," he replies, "but for me, personally, the background music and special stage made *Sonic 2* stand out even more."

It wasn't just a superb game, but a superb piece of gaming business. In order to have the game out in time for Christmas 1992, the company needed to co-ordinate its international launch strategy. While it wasn't a simultaneous worldwide launch, it was as close as you'd get in those days. For the sake of comparison, the comparable blockbuster launch *Super Mario Bros 3* took almost three years to complete its international release – *Sonic 2* took a matter of days. There was no time for hype to dissipate, and six million sales resulted.

THE GANG'S ALL HERE

Meet some of Sonic's weird and wonderful friends

ROUGE THE BAT

■ A treasure hunter and spy who stakes a claim on all the world gems, the only thing more obnoxious than Rouge herself is her painful hotter/colder Easter-egg hunt gameplay. Do yourself a favour and don't Google her without SafeSearch on.

SHADOW THE HEDGEHOG

■ If you've ever wondered what Sonic would look like if drawn by a Linkin Park fan, wonder no more. Shadow is Sonic's edgy nemesis and even got his own game, in which he uses guns and glitches through stuff.

CHARMY BEE

■ 'Why not Charmy *The* Bee?' we hear you cry. While we're not entirely sure what Sega's line of thinking was, we'd suggest it's because the little fool doesn't deserve it and anyone who has heard him witter on in *Sonic Heroes* will probably agree. Charmy is the worst. The *worst*.

KNUCKLES THE ECHIDNA

■ Guardian of the Master Emerald and a friendly rival to Sonic, although Sega took even more liberties with echidna physiology than it did with Sonic – instead of waddling around eating ants as he should, Knuckles is a hard-punching badass

MILES 'TAILS' PROWER

■ A plucky little fox with two tails, which can be spun at high speeds to allow limited flight. He's Sonic's best friend and a master mechanic, hence why he frequently turns up in mechs or planes. He can be a bit of a know-it-all, but he's a loyal sidekick to Sonic all the same.

BIG THE CAT

■ The single greatest character ever created, this lumbering slab of brilliance makes up what he lacks in smarts with sheer determination. His best friend is a frog called Froggy, who frequently runs away – that's why *Sonic Adventure* sees him repeatedly going fishing to find his missing buddy.

E-100 SERIES

■ There have been several playable Robots over the course of the series, but we didn't start playing *Sonic* games to mess around with machine guns and flamethrowers… but then again, *Shadow The Hedgehog* exists so all bets are off.

ESPIO THE CHAMELEON

■ After a few years of designing anthropomorphic animals, Sega decided to pay attention to what the relevant creatures actually look like and how they behave. As a chameleon, Espio is able to disguise himself – he's a self-proclaimed ninja warrior and pretty cool.

VECTOR THE CROCODILE

■ Vector is secretly one of the oldest *Sonic* characters, having originally been designed as the keyboard player in Sonic's band for an unused Sound Test feature in the first game. Still, he finally emerged in *Chaotix* before returning as the muscle on his team in *Sonic Heroes*.

SONIC THE HEDGEHOG

■ The star of the show and Sega's enduring mascot. Factual accuracy was clearly of no concern when designing him – real hedgehogs have a top speed of around 12mph, are not blue and do not wear sneakers. Before his playable debut, he appeared as a mirror ornament in arcade driving game *Rad Racer*.

AMY ROSE

■ Sometimes mistaken as Sonic's girlfriend, Amy is simply besotted with him and while the two are good friends, there's nothing more going on unless you delve into the plentiful fan fiction (for the love of god, never do that). She wields a massive hammer, which she's surprisingly handy with.

CREAM THE RABBIT

■ No, that isn't an instruction. Cream made her debut in the GBA spin-off series, her flappy ears working like Tails' tails in allowing brief flight. She's usually accompanied by the brilliantly named Cheese The Chao, a dapper little chap who is much more likeable than Cream herself.

» The official artwork for *Sonic Spinball*, which was released on the Mega Drive in 1993.

» This early *Sonic* concept art can be found in the rather good *Sonic Gems Collection*.

» [Wii] We'd go as far as to say that *Sonic Colors* is one of the best of the recent *Sonic* games. If you're not played it, you really are missing out.

▶ The following game would prove to be the most ambitious of the lot – and it was the point at which Iizuka joined Sonic Team. For the young designer who was just coming off of *Golden Axe III*, it was a huge moment. "As noted previously, I did have a feeling that I wanted to make *Sonic* even before I joined Sega, so when I was told that I will be able to work on *Sonic 3*, I was very delighted," he remembers. "Before I went to the USA, my thoughts of *Sonic 3* were expanding, and after I officially joined the team, I was writing several notebooks filled with game design ideas.

"At that time, the very new technology of 3D expression using polygons was investigated," Iizuka continues. It's a surprising admission – the Mega Drive wasn't a machine that was particularly gifted with 3D capabilities, even with additional technology involved. "We weren't able to achieve the goal of having *Sonic 3* be '3 for 3D' but we did achieve 'three for three characters and three routes'."

Sonic and Tails were joined by Knuckles, a feisty echidna with the ability to glide and climb walls. "From the beginning of *Sonic 3*'s development, when Knuckles became a playable character, the idea to have his own particular route where only he can go in each stage was confirmed. So to create an ability that makes Knuckles go to places where Sonic and Tails can't go was wall climbing and gliding."

Additionally, players gained the ability to control Tails during flight, allowing for greater exploration of levels. The level designers were stretched thin to accommodate it all. "From a game design perspective, we needed much bigger levels compared to previous titles, and we were challenged to create the multiple routes which can be changed depend on the player character you are using," says Iizuka. What's more, Iizuka notes that the new features created some level design problems that were hard for the team to accommodate for. "It was very fun to create those Knuckles-only routes, but as his ability was too strong, he could climb to where he shouldn't go, and/or use the glide and ignore everything and get to the goal easily… so the debug was very tough."

From a character design perspective, Knuckles stands out as being even more aggressive and hard-edged than the already edgy Sonic, which was a deliberate choice. "He's actually not a villain, but was his first rival," Iizuka points out. "Tails in *Sonic 2* was on Sonic's side and was his little brother-like character, so in *Sonic 3* the idea of creating a rival came very quickly. But we didn't want to have just an enemy character, and we wanted to make him playable too, so we added the story of 'was tricked by Eggman'," – or, for the retro purists, Robotnik. "Knuckles was not made to be a cute character unlike Tails, so we made him look strong and cooler by having dreadlocks. After more than 20 years he is also still one of the popular characters."

The eagle-eyed amongst you will note that Knuckles was not playable in *Sonic 3* – he remains firmly in the antagonistic role from the second you meet him in Angel Island Zone to the moment you topple him in Launch Base Zone. However, that's got

"We needed much bigger levels compared to previous titles, and we were challenged to create the multiple routes"
Takashi Iizuka

» [Mega Drive] By *Sonic & Knuckles*, abstract checkerboards were out and more realistic brickwork was in.

a lot to do with the scale of the game. "*Sonic 3* was aimed to be more epic with larger level and various stages. But because of this, development took longer than expected, and we found out that the amount of the data may exceed the cartridges used at that time," Iizuka remembers. "Unfortunately, we decided to divide the game into two titles." You can see this in *Sonic 3* alone – the level-select screen lists levels that don't exist and Knuckles appears on the end post of every level but can't be played.

"We really wanted to make a complete version with first part and second part combined," Iizuka recalls. Of course, doing so would have been prohibitively expensive – a 32MB cartridge with save memory was enormously costly at the time. "Then Naka-san, who was the main programmer at that time, suggested docking the two cartridges. First we were very worried if that could really happen or not, but when the hardware development team achieved this idea, we were very happy." The second half of the game was thus released as *Sonic & Knuckles*, a cartridge with a cartridge slot on top. It could be used as a standalone game, or combined with *Sonic 3* to make the complete game. There were bonus features, too – owners of both *Sonic 3* and *Sonic & Knuckles* could play the Doomsday Zone, a final battle that was only accessible through the combined game, and Knuckles could be added to *Sonic 2* ▶

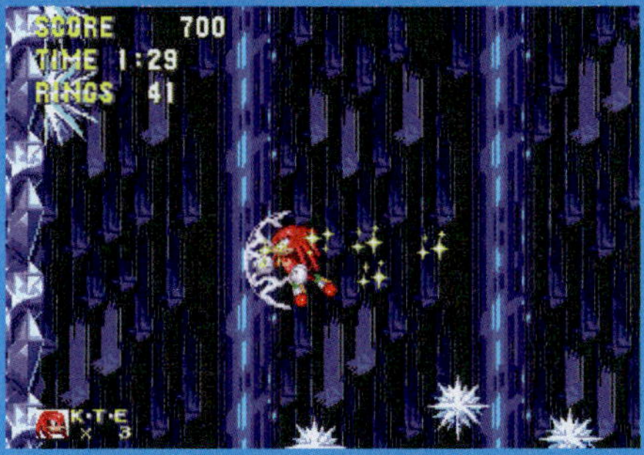

» [Mega Drive] Knuckles was always intended for *Sonic 3*, but finances and deadlines made this impossible, he was made playable in *Sonic & Knuckles*.

SUMMER OF SONIC

2016 marked the return of Sonic's own convention – we speak to its organisers to find out more

How and when did Summer Of Sonic originate?

Svend Joscelyne: Summer Of Sonic originally started in 2006 as a one-off fan project I created to celebrate Sonic's 15th Anniversary. Back then, it was just a website, not a live convention – a collaboration between different fan sites that wrote interesting articles, interviewed Sega and Sonic Team celebrities, and held contests. We even had a virtual birthday card for Sonic that users could sign.

What prompted you to turn the event into an offline convention?

SJ: It wasn't really our intention to pivot from an online website to a live convention; we just reused the name for the 2008 event because it was too good to use for a two-week project!

The idea for a live event came when a meeting of like-minded *Sonic* fans, who previously only knew each other online, got a bit out of hand. What started out as four guys turned into about 30 people dominating a pub, after word had spread. It made me realise that Sonic was actually bringing people together, years after we were all playing the games on our Mega Drive consoles.

With the help of Adam and Kevin Eva (who was the Sega community manager at the time), we set out a plan in 2008 to hire a hall and decorate it so these 30 people could have their own space to hang out. Of course, word spread again and we ended up having to fit 300 people in a 200-capacity space! Good times.

What sorts of things generally take place at Summer Of Sonic?

Adam Tuff: A wonderful aspect of the *Sonic The Hedgehog* universe is the variety of media he has appeared in. The result is that Summer Of Sonic has become a celebration of a multitude of aspects – not just the videogames! The fanbase is extraordinarily talented, and so we encourage guests to show off their skills with art and cosplay contests. We have been extremely fortunate to be able to use Summer Of Sonic as a platform to show off new and upcoming titles – a feature that always attracts large crowds. We also have an incredible line-up of Sonic celebrities from every corner of the franchise, including members of Sonic Team, composers, artists and voice actors. We have even attracted big *Sonic The Hedgehog* names like Yuji Naka, one of the creators of Sonic, and the current head of Sonic Team, Takashi Iizuka.

Do you get any support from Sega?

AT: Sega have been such an incredible source of support financially and logistically. We've worked with so many enthusiastic people from Europe, America and Japan, and every event always feels like such an immense team effort. We cannot thank all those involved enough!

How has the event changed over the years?

SJ: We've really come a long way since 2008. Back then, we just had a small hall, a stage and a Mega Drive hooked up to a projector. As the years went on, the venue has increased five-fold and Sega's support became stronger as we became a pseudo-official event. This fan project is often listed in press releases alongside official Sega America events, it's mad! The Sonic team is especially appreciative of the event, which for us is incredibly humbling.

Just as important are the things that haven't changed. The Summer Of Sonic crew has largely been the same since 2008, so we now have the experience and camaraderie to put on a good show. It just feels like a group of best friends throwing a party.

We've also never taken our sights off of what makes Summer Of Sonic the exciting show it is. For us, it's all about fans meeting up in one place to make friends and have fun. Everything else is gravy, but as long as we focus on that core element, we always have a show that makes *Sonic* fans feel welcome.

THE BEST OF SONIC TODAY

It's fair to say the Sega mascot has had his ups and downs, but the present and future of the Blue Blur is looking very bright indeed

SONIC THE HEDGEHOG MOVIE

2020

■ Despite being ridiculed and delayed almost immediately after the first trailer debuted, this big-screen adaptation of *Sonic The Hedgehog* managed to turn around its fortunes and become the highest grossing videogame movie adaptation of all time. It stars Sonic (voiced by Ben Schwartz) as an interplanetary traveller who ends up on Earth, enjoying a hidden life in Green Hills, Montana. This is disrupted once Dr Robotnik (played by Jim Carrey) learns of the hero and his powers, and goes on the warpath in order to capture him. The film works at being a pretty good kids film, while paying the occasional lip service to long-term *Sonic* fans. If you enjoyed the film, you'd be pleased to know a sequel was announced in 2020, for a 2022 release.

SONIC MANIA

PS4, XBOX ONE, PC, SWITCH

■ This 2D game celebrates *Sonic*'s past with redesigned versions of classic levels from Sonic's 16-bit platform games, alongside brand-new levels, enemies, bosses and the 'Drop Dash' move that allows Sonic to rocket forward as soon as he hits the ground. Visually, it could pass for a lost 32X or Saturn game, with extra colour and smoother animation pushing *Sonic Mania* past what the Mega Drive could do, and the music is reminiscent of *Sonic CD*.

Green Hill Zone has received a makeover, with Batbrains lurking in an enormous new cavern section. A new boss has been added to the stage, which adds a twist to the old Robotnik wrecking ball template – the two tethered spheres can switch between being the attacker and the target, and swing from a central pivot. However, the big attraction is the brand-new Hollywood-themed Studiopolis Zone. The level is filled with spring bumpers, launch pads and breakable windows, as well as broadcast trucks that can transmit Sonic through satellites. Better yet, the game is also packed with references to classic Sega games – we've seen nods to *Streets Of Rage*, *Dr Robotnik's Mean Bean Machine* and even an old *Sonic* popcorn machine.

Sonic Mania arrived in August 2017 to critical acclaim from the press. There's been no word on a sequel, so let's keep our fingers crossed for Sonic's 2021 celebrations...

» [Xbox 360] *Sonic The Hedgehog 4* was an episodic release across two separate downloads. This is *Episode 2*.

if you also owned that game. Expansion packs had been commonplace in computer gaming, but not on consoles, and the execution was widely accepted as a good thing. Of course, the team can rest happy too – many fans consider both games part of a whole, rather than two games with a gimmick.

Of course, those things weren't all that *Sonic 3* and *Sonic & Knuckles* brought to the table – new elemental shields gave additional abilities to Sonic, including a double-jump, an air-dash and a bounce attack. Hiding gigantic rings throughout each level for special stage access encouraged players to explore a bit as well as perfecting their fastest routes. Oh, and a new, less abstract art style pointed towards Sonic's future direction, in which he'd visit realistic cities and interact with humans.

The change of direction in the 3D era has often been a point of contention amongst long-term fans of the series, but in recent years Sonic Team has been using the Mega Drive games as reference material with increasing frequency. Side-viewed gameplay has been employed commonly since *Sonic Unleashed*, *Sonic Generations* gave us glorious updates of classic stages, and *Sonic Lost World* featured an abstract art style that hadn't been seen since the very first games in the series. "3D games are dynamic and the visuals are grand too, but personally I like the 2D game from the Mega Drive era, too, as it is easy to play," says Iizuka when asked about this trend. "We brought up various ideas in the past but with limited hardware spec, so we do have ideas that we weren't able to apply at that time. Even now when I think about creating a new game, I always try to think applying the good part of 3D and good part of 2D to be applied in that new game."

Of course, the influence of Sonic's earlier outings goes much further than that too. Every E3 conference dig can be traced back to the console war that truly fired up when Sonic and Mario were put side by side.

» [Mega Drive] Sonic dashes his way through Marble Garden Zone because he suddenly remembered he left the kettle on.

» [PS3] *Sonic & All-Stars Racing Transformed* is easily the best spin-off from the *Sonic* franchise.

Every time console games have pushed to obtain an older target age group, that's something that *Sonic* was on the leading edge of – and broadening demographics has been important to the growth of the games industry, whether for reasons of content (such as *Grand Theft Auto*, a game that couldn't be sold to the under-18 audience in good conscience) or appeal (games like *Dr. Kawashima's Brain Training*). Five years prior to the co-ordinated international launch of *Sonic 2*, your gaming experience depended heavily on where you lived – you might be playing a NES, a ZX Spectrum, an MSX or something else entirely depending on region. These days, with same-day global launches and region-free consoles, that seems like a lifetime ago. And of course, every time you buy DLC, you might want to spare a thought for *Sonic & Knuckles*. And, of course, all of that is to say nothing of the legion of mascot platform games that came in the wake of the *Sonic* series.

Likewise, the games have brought a generation of creators into the fold. The kids who grew up idolising *Sonic The Hedgehog* are now the kids making games like *Freedom Planet*, and in some cases even working closely with Sega – people like Christian Whitehead and Simon Thomley were raised in the fan scene and have taken a key role in continuing the legacy of those early Mega Drive games, both through direct conversions and with projects like *Sonic Mania*, a love letter to the 16-bit heritage of the *Sonic* series. Whatever Sonic is up to in the present day, the historical significance of that quartet of Mega Drive games is assured.

But for all of our assessment of Sonic's legacy, it's Iizuka as the guardian of that legacy who truly matters. "I do not want say anything too exaggerated, but I think the *Sonic* games were one of the titles that energised the videogame industry of the Nineties," he concludes. "Especially in the west, by having *Sonic* in the market, the hardware competition of Nintendo versus Sega was very clear, and that lead to the result of having more hardware in the market and many third parties joining to create games on Mega Drive and/or SNES. Of course, this wasn't just because of *Sonic*, but to Mega Drive, I think *Sonic* was a great trigger." A trigger is a fine way to think of it – the Mega Drive was always potent, but *Sonic* propelled it like a speeding bullet into the realm of the all-time great consoles. All these years later, the impact of that shot is still being felt. *

THE 2000s

A DECADE OF EXPANDING HORIZONS AND ARTISTIC AMBITION

It was an interesting decade for gamers during the Noughties. 3D gaming continued to evolve with systems like the Dreamcast, PS2 and Xbox greatly improving on the capabilities of the earlier 32-bit machines and bringing online gaming into the mix. After the GameCube continued Nintendo's trend of selling fewer systems than its predecessor, Nintendo turned into an innovator and courted the casual market with its DS handheld and Wii home console. While that was happening, Microsoft and Sony's next consoles pursued the hardcore by delivering high definition games on the Xbox 360 and PlayStation 3. This decade was a good era for the 'Big Three' and gamers, as there really was no losers.

GAMES OF THE DECADE

2000
THE SIMS

After tinkering away with various simulator titles throughout the Eighties and Nineties, Will Wright and his talented Maxis team eventually created the ultimate life simulator. It went on to become one of the biggest PC games of all time and has led to countless expansions and sequels over the years.

2001
HALO: COMBAT EVOLVED

Bungie's excellent Xbox debut not only helped put Microsoft's new console on the map, but also redefined first-person shooters in the process. Levels like The Silent Cartographer felt like nothing else that was available at the time, while you were just as likely to be enthralled by the grass textures as you were the on-screen action.

2002
ELDER SCROLLS III: MORROWIND

The third *Elder Scrolls* game is considered by many to be the best. Vvardenfell was a truly alien-like setting to explore, while the free-form design established in *Daggerfall* is honed to an exceptional degree. Such is *Morrowind*'s success that Bethesda made it a template for its future games.

2003
WARIOWARE, INC: MEGA MICROGAMES!

Nintendo's collection of minigames felt oddly prescient as it mimicked the short bursts of play that would go on to define the mobile games industry that would fully rear its head in the next decade. *WarioWare*'s special, though: a truly wacky experience that never failed to raise a smile.

2004
HALF-LIFE 2

Gordon Freeman's second adventure was a long time coming, but was definitely worth the wait. Valve once again made strides with storytelling, engine physics (check out that Gravity Gun) and cutting-edge tech. It cleverly stepped into horror, too, as anyone who has experienced Ravenholm will testify.

2000 JANUARY
Lost Boy Games is founded in Amsterdam, it will later become known as Guerrilla Games and be known for its *Killzone* series.

2000 JANUARY
After tinkering with all sorts of prototypes, Will Wright and Maxis release the ultimate life simulator, *The Sims*.

2000 MARCH
Realising it needed its own games division to take on Sony, Microsoft sets up its own studio in Redmond, Washington.

2000 MARCH
Tameem Antoniades, Mike Ball and Nina Kristensen set up Just Add Monsters, only to later change its name to Ninja Theory.

2000 MARCH
The PlayStation 2 hits Japan. Games include *A-Train 6*, *Fantavision*, *Ridge Racer V* and *Dead Or Alive 2: Hardcore*.

THE NOUGHTIES...

AS TOLD BY MARK CERNY

THE INDUSTRY VETERAN LOOKS BACK AT AN ERA OF HUGE TECHNOLOGICAL ADVANCES

If the Nineties had been about pursuing the possibilities of 3D games then the Noughties was about perfecting them. The visual advances weren't lost on PlayStation 4 lead architect, Mark Cerny. "Games took huge steps towards photorealism, helped by a massive increase in hardware capability that not only allowed each individual pixel to be rendered much more intelligently, but simultaneously supported an increase in the resolution of the games to HDTV levels (albeit 720p for the most part). I think also our narrative skills grew as an industry to the point where large, story-based titles could really hold their own. Early in the decade *Metal Gear Solid 2* really stands out, followed by the *Grand Theft Auto* titles and others."

Diversity was certainly the name of the game during the Noughties, with all sorts of weird and wonderful titles making it to market. It's hard to imagine a game like *Gitaroo Man* receiving a physical release today, but they thrived during the Noughties. "Frankly, my favourites from that era are pretty random," continues Mark when we ask him about the games that left an impression on him during this period. "I just fell in love with *Pikmin* and *Katamari Damacy*. I think the appeal was the unique world feel, for very different reasons – mobs of ambulatory flowers in the former and some wonderful music in the latter. I also got caught up in the rhythm game boom, and spent many hours on *Guitar Hero*. It made me feel like I was performing even though, of course, I wasn't doing much beyond hitting buttons on a plastic guitar. The Noughties also were a great era for fans (like me) of single-player campaigns. The decade kicked off with a bang with *Halo: Combat Evolved* and its wonderful level design, and later on *Half-Life 2* very successfully added physics to the mix. *Uncharted 2* closes out the decade nicely with its deep and involving story."

While the Noughties was an excellent period for gamers, it's worth remembering that it presented a far tougher challenge for game developers. "The learning curve was just brutal for the development community, they had to master two full generations of hardware advances," concludes Mark. "To give an example, Naughty Dog started the decade in a transition away from *Crash Bandicoot* – where individual polygons had to be counted and accounted for – to *Jak & Daxter*'s wide-open seamlessly connected world. And after just five years, for the *Uncharted* series they had to transition again to realistic human characters and movement, and the complexity that human stories bring to game creation. Also, it's been estimated that development budgets for triple-A games grew by a factor of ten over the course of the decade; that might seem great for the developers but brings a tremendous amount of chaos as brand-new company structure and new approaches to game development are needed."

2005
RESIDENT EVIL 4

Capcom's superb action game didn't just reinvent its own franchise, but the survival horror genre in general. Its influence reaches far and can be seen in countless third-person action games today, while its dramatic setpieces and memorable boss encounters still land with plenty of impact.

2006
GEARS OF WAR

Epic's bombastic third-person action game refined the cover mechanics of earlier shooters like *Kill Switch*, turned Cliff 'Cliffy B' Bleszenski into a gaming superstar and felt like a proper next-gen game compared to anything else on the Xbox 360 at that point. The infamous 'brown era' of gaming started here, too.

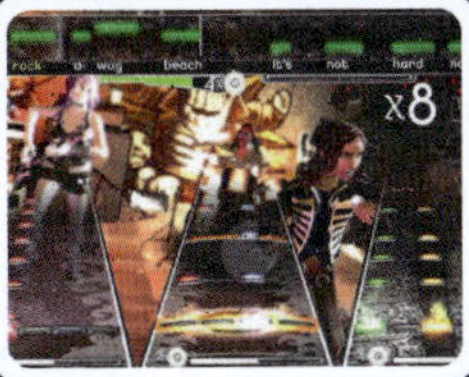

2007
ROCK BAND

While Konami dominated Japanese arcades with its numerous musical peripherals, Harmonix sewed up the console market with this, the definitive way to rock out in your home. The entry level wasn't cheap, but those that dived in discovered the ultimate rhythm action game that remains the highlight of the genre.

2008
FIFA 09

While it made its debut in the Xbox 360 version of *UEFA Champions League 2006-2007*, it was *Fifa 09* which brought the brilliance of Ultimate Team to a far wider audience. Collecting cards was tremendously addictive, with gamers going to any length to create the best footy team possible.

2009
ANGRY BIRDS

This zany destruction game appeared to be on everyone's mobile device when it launched in December. Granted, it wasn't the most original of titles, but it proved that a good theme implemented in a new way could effortlessly catch on with casual gamers. It's gone on to be downloaded over 2 billion times.

2000 APRIL
Nintendo follows up its acclaimed N64 *Zelda* title, *Ocarina Of Time*, with an ambitious sequel, *Majora's Mask*.

2000 JULY
After leaving his role at LucasArts, Tim Schafer decides to start Double Fine Productions in San Francisco, California.

2000 OCTOBER
SSX launches on PlayStation 2 and gives extreme sports fans an alternative to the *Tony Hawk's* franchise.

2000 NOVEMBER
After starting in 1999 as a *Half-Life* mod, Minh Le and Jess Cliffe's *Counter-Strike* receives a commercial release.

2000 DECEMBER
Bandai takes on the Game Boy for a second time by releasing the WonderSwan Color. It doesn't topple Nintendo's handheld.

GAMING CONQUERS THE LIVING ROOM

The first decade of the 21st Century saw the humble games machine become a fixture of the living room. The PlayStation 2's ability to play DVD movies signified a shift, as games consoles increasingly became all-purpose entertainment devices. Beyond that, the hardware of the decade was defined by new possibilities in connectivity – wires became passé and internet connections became the norm, prompting an increase in online multiplayer and the dawn of Achievements and Trophies. We also began our move away from the old TV formats, towards a high-definition future, during a unique generation where every manufacturer could claim success.

1

2

3

4

5

1 PLAYSTATION 2 SONY • 2000

Sony's second console arrived on an enormous wave of hype, fuelled by wild technological claims and amazing footage of games like *Gran Turismo 3* and *Metal Gear Solid 2*. The system also capitalised on the popularity of its predecessor by including backwards compatibility, and hastened the adoption of DVD movies. The early demise of the Dreamcast and late arrival of other rivals gave the console a clear run at the market, and it established an indomitable early lead. A steady supply of classic games followed, and the PlayStation 2 became the best-selling console of all time with 155 million units sold.

2 GAME BOY ADVANCE NINTENDO • 2001

Where the Game Boy Color had been an evolution of the Game Boy line, this 32-bit console was a revolution. As 2D games had fallen out of fashion on home consoles, the Game Boy Advance provided a great home for them, as well as a whole variety of hits from the past (many of which originated on the SNES). The original model suffered from an unlit screen, but subsequent revisions fixed that issue. 81.5 million consoles were sold, of which 53% were the Game Boy Advance SP model and 3% were the late Game Boy Micro version.

3 GAMECUBE NINTENDO • 2001

Nintendo's purple box aimed to conquer the market by combining capable hardware with an affordable price point. It certainly had the graphical grunt, as one look at *Star Wars Rogue Squadron II: Rogue Leader* confirmed, and the expected Nintendo magic was evident in games like *Super Mario Sunshine*, *Metroid Prime* and *The Legend Of Zelda: The Wind Waker*. But third-party games suffered on the system's slightly odd controller, and sluggish game sales led to difficulties with publishers and retailers dropping the console. 21.7 million systems were sold, and Nintendo was beaten into third place in the market for the first time ever.

4 XBOX MICROSOFT • 2001

Even with Microsoft's vast financial resources, there was no guarantee that the company's console debut would be a success, and early on it looked set to struggle. However, a huge early price cut and the drawing power of the superb first-person shooter *Halo: Combat Evolved* stabilised the system, and it became the platform of choice for online console gaming thanks to its excellent Xbox Live service. The Xbox never really took off in Japan and actually lost a lot of money overall, but it established its manufacturer as a key player in the console market for years to come.

5 DS NINTENDO • 2004

Faced with its first real handheld competition in years, Nintendo delivered its best-selling handheld of all time. Although the dual screens of the system grabbed attention, the bigger selling point was the touchscreen that simplified controls, allowing casual audiences to latch onto games like *Dr Kawashima's Brain Training*. 3D games became properly viable, leading to excellent handheld instalments of *Mario Kart* and *Metroid Prime*, while 2D games like *New Super Mario Bros* were still welcome.
The later DSi revision added a camera and downloadable games. Over 154 million DS consoles were sold, making it the second best-selling games machine ever.

2000 DECEMBER
Sonic Team takes a break from making games about hedgehogs and releases *Phantasy Star Online* on the Dreamcast.

2001 MARCH
The Game Boy Advance is released in Japan. Launch games include *Konami Krazy Racers* and *F-Zero: Maximum Velocity.*

2001 MAY
PopCap Games releases its puzzler *Bejeweled* and proves that you don't need flashy graphics to create a hit videogame.

2001 JULY
Final Fantasy X releases on PS2 in Japan and becomes a commercial success for Square, even with Tidus' annoying laugh.

2001 AUGUST
After starting off as a *Resident Evil* game, Capcom unleashes *Devil May Cry* – Goths and gamers fall in love.

6 PSP — SONY • 2004

Sony's sleek handheld promised to bring games with console quality graphics to the palm of your hand – and impressively, it delivered on that promise while providing acceptable battery life and affordable hardware. Despite uneven support over its lifetime, the PSP received both excellent ports and great original games such as *Lumines*, *WipEout Pure* and *LocoRoco*. However, its proprietary UMD movie format flopped and Sony spent much of the system's life fighting security flaws that enabled the running of homebrew software and pirated games. Despite its problems, the system became the most successful non-Nintendo handheld ever, with 76.4 million units sold.

7 XBOX 360 — MICROSOFT • 2005

Starting the next generation early proved advantageous for Microsoft, which managed to sell millions of consoles before its rivals got off the ground. Huge franchises like *Final Fantasy*, *Resident Evil* and *Tekken* made their Xbox debuts thanks to improved relationships with Japanese developers, and games like *Gears Of War* headed the exclusive line-up. However, design flaws resulted in the notorious and widespread 'red ring of death' hardware failure, which ultimately cost Microsoft $1 billion in repair and replacement costs. Sales remained strong throughout the generation, in part due to the family-friendly Kinect motion control device, and 84 million consoles were sold.

8 PLAYSTATION 3 — SONY • 2006

Unlike Sony's first two consoles, the PS3 was not an immediate smash hit. The multimedia focus of the machine had detracted from gaming features, the complex Cell processor was tough for developers to work with, and the high cost of the machine put off prospective buyers. The system even felt somewhat unfinished – the initial Sixaxis control pad lacked rumble, the Trophy system wasn't implemented until 2008. However, hardware revisions made the right cuts to get the cost down (including, controversially, PlayStation 2 backwards compatibility), and the tide was ultimately turned by strong first-party games like *Uncharted*, as well as third-party exclusives like *Metal Gear Solid 4*. The console overtook the Xbox 360 at the end of the generation, selling 87.4 million units.

9 WII — NINTENDO • 2006

After years of declining fortunes, Nintendo abandoned the technological arms race and focused its hardware engineering efforts on control innovations. The motion controls of the Wii Remote demystified games for legions of casual players, with intuitive actions replacing button-based commands in games like *Wii Sports*. The console also marked Nintendo's first sustained retro gaming program, with the Virtual Console service offering downloadable games from a variety of its own past consoles and others. However, some core gamers resented the system, perceiving it as a machine with dated graphics and gimmick-driven games. Sales were explosive but peaked early, with numbers declining at the new decade's beginning as rivals held steady. Even so, over 101.6 million Wii consoles were sold – the most of its generation. It was still supported late into the Tens, too – thanks to Ubisoft's long-standing *Just Dance* series, which amazingly received its 20th Wii version in 2019.

6

7

8

9

OTHER SYSTEMS FROM THE NOUGHTIES

N-Gage • Nokia, 2003

Nokia was ahead of the game in combining mobile phones with handheld gaming, but its inelegant technical execution doomed the unique platform.

iQue Player • iQue, 2003

This odd venture attempted to introduce Nintendo 64 games to the piracy-heavy Chinese market, but less than 20 games eventually saw release.

Gizmondo • Tiger Telematics, 2005

This fascinating handheld promised innovative GPS-enhanced game experiences, but the system quickly collapsed under the weight of its parent company's controversies.

Tapwave Zodiac • Tapwave, 2003

This Palm OS PDA with game-focused hardware received some interesting support early on in its lifespan, but it couldn't compete against the might of the established players.

iPhone • Apple, 2007

Though core gamers scoff at its scores of casual games, the iPhone revolutionised mobile gaming and remains popular today.

2001 SEPTEMBER
The GameCube launches in Japan alongside *Luigi's Mansion*, Sega's *Super Monkey Ball* and *Wave Race: Blue Storm*.

2001 OCTOBER
DMA Design releases *Grand Theft Auto III* and redefines what gamers can expect to discover in open world games.

2001 NOVEMBER
Microsoft releases the Xbox in the US. Launch games include *Project Gotham Racing* and *Halo: Combat Evolved*.

2001 NOVEMBER
Future Publishing launches the *Official Xbox Magazine* in the UK. It becomes affectionately known by readers as *OXM*.

2001 DECEMBER
Panasonic releases the Panasonic Q, a hybrid GameCube that can play DVDs. It will become extremely collectible.

World of Warcraft

For over 15 years, World Of Warcraft has been home not only to the eternal clash between orcs and humans, but also to new alliances, virtual relationships, a digital virus wiping out servers and, of course, Leeroy Jenkins. We explore one of the most important games of the Noughties

Words by Adam Barnes

Kevin Jordan
Kevin was one of the designers of *WOW* who started work on the project in its early days.

"There are 10 million people in the *World Of Warcraft*, because Chuck Norris allows them to live." So goes the iconic advert that came alongside the success of *World Of Warcraft*, and Chuck Norris wasn't the only famous face giving the game their stamp of approval. Ozzy Osbourne, Mr T, Aubrey Plaza, Verne Troyer and William Shatner are just some of the celebrities that put their names – and likenesses – to Blizzard's MMO, and those are just the ones that featured in the ads. Vin Diesel, Ronda Rousey, Mila Kunis, Robin Williams and Jamie Lee Curtis have all vouched for the time they've lost in Azeroth. Matt Stone and Trey Parker loved it so much they made an episode of *South Park* devoted to it. There's no muted way to put it: *World Of Warcraft* is a phenomenon. It has the broad appeal that only a handful of games have been able to achieve, and the cultural significance within and without the games industry that arguably no game has had before or since. But what's more, though the game launched over 15 years ago, *WOW* is still an active and incredibly popular game, even now. It's one of those increasingly rare classics that permeates society so deeply that even non-gamers will know what you mean when you say, 'I play *World Of Warcraft*.' But there was a time, as hard as it may be to remember, when the concept wasn't so recognisable.

Towards the end of the second millennium and coming off the back of *Warcraft*, *StarCraft* and *Diablo*, Blizzard had a luxury that not many developers of the era had: it had time to fail.

THUNDER BLUFF

The cow-like Tauren people have it good because their starting zone of Mulgore and city of Thunder Bluff are gorgeous places to be – they're overlooked because of the disinterest in the race, though.

There was a game in the works behind the scenes at the studio known as 'Project Nomad', a top-down action RPG-like game that would allow players to switch between three active characters from a very long list, each with their own distinct and varied playstyles. "The project didn't really go anywhere," says Kevin Beardslee, who was working on Project Nomad for its short life. "For a while I got pulled off to work on *StarCraft: Brood War*, so I helped finish that up before going back to this project that wasn't going anywhere." This, combined with the release of and subsequent enjoyment of *EverQuest*, led Kevin to believe that the burgeoning MMO genre was an avenue that the company should be heading down. Even if the game amounted to little more than '*EverQuest* done Blizzard-style', it would likely still be another winner to add to the studio's already stellar reputation. Beardslee pitched it to the relevant person until it was carried up the chain of command; within the space of a week, Project Nomad was cancelled and development on an MMO began. "I actually pitched *World Of Warcraft* or *StarCraft*," adds Beardslee, who wanted to leverage a Blizzard IP but didn't really mind which one.

"I worked in tech support," explains Kevin Jordan, one of the designers that would join the *WOW* team early on. "I answered phones, I did some online support emails: you know, that kind of thing." Jordan remembers the team that was working on Project Nomad came to speak with each of the departments within Blizzard to discuss a potential new project. "They sort of had this chat and were saying, 'We're going to stop development on what we're working on, we're going to make an MMO,' and they sort of pinged everyone and what they felt would be better, a fantasy MMO based on *Warcraft* or a sci-fi MMO based on *StarCraft*. It was probably 80% or 90% of people that said they wanted a fantasy MMO." Kevin Jordan, who was a diehard MMO player since *Ultima*

2001 DECEMBER
Tecmo releases *Fatal Frame*, an interesting take on the survival horror genre where a camera is your only protection.

2002 JANUARY
Smilebit and Sega team up to bring us *Jet Set Radio Future*. Its soundtrack will keep Darran tapping his feet for years.

2002 MARCH
Capcom remakes *Resident Evil* on GameCube. The new game tones down on the cheesy dialogue and is a great success.

2002 MAY
Developer Infinity Ward is established by Vince Zampella, Jason West and Grant Collier in Woodland Hills, California.

2002 MAY
The Elder Scrolls III: Morrowind wows PC gamers thanks to its ambitious, open-ended game design.

2002
OCTOBER
After 17 years at Interplay, Brain Fargo resigns and starts up inXile Entertainment in Newport Beach, California.

2002
NOVEMBER
Retro Studios and Nintendo create *Metroid Prime*, a 'first-person adventure' game for the GameCube that wows critics.

2002
DECEMBER
Highbury Entertainment launches *games™*, a multiformat magazine which includes a unique retro section.

2003
After Infogrames Studios closes, Carl Cavers, Darren Mills, James North-Hearn and Paul Porter form Sumo Digital in Sheffield.

2003
FEBRUARY
The Game Boy Advance SP is launched in Japan, its clamshell design and backlit screen are well-received.

IRONFORGE

An underground railway connection with Stormwind means that the dwarven stronghold of Ironforge at least has a good deal of footfall from Alliance players.

STORMWIND

The de facto capital of the Alliance, Stormwind is the Human city, and by and large your run-of-the-mill fantasy castle settlement. It isn't the easiest to navigate, but the sheer number of players picking the human race means it's number one.

WORLD OF WARCRAFT THEN AND NOW

16 YEARS IS A LONG TIME... BUT WHAT HAS CHANGED?

CHARACTERS

THEN

As the years have rolled on, Blizzard has been all too ready to make big changes to the key characters of the game – and actually this has been to its benefit. Yes, it has meant that beloved and long-lasting characters have been killed off from time to time, but it has also given room for others to grow and become more prominent. Young prince Anduin is a prime example of this, as the forgettable child NPC in Stormwind is now a prominent character; his own personal growth into an adult has been a significant topic of each new expansion pack, perhaps mirroring the game's own audience?

NOW

GRAPHICS

THEN

While there was only one instance (so far) of *WOW* getting a graphical overhaul when *Cataclysm* released, with each new expansion pack the artists at Blizzard get better and better at fine-tuning and honing the visual flair of the game. Not too long ago, the character models were reworked, too, and it brought a whole new level of quality to the game. However, that semi-cartoon, exaggerated look to *WOW*'s art style has never gone away, and that has only helped to keep Azeroth looking familiar.

NOW

COMBAT

THEN

The part of the game that perhaps changes the most often is the gameplay, since with each new expansion pack a big change is often thrown into the mix to keep things feeling fresh. However, while it's true that Blizzard has made great steps towards making every class feel viable in all its specialisations, nowadays there's a greater identity to each class and its specialisation than there ever was in vanilla *WOW*. As distinct as they were originally, some classes were just a chore to play in certain specs.

NOW

AREAS

THEN

Aside from the obvious graphical improvements that have been made over the years, perhaps the aspect that Blizzard has learnt the most in is in the way players progress through the game. The breadcrumb trail of quests now more effectively guides players around each new area to ensure they don't miss anything – which was a very real problem before. Vanilla *WOW* arguably felt more like a world since it was necessary to explore everything on foot to find every quest, but it was hard work finding your way around.

NOW

Online, made strides to speak to the relevant people so that his interest in the growing genre could help the project.

The amount that *World Of Warcraft* owes to *EverQuest* isn't big news, but it only acted as a foundation for what Blizzard wanted to achieve. As has historically been the case, Blizzard wanted to use its unique ability to take a popular yet complex concept and open it up to a broader audience. A large part of doing so meant adapting the frustrations that *EverQuest* had built. "The biggest thing that I pitched was instanced dungeons," says Beardslee, referring to the engine's ability to create personal sessions for a dungeon based on each group accessing it, rather than *EverQuest*'s method which meant that players were often left unable to take on a boss since they were always waiting for the server reset. "I made the analogy of getting let into Disneyland and trying to run to whatever your favourite ride is and someone saying, 'Nope, sorry, someone already rode it – ride some other ride.' Everyone wants to try the encounters and bosses, and they shouldn't be limited just by the fact that it's not available." This wasn't the only concept that Beardslee had hoped to improve upon, however, with WASD-based movement rather than mouse control, better questing with more visible quest givers and a 'rested' state for catching up with friends who can play more often than you being just some of the suggestions that the developer included in his pitch. The fact that it was a Blizzard game

[PC] Outside of questing and killing, there are more relaxed pastimes like fishing, cooking or any one of the many professions.

2003 MARCH Nintendo releases *WarioWare, Inc: Mega Microgames!* a crazy speed dating-like selection of minigames.

2003 JUNE Chris Parker, Feargus Urquhart, Darren Monahan, Chris Jones and Chris Avellone form Obsidian Entertainment.

2003 JULY BioWare releases *Star Wars: Knights Of The Old Republic* on Xbox. Its revelatory twist shocks gamers to their core.

2003 OCTOBER Nokia launches the N-Gage, a bizarre cross between a games machine and phone. 'Side talking' becomes a thing.

2003 OCTOBER *Prince Of Persia: Sands Of Time* is released and sees Ubisoft Montreal completely overhauling the series.

This zone is like a big old nostalgia blanket for *World Of Warcraft* players. Whether it's talk of Mankirk's wife or the regular Alliance raids, it's perhaps the MMO's most iconic area.

» Navigating longer distances requires using flight paths via griffons (Alliance) or duskbats (Horde). It takes time, but the bird's-eye view offers a glimpse of zones to come.

meant there was also going to be a bigger focus on the visuals of the game, too, as well as a much more involving and interesting storyline.

The team began development by splitting each day into two: the first half was just sat at the couches chatting about design decisions, while the second half was building the world itself. When it came to the latter, Blizzard began with just one zone, which it built, tested and refined to ensure the core gameplay loop was working perfectly. This first zone would become Elwynn Forest, the human starting area, and from there it would go on to define how the rest of Azeroth would look, feel, play and act. But Azeroth was going to be a big place, there needed to be more hands on deck. "They got us to do a map test," says Bo Bell, one of the QA members that was given a task to appraise their ability to design a level. This process was to find out who in the other departments of the studio had what it took to create a compelling an interesting world. "Something like 47 people turned in a map," adds Bo. "Initially there was only one position available, but they were blown away by all the submissions. The team wasn't quite sure what they were looking for, because the entire concept was completely fresh ground for them."

Initially, the engine was built on a tweaked version of the *Warcraft III* engine, the idea being that the two teams could just share the assets. Quite quickly *WOW* grew beyond this scope, however, and the engine became all its own thing, able to handle a closer, third-person perspective. Because of this increased scale, there was a necessary on-the-fly approach to development. If a spider-infested forest was needed, Bo suggests, then it was requested and the art team would go on to make it, an ad hoc process that simply wouldn't work in game development these days. "I tell people that that's how we did things," he adds, "and they look at me like we were insane, they're like: 'You don't have time to stop and do stuff like that.' I always say, 'I know but everyone was passionate and everyone wanted this awesome product.'"

This natural growth of a world continued over the course of the game's development, and with Chris Metzen finessing every aspect of the game's lore to really build upon the stories told in the RTS *Warcraft* games, Azeroth itself became a key part of why *WOW* was so iconic. Any *WOW* player will be able to recall fond memories of particular quests or iconic zones, and everyone

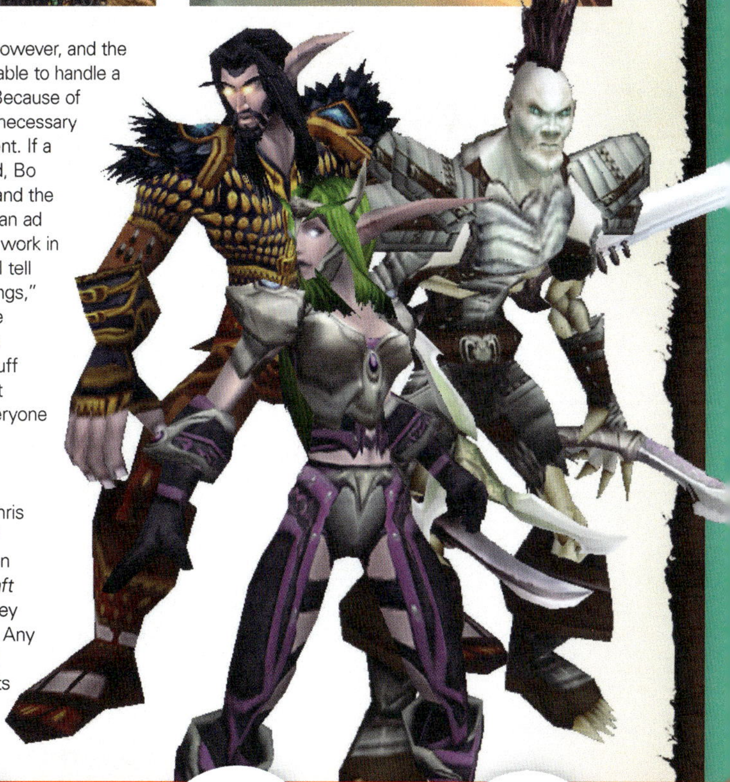

2003
NOVEMBER
Niklas Hed, Kim Dikert and Jarno Väkeväinen set up Rovio Entertainment. It will go on to make a hit game about irate avians.

2004
JANUARY
Live Publishing launches **Retro Gamer** a quarterly magazine devoted to nostalgia. Whatever happened to that, then?

2004
MARCH
Team Ninja reboots the *Ninja Gaiden* franchise on Microsoft's Xbox, taking a bloody leaf out of *Devil May Cry*'s book.

2004
MAY
Sammy Corporation spends $1.8 billion on acquiring Sega Corporation to form Sega Sammy Holdings Inc.

2004
JUNE
Spider-Man 2 proves you can make great games based on movies, particularly if you style them around *GTA*.

TOP OF THE CLASS

A GUIDE TO WORLD OF WARCRAFT'S ORIGINAL CLASSES

WARRIOR

As the basic melee character, Warriors can either deal damage or take it. They're best suited as tanks, however, and except for those irritating moments when a player charges in to steal your quest enemy, are often the most in-demand class when it comes to co-op play.

PALADIN

In classic *WOW*, the Paladin is exclusive to the Alliance and combined tankiness with healing. In solo levelling it is an abomination to play since it is so slow and uninteresting, but a free mount, useful auras for raiding and the ability to make yourself immune to damage and then simply Hearthstone away certainly made up for all of the hassle.

HUNTER

As one of two classes capable of using companions, the Hunter is actually a very safe choice in pretty much any aspect of the game. It's also one of the best solo levelling classes since a Hunter's pet can tank mobs while they safely deal damage from a distance. The traps, too, are great in both player-versus-player and raiding.

ROGUE

Arguably the best damage dealers in the game, a good Rogue player is invaluable to any raid, dungeon or PVP match. Its stealth skills make it one of the more fun classes to play, too, since it is able to approach situations in a way that few other classes in the game can.

» [PC] Vanilla *World Of Warcraft* was not quite as easy as it is today, and you could easily spend a lot of time running back to your corpse.

» [PC] It's possible to 'try on' items that were linked in chat, a smart move that gives players something to work towards.

certainly had their favourites: some might warmly recall racing naked through the Wetlands at too low a level just to join their Night Elf friend on a quest, others will remember the inane chat of The Barrens or the repeated Alliance raids, while everyone will remember teaming up for their first Elite kill – Hogger. Regardless of what that memory is, there's one thing that ties it all together: the community. "On the social side, I wanted to be sure there were lots of things players could do for each other," says Kevin Jordan, who was focused more on the design of the combat and the gameplay side of things. "You know, the simple buffs and the cures and things that you could do while you're passing someone. Because it was no skin off your back and it had the potential to be a friendly gesture that could spark a conversation, right?" The sound of Arcane Intelligent is a familiar one, since Mages would cast it on any player that they came across in the world. Priests had Fortitude, Druids had Mark Of The Wild, Paladins had Blessing Of Kings; but it was all designed to foster a little bit of social interaction. "Another thing was that we had this concept of communal areas. So, instances required five people but out in front of the dungeon area was a lot of non-elite content that you can do solo and quests will point you there. It would be this kind of thing where people were frequently bumping into each other and this would seamlessly transition people into getting into a group."

World Of Warcraft became a behemoth team for Blizzard, with over 60 people working on it – at the time that was an exceptional amount – and chipping away at making it the best it could be. There were designers for every part of the game, and since the game was so huge it needed the manpower. But despite moments during alpha where the team itself were getting excited, there were still doubts over *WOW*'s potential. "It was like, we knew we were good," says Bo, "we knew that we were making an awesome game, but we were still like… this might not sell real well, this may not be this awesome thing we think it is." Despite the excitement surrounding the game, the devs didn't truly know what they had on their hands until the open beta test. "The number of people that came in during the open beta, we were blown away. Everybody was talking about it, everybody wanted to get in on the *WOW* beta and at that point I knew we were going to blow *EQ* away."

And, of course, this was just a taster for things to come. The open beta didn't just prove there was a demand to Blizzard, it reinforced the hype that was building around *WOW*. There was a tangible excitement about its release, and gamers – MMO fans, *EverQuest* players and everyone in between – was eager to play when it launched in November 2004. And despite this hype, Blizzard was not prepared. "Our goal was 325,000 units," says Beardslee of the humble expectations for the game, "if we could sell that from November to the end of the year, then we felt like we were would be doing really well. We basically would have more than half of *EverQuest*'s userbase, and we did that. And then it doubled and doubled." The improvements it made to the *EQ* template were noticed, and players around the globe became absorbed by what was being termed 'The World Of Warcrack'. It ate up lives and players became devoted to their guilds, their levelling friends

DARNASSUS

Despite its gorgeous, nature-inspired design and relatively easy-to-navigate layout, the elven capital of Darnassus is shoved off in the corner of the world and, as a result, is mostly abandoned.

ORGRIMMAR

The Horde doesn't get quite as much choice when it comes to the cities that players would choose to call home, making the orc capital of Orgrimmar the go-to city destination. Its inventive design, built into the rocky environment of Durotar, make it a fun place to be.

2004 AUGUST id Software releases *Doom 3*. It's basically a reboot of the original, but with a bigger emphasis on story and horror.

2004 SEPTEMBER Big Blue Box Studios' ambitious action RPG *Fable* finally arrives on Xbox after a lengthy development period.

2004 OCTOBER Ex-LucasArts staff, Dan Connors, Troy Molander and Kevin Bruner start up Telltale Games in San Rafael, California.

2004 NOVEMBER After five years, Valve Corporation launches *Half-Life 2* to huge acclaim. A long wait for a third game begins here.

2004 NOVEMBER Nintendo releases the DS in North America. Launch games include *Super Mario 64 DS* and *Feel The Magic: XY/XX*.

UNDERCITY

Buried beneath the once-great human city of Lordaeron, the novel concept of the Undercity is important because of its lore. It's a disaster to navigate, however, meaning most undead hop the nearest Zeppelin to Orgrimmar.

and their online avatars. All the while, Blizzard was struggling to keep up: "The biggest hurdle was that we didn't realise the concurrency of the number of players," says Beardslee, who recalls the queues that players had to endure just to play. "We had a bunch of numbers so we could figure out what a server could accommodate. We thought maybe people would get on and play for one to two hours a night but people were playing four to six hours every night and the same people were playing every single night."

The popularity didn't stop there, either. While more and more content was brought into the game after its launch with core features like player-versus-player or additional endgame content being added, in many ways Blizzard had to spend its time putting out fires, balancing the game, giving its voracious community additional things to do and ultimately maintaining its booming popularity. Despite launching just over two years after the vanilla release, the first expansion pack, *The Burning Crusade*, struck at a time when excitement for *WOW* was at its highest. It brought with it flying mounts, two new playable races and a chance to explore the original orc homeland of Outland. *The Wrath Of The Lich King* followed only a year later, tying off the beloved story of *Warcraft III*. This is widely considered to be the pinnacle of *World Of Warcraft*, which resulted in the game's height of subscribers at over 12 million by the end of the expansion's life. In December of 2010 *Cataclysm* was released, forever changing Azeroth by having the slumbering dragon Deathwing lay waste to the original world map. This allowed Blizzard to overhaul the graphics, but also to streamline the levelling experience in the process; it was a bold move, and a well-liked one, but many will say it was the death knell for the MMO. Since then the total number of subscribers has dropped and never quite recovered, with the *Mists Of Pandaria* expansion pack acting as a sort of nail in the coffin: though the expansion pack was well-designed, the shift in style and tone left many considered about the direction the series was beginning to take. *Warlords Of Draenor* (2014) rectified that by reigniting the Alliance and Horde war, while *Legion* (2016) felt like it was trying to encapsulate the same feelings that players had when they first played *The Burning Crusade*. *Battle For Azeroth* (2018) proved Blizzard's consistency when it comes to *Warcraft* content, and it sold 3.4 million copies on its first day alone – the fastest selling *WOW* expansion pack of all time. The most recent expansion, *Shadowlands*, marks a new chapter for the MMO, as well as an overhauled levelling system.

But perhaps the most exciting thing that Blizzard has done, at least for retro gamers, is its release of *World Of Warcraft: Classic*. After years of demands from fans, the studio re-released the 'vanilla' *WOW* experience, warts and all, for players to get wistful over. "I think it's good to release *Classic*," says Kevin Jordan, "because there aren't a lot of high-quality games out there that provide the experience that vanilla *WOW* provided. A lot of MMOs, *WOW* included, have gone to a more streamlined approach and they don't cater this much to the social environments. I think it has potential to be very successful again." In a sort of ironic twist of fate, *Classic* was met with long server queues as Blizzard underestimated player interest. The developer was a little quicker to respond than before, but perhaps it says something of the love that players still have for vanilla *World Of Warcraft*. *

WORLD OF WARCRAFT

SHAMAN

These masters of the elements are restricted to the Horde and are very valuable additions to any team. They can heal, they can deal damage and they can even help to tank damage in a pinch. By leveraging deployable totems, Shaman play is more about kiting the enemy to a specific area, and players will get a good deal of self-sustain while doing so.

MAGE

Commonly referred to as the 'glass cannon' of the game, the Mage class is capable of pumping out some serious damage, which makes them desirable teammates. If player-versus-player is more your scene, then the Frost skill tree is going to be essential.

PRIEST

Obviously the primary healing class of the game, Priests are actually the only class in the game with two healing specialisations. The damage-focused Shadow Priest is severely lacking, but play as a healing Priest and you'll be guaranteed a slot in any dungeon or raid group, so long as you don't let those wipes happen…

DRUID

The ability to shapeshift into different animal forms – and through that fulfil any role in the game – makes the Druid a very tantalising class since it's such a cool concept. The problem is, however, that the Druid is the epitome of the jack-of-all-classes; fun to play, perhaps, but not in demand at all.

WARLOCK

Where the Mage is about high-damage spells with long cast timers, the Warlock is more about stacking numerous damage-over-time curses to whittle away at the enemy. Their damage is among the highest in the game, but it's arguably their Soulstone ability – which allows a group's tank or healer to resurrect themselves in battle – that makes them so popular.

2004 NOVEMBER
Blizzard releases its MMORPG *World Of Warcraft*. You can read about it right here on these pages!

2004 DECEMBER
Sony releases the PlayStation Portable in Japan. It's more powerful than the DS, but will that be enough?

2005 JANUARY
Resident Evil 4 not only shakes up Capcom's horror franchise, but will also influence action games for years to come.

2005 MARCH
God Of War debuts on PlayStation 2. The action-packed game introduces gamers to the angry antihero Kratos.

2005 APRIL
Hideo Kojima forms Kojima Productions, a subsidiary of Konami in Tokyo, Japan. Let's see if that partnership lasts…

ONLINE GAMING GETS HUGE

WORDS BY DARRAN JONES

THE ABILITY TO PLAY GAMES ONLINE HAS EXISTED SINCE THE EARLY DAYS OF GAMING, BUT IN THE NOUGHTIES SERVICES LIKE XBOX LIVE ALLOWED IT TO REACH THE MASSES, AND THEN IT REALLY TOOK OFF

TOM HALL

» Tom worked on a number of early important online games, including *Doom* and *Rise Of The Triad*.

STEVE LYCETT

» Steve has worked on a number of online games at Sumo Digital.

MARTYN CHUDLEY

» Bizarre Creations' founder, Martyn Chudley worked on the *Project Gotham Racing* series.

It's easy to take online gaming for granted nowadays. Industry juggernauts like Microsoft, Sony and Valve have integrated it into their systems and services seamlessly, and it allows us to do whatever we want, from taking part in massively multiplayer experiences, to pitting our wits and skills against a friend in one-on-one battles. Most online services make it incredibly easy to chat with friends, access high scores and find out more about the games you want to play, but it hasn't always been like this, as *Doom*'s director Tom Hall remembers. "I played a primitive deathmatch game called *MazeWar* in the CompSci Building of the University Of Wisconsin-Madison," he tells us. "It had networked multiplayer for free – the computers were already connected to the mainframe. It was pretty cool to see another player, but 'battles' were usually over quickly."

Online gaming largely progressed in those early days of gaming, thanks to games like *MUD* (*Multi-User Dungeon*) but as the Seventies gave way to the Eighties, progress slowly continued to be made. However, it wasn't until the Nineties that more gamers began to venture online, and even then it wasn't easy. "Early on, it was getting networking working of course," continues Tom when we ask him about the biggest obstacles developers faced when taking games like *Doom* online. "Also educating players on how to connect, since it was a little arcane, with all the IPX (Internetwork Packet Exchange) stuff. Then the challenge was matchmaking, which was a business for DWANGO until the internet properly took off. Remember, folks might not have the hardware to talk to other computers, or they were downloading games off bulletin board systems, which took forever. This was taking the early baby steps from stuff that computer nerds played in computer labs and starting to get it to the (still tech-savvy) public)."

While the Nineties made a lot of advancements and helped expand the popularity of genres like first-person shooters, MMORPGs and real-time strategy games, it could still feel like pulling teeth from a developer's point of view. Steve Lycett has worked on several online racing games and is well aware of those challenges. "We now live in an age where the internet connection is almost a human necessity taken for granted as much as water and electricity," he begins, "but back then just getting connected was a major challenge. You'd need to sign up to an ISP or a service like Wireplay and a modem, starting each session listening to squawks and beeps, and you'd pay per minute for however long you were connected! You could either take calls or use the internet, not both and you'd need to arrange to have someone to play with in advance. Even with a 'connected console' such as a Dreamcast, you had some real-world technical and logistical challenges to overcome just to play online games with your friends."

Those challenges were largely overcome, however, and as videogames continued to mature, services like Xbox Live helped change how we consumed and enjoyed online games. "Xbox Live gave us a whole new way of playing console games, building on some of the Dreamcast advances and giving a solid, formalised online experience – until then PC online games were utterly disparate, with no crossover to other games at all," continues Martyn Chudley, who helped create *Project Gotham Racing 2*, one of the service's first online racing games. "With a very tightly controlled ecosystem, (and apart from network latency and speeds) you

» [Xbox] *Halo 2* utilised innovative matchmaking technology and was a huge reason for signing up to Xbox Live back in the day.

2005 APRIL
Nintendogs sells the DS to casual gamers who love grooming and petting their dogs and taking them for walks. Aww.

2005 JUNE
Killer7 causes a stir on GameCube. Grasshopper's odd game lets you play as a group of assassins. A PS2 version follows.

2005 SEPTEMBER
GBA owners in America are treated to the superb *Rebelstar: Tactical Command* by strategy king Julian Gollop.

2005 OCTOBER
Rockstar Games releases *The Warriors* 26 years after the actual film, proving a good licence can be published anytime.

2005 OCTOBER
Team Ico's beautiful *Shadow Of The Colossus* lands onto PS2. Despite its technical flaws, it astounds reviewers.

1

2

3

4

5

"XBOX LIVE GAVE US A WHOLE NEW WAY OF PLAYING CONSOLE GAMES, BUILDING ON SOME OF THE DREAMCAST ADVANCES AND GIVING A SOLID, FORMALISED ONLINE EXPERIENCE"

MARTYN CHUDLEY

knew that everyone had 'exactly' the same setup, and we could exploit the Live matchmaking, Achievements, Gamertags etc that Live provided. We'd not done much PC coding at that time, other than ports, mainly because it was such a fractured space – machine specs varied wildly across all elements – graphic capabilities, resolutions, controls, performance. Everything. Consoles *fixed* all that to one standard."

Even though services like Xbox Live and PSN have made online gaming easier, the internet is still a challenge for developers. "We still fight the core technical fundamentals of latency and bandwidth," highlights Steve. "Modern games need to send not only information from other players, but you also have voice chat, streamed video and more. That's great if you've got a low-latency/high-bandwidth connection, but it's only as good as the player in the session with the worse connection, so we spend a lot of time mitigating that with server locations and code solutions like client-side prediction. The complexity of networking has jumped, too, over the years. In *OutRun 2*, we only really needed to update the position of the players' cars over the network as the traffic pattern was fixed. Compare that to a modern open world game like *Crackdown 3*, now we have to be able to synchronise and update thousands of objects from players, to enemy AI, to complex traffic and prop object placement. Which is even more challenging when the player is busy making it all blow up in a myriad ways!"

Those challenges are worth it, though, when you consider how much satisfying online gaming is today. And Martyn Chudley believes its popularity today can be summed up with one simple word. "Social," he concludes. "Games are now perceived as a million times cooler than back in the day and this is because they are pretty much *all* connected in some way now, though the various online services that the hardware manufacturers have created. If gaming was still a completely solitary experience I believe games would still be as geeky and nerdy as they were when we all started out!"

GENRE-LY GREAT ONLINE

EXPERIENCES BEST ENJOYED WITH OTHERS

SURVIVAL

1 Games like *DayZ*, *Minecraft* and *Ark: Survival Evolved* fall into this category and they often feature mechanics like crafting and are typically set in procedurally generated environments and can often have a hostile theme. They're far more entertaining online, as you're often surviving at the expense of others.

ARENA SHOOTERS

2 *Unreal Tournament* and *Quake III* helped popularise this genre and it's easy to understand how. Taking on living opponents in tight, constricted areas is so much more satisfying than when you play against a group of AI bots. It's technically the same game, but the experience is massively diluted.

MMOs

3 While you can technically play games like this on your own, they're rarely that satisfying to play. Games like *World Of Warcraft*, *Final Fantasy XIV* and *EVE Online* are all about engaging with other players (peacefully or otherwise), rather than just moving around in your own space, and they're all the better for it.

MOBA

4 While these games can be extremely difficult to get into compared to many of the genres we're featuring here, the enjoyment factor has the potential to become even more intoxicating. Working as a cohesive unit is often the only way of true success and a single-player game simply can't replicate that.

BATTLE ROYALE

5 This is a relatively new genre, thanks to the rise of games such as *PlayerUnknown's Battlegrounds* and *Fortnite Battle Royale* (although some may argue *Bomberman Online* is an earlier contender). Regardless of how new the genre actually is, it's certainly pointless if you're not playing against human opponents.

2005 NOVEMBER
Harmonix channels arcade game design and creates *Guitar Hero*. Plastic guitar peripherals start selling like crazy.

2005 NOVEMBER
Microsoft's latest console, the Xbox 360, launches. It offers HD gaming, advanced online... and the Red Ring Of Death.

2005 DECEMBER
Sega releases *Yakuza* in Japan, and introduces the world to the gangster with a big heart, Kazuma Kiryu.

2006 FEBRUARY
Criterion Games takes a break from arcade-style racers and unloads the excellent chaotic *Black* on PS2 and Xbox.

2006 MAY
New Super Mario Bros leaps to DS. Nintendo's inventive platformer does well, selling over 31 million units.

» [PC] *Shadow Of Mordor*'s Nemesis systems shows there's room for open worlds to evolve.

BRAVE NEW OPEN WORLDS

by Paul Walker-Emig

» [PC] CD Project Red's *The Witcher 3: Wild Hunt* mixes rural wastelands and dense urban locales effectively.

Michael de Plater

Kelsey Beachum

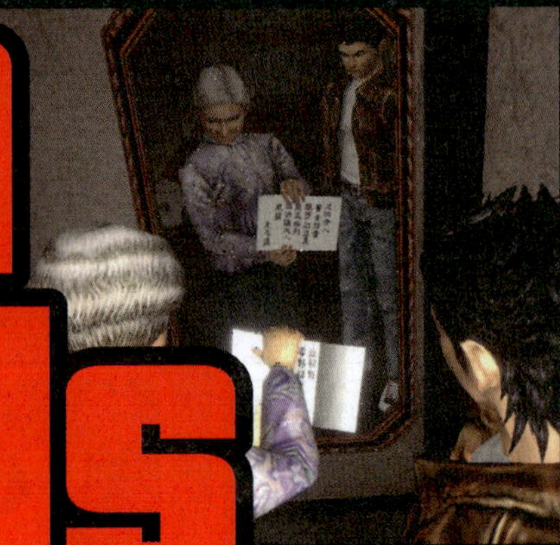

» [PS2] *GTA: Vice City* iterates on the advancements made in *GTA III*, and takes us back in time to the Eighties.

2006 JULY Future Publishing releases *Nintendo Gamer*, a new Nintendo-focused magazine with distinctive Wil Overton art.

2006 AUGUST Volition creates *Saints Row* in an attempt to take on *Grand Theft Auto*. The series will later lean into the absurd.

2006 SEPTEMBER Clover Studio reinvents the scrolling fighter with the incredible *God Hand*. Sadly, the public doesn't realise its brilliance.

2006 NOVEMBER Sony's PS3 arrives to a lukewarm reception. Shortly afterwards, Nintendo releases its innovative Wii.

2006 NOVEMBER Epic Games releases *Gears Of War* as an Xbox 360 exclusive. It helps to establish the cover shooter and HD era.

Before GTA III...

EXAMINING THE DNA OF EARLY OPEN WORLDS

How the turn of the century gave us a boom in open world gaming and set the template for the modern blockbuster

The rise to prominence of 3D gaming in the Nineties triggered an era of experimentation that gave birth to new ideas, genres and styles. Out of that crucible emerged a handful of influential games that laid down the template for the modern blockbuster, their influence still keenly felt today. We are talking about the emergence of the modern 3D open world.

Before we pay tribute to the legacy of those games, we must acknowledge that open world titles existed well before the era of 3D gaming. "The genesis of the open world happens entirely in the United Kingdom in two key years, 1984 and 1985," explains Chris Bateman, founder of ihobo, the studio behind *Silk*, an open world game inspired by games like *The Lords Of Midnight*, *Eye Of The Beholder* and *The Bards Tale*. "*Elite*, *The Lords Of Midnight*, *Paradroid* and *Mercenary* all laid out ways of giving the player maximum agency with the relatively minimal resources of the ZX Spectrum, Commodore 64 and Amstrad." Chris points out that *Elite* "directly inspired DMA in making the *GTA* franchise".

However, we can't ignore that the titles that emerged around the turn of the century were markedly different. The likes of *Shenmue* and, most significantly, *Grand Theft Auto III* gave us a vision of what the future of games might look like. It's a vision that proved to be remarkably accurate, the hallmarks that the games of this era established are still evident in some of the biggest games of today.

"Two of my favourite games at the turn of the last millennium were *The Legend Of Zelda: Ocarina Of Time* and *Grand Theft Auto III*," recalls Michael De Plater, vice president at Monolith Productions. "And two of my favourite games at the dawn of the Twenties are *The Legend Of Zelda: Breath Of The Wild* and *Red Dead Redemption II*. So, there's a pretty straight line from those breakthrough games to their direct successors today," he continues.

The aforementioned *Ocarina Of Time*, which came out in 1998, made important steps towards what we would come to understand as the modern open world game – its open structure was cited by *GTA III* producer Sam Houser as an influence. 1999's *Shenmue* was also a pioneering title which deserves credit for introducing a host of revolutionary systems – the game included the now-common feature of a day/night cycle, changing weather and gave us an incredibly detailed 3D city in which to roam freely. Its level of realism was stunning at the

ELITE

David Braben and Ian Bell's legendary 1984 space sim was revolutionary, and a case can be made that it is the first true open world game.

ULTIMA IV

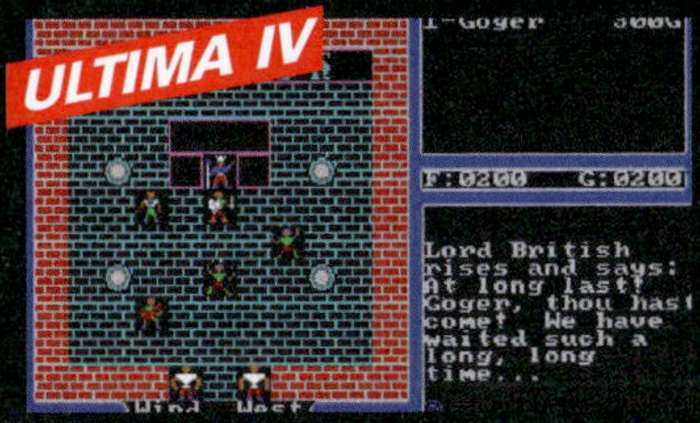

This influential series is known for its open nature. *Ultima IV* expands on that by allowing you to align with different factions.

GRAND THEFT AUTO

1997's *Grand Theft Auto* might look very different to the *GTA* we know now, but that formative DNA still persists in the franchise today.

HUNTER

This 1991 Amiga and Atari ST title is notable for allowing you to use a number of vehicles to navigate its 3D world.

THE LEGEND OF ZELDA

While this iconic NES title is not an open world game per se, this game, and its sequels, were a big influence on the genre.

URBAN CHAOS

Though it wasn't particularly well-received, this free-roaming fighting game from 1999 was a taste of what was to come.

MERCENARY

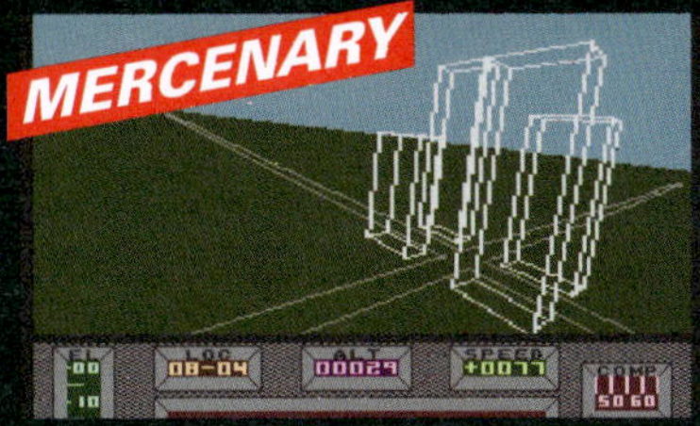

Your goal in *Mercenary* is to escape from a wireframe planet, with the game offering multiple open paths to achieve that end.

THE SEVEN CITIES OF GOLD

After sailing to 'the new world', *Seven Cities* lets you explore the coast, interacting with the natives and setting up missionaries and forts.

SKOOL DAZE

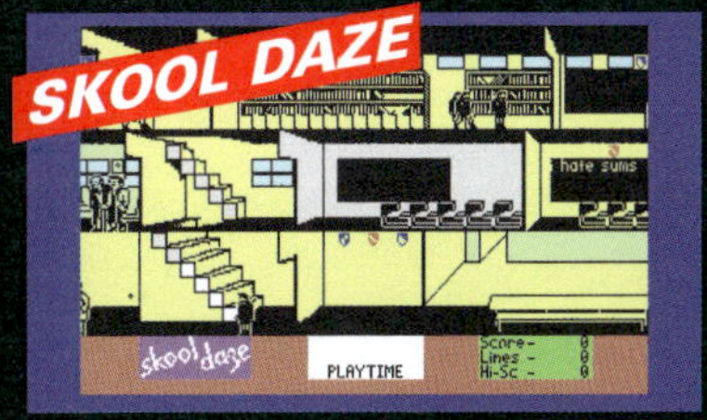

The concept of the 'sandbox', is on show in an early form in this title that has you play as a schoolboy trying to steal his report card.

SID MEIER'S PIRATES!

Allowing you to journey to different countries, this game gestures towards the scale that would become such a big feature of modern open worlds.

2007 MARCH *STALKER: Shadow Of Chernobyl* blows in. The first-person shooter takes inspiration from the real-life incident.

2007 JUNE Apple releases the iPhone and its new iOS operating system. The innovative phone changes the mobile market significantly.

2007 AUGUST Ken Levine's *BioShock* releases. Its unique underwater setting and distinct Art Deco look make big waves.

2007 SEPTEMBER Over a million gamers play *Halo 3* online during its first 24 hours of life. It makes $300 million in its first week of sale.

2007 OCTOBER Japanese luminaries Shinji Mikami, Tatsuya Minami, Atsushi Inaba and Hideki Kamiya create PlatinumGames.

ADDING A NEW TWIST TO AN ESTABLISHED GENRE

OPEN WORLD INNOVATORS

STALKER: Shadow Of Chernobyl

This 2007 post-apocalyptic open world can be credited as a huge influence on the survival and simulation mechanics that would later appear in many other games. *STALKER* requires you to eat when your character becomes hungry and dress bandages to stop bleeding in a dangerous world with sparse resources.

Minecraft

What makes *Minecraft* stand out from the open worlds that preceded it is the fact that its world is one you are given the tools to shape yourself through mining, building, crafting and so on. It's hard to overstate the impact this game has had on the industry.

No Man's Sky

Opinion is divided on how much fun *No Man's Sky* is as a game, but you can't deny how impressive it is as a piece of technical innovation. Taking procedural generation to the next level to give us an impossibly huge universe to explore, no one had dreamed that an open world this large was possible.

DayZ

Taking inspiration from a variety of genres, including open worlds, MMOs and survival games, *DayZ* sparked a trend for multiplayer gameplay built on unpredictability, conflict and cooperation. It also served as the genesis of the 'battle royale' concept, which has become a big trend in gaming.

Zelda: Breath Of The Wild

Breath Of The Wild takes inspiration from open worlds to give new life to the *Zelda* series and, in turn, has given something back. The game eschews the icon-driven approach of many other open world titles in favour of discoveries that emerge naturally through exploration.

time, though the game didn't always hit the mark with its groundbreaking ideas. *Shenmue* left an indelible legacy, but its unevenness, and the series financial failure, was perhaps indicative of the fact that this was a genre still finding its feet. It wouldn't be long, however, until the gaming world was shaken to its core by a monumentally successful sequel.

By the time 2001 rolled around, the *Grand Theft Auto* series had already established a solid foundation with its successful 2D top-down titles. But it was *Grand Theft Auto III* which took that foundation and radically reimagined it to deliver us a 3D rendition of Liberty City that took the series, and open world videogames, to a whole new level.

"In the Nineties, there began a publishing battle on presentation values that lead to more film-like techniques appearing in games, larger team sizes and greater development budgets," says Chris. "It was a war for the so-called 'triple-A market' – which is to say, for the prestige of big budget games. *Shenmue* is an example of the escalating cost of development and the battle for that 'prestige' status at the turn of the millennium. Yu Suzuki's magnum opus was an astonishing piece of work, and one of the most interesting narrative designs we've ever seen, but unlike *GTA*, it lacked mainstream popular appeal. A lot of the budget in *Shenmue* went on establishing the atmosphere of its setting; most of the budget in *GTA* went on toys for the player to crash, smash and shoot up. As much as I love *Shenmue*, I can't deny that DMA had uncorked the commercial genie of the open world genre while Suzuki-san was making a grand folly."

Grand Theft Auto III perfectly captured the giddying excitement of what would come to be known as 'sandbox' gaming, allowing us to make our own fun by stealing cop cars and getting in epic chases, scrapping with pedestrians, diligently lining up stolen cars and then blowing one up with a rocket launcher to create an explosive domino effect that would cascade down the street, or whatever else popped into your imagination. There was a liberating sense of possibility in this huge city (well, for the time) and a formative experience to an audience which was not accustomed to being given that much freedom in a game space that big.

This freedom not only made *GTA III* a hell of a lot of fun to play, it became the basis for the media hysteria which only helped raise its profile. The idea that players could do whatever they wanted, including embarking on murderous rampages, had the media, pundits and politicians frothing at the mouth about the way the game might indulge and foster the worst impulses in the young minds playing it. There was certainly room for legitimate debate. Particular focus was placed on the fact that the game allowed you to hire sex workers and then murder them to get some of your money back, which mirrored

2007 OCTOBER
Valve's acclaimed *Portal* is released. It's a unique first-person puzzler where you're at the mercy of the villainous AI, GLaDOS.

2007 NOVEMBER
Harmonix and MTV Games release *Rock Band*, a rhythm action classic that lets you play songs with your friends.

2007 NOVEMBER
Ubisoft Montreal creates *Assassin's Creed*, kicking off one of the most successful franchises in videogaming.

2007 DECEMBER
The *Wii Fit* craze starts off in Japan. Gamers go mad for the new Balance Board and the focus on yoga strength training.

2008 FEBRUARY
Space Invaders Extreme reinvents the franchise on PSP and Nintendo DS, adding fast-paced gameplay and electronic music.

real-world violence against these vulnerable people in a way that is uncomfortable. However, the media's characteristic immaturity when dealing with the topic of videogame violence and the self-serving performative morality of the conservative observers attacking the game helped ensure that there was little room for considered reflection.

Rockstar quickly built on the success of *GTA III* with *Grand Theft Auto: Vice City* in 2002 and *Grand Theft Auto: San Andreas* in 2004, each adding new features to the series, though very much based on the building blocks established by *GTA III*. The series was an incredible critical and commercial success, signalling a major shift in the landscape of videogames. Where the kind of player freedom and agency the series thrived on had once been a preserve of relatively niche genres and titles – the likes of *Deus Ex* and *Baldur's Gate*, to give a couple of examples – *GTA* established it as a core element of the big budget blockbuster. Additionally, once players had experienced a game that took place in a believable world, as opposed to a linear, directed level, the old way of doing things quickly seemed old fashioned. The mainstream audience had a taste of something new and never looked back.

"The influence of the open world approach is felt everywhere now," Chris reflects. "Any game that is targeting the core market for games wants to tap into the appeal of agency, and the flexible play of the big sandboxes."

» [PC] *GTAV* shows the huge leap forward the series has taken, but it's still a recognisable evolution from *GTA III*.

"Right from the start the genre was founded on the synthesis of elements and features from other genres with Grand Theft Auto combining driving and shooting"
Michael de Plater

» [PC] *Silk* (left) mimics games like *The Lords Of Midnight*. The *Red Dead* series (below) highlights how Rockstar's *Grand Theft Auto* formula can successfully be lifted and applied to a new setting with a few tweaks.

GTA defined the contours of what a modern 3D open world game looks like, establishing conventions that are still adhered to. Think of the minimap, the idea of picking up different missions from characters across the game world, the mix of a structured missions and free-roam gameplay, even the way these games tell their stories.

"It's worth noting *Grand Theft Auto* handled the nonlinear aspects of its story by gating the player in a particular area until the player indicated they wanted to move on to other sections of the map/game," says *Outer Wilds* writer Kelsey Beachum on the approach *GTA* took to the challenge of open world storytelling. "This isn't 'bad', per se; it's just a way of telling a linear main story that allows other less linear subplots and arcs to unfold without conflicting with major story elements. Many open world games rely on some degree of gating in order to simplify the challenges of storytelling, player agency and gameplay progression inherent to open world settings."

The vital role that the *GTA* series played in establishing what a modern open world game looks like in the years following the millennium was immediately evident in the spate of similar titles that followed, initially dubbed '*GTA* clones' in a move that mirrored the impact *Doom* made on the FPS with the emergence of the term '*Doom* clones'. 2002's *The Getaway* was an attempt to bring the *GTA* formula to gangland London, the first *Saints Row* game a clear move to cash in on the *GTA* craze and 2005's *Yakuza* showed a willingness to incorporate the legacy of its native *Shenmue* with influences pulled from the more financially successful *GTA* series.

None of this is to suggest that open world games did not also take their own paths or find ways to evolve the genre. "I think open world games are an umbrella which can support almost any type of genre or experience from just about any other game," Michael argues. "Right from the start, the genre was founded on the synthesis of elements and features from other genres with *Grand Theft Auto* combining driving and shooting."

Indeed, the fact that open world games were not a flash in the pan and that so many other titles have been able to take the template laid down by the open world games that emerged around the year 2000 and find their own twist is a testament to the genre's flexibility. Think of how *Forza Horizon* has used it with racing, or how, in 2007, the first *Assassin's Creed* took the open world concept to a historical setting and added parkour, making the navigation of the world's architecture a key feature. "With *Middle-earth: Shadow Of Mordor* and later with *Shadow Of War*, we brought in systemic design influences and player-driven story features from sports games and strategy games," says Michael on Monolith's own innovations. *The Outer Wilds* provides yet more evidence that the genre is far from stagnant. "The idea of exploring a world that changes over time was one of the main motivations behind the game's creation," says *Outer Wilds* creative director Alex Beachum. "Not only did we want players to explore time in addition to space, we wanted to create a world that felt like it would go on existing with or without the player (as opposed to many game worlds that feel static or player-centric). Through exploration players can come to understand the systems governing the world, but they can never truly control it."

Acknowledging the ways in which game designers have taken fresh approaches to an established genre does not undermine the debt games still owe to that vital period around the year 2000. Open world games still dominate our sales charts: *Red Dead Redemption II*, *Ghost Of Tsushima*, *Assassin's Creed* and *The Witcher 3* are all blockbusters. And with upcoming games like *Horizon Forbidden West*, that trend is likely to continue. These games clearly don't deserve to be called '*GTA* clones'. Nevertheless, from the icon-speckled maps, to the sandbox gameplay and the vast worlds, they are still recognisable as games that emerged from the template established by *GTA III* and its contemporaries. *

2008 JUNE
Metal Gear Solid 4: Guns Of The Patriots launches on Sony's PlayStation 3. It will go on to sell over 6 million copies.

2008 JULY
After an extended break, Capcom releases *Street Fighter IV*. It arrives in arcades and becomes a gigantic success.

2008 AUGUST
Afrika marks a break from the usual PS3 games by offering a safari sim and the ability to photograph animal subjects.

2008 OCTOBER
An enhanced version of Ultimate Team is packaged with *FIFA 09*. EA orders a Scrooge McDuck-sized money vault.

2008 OCTOBER
Bethesda releases *Fallout 3*. The apocalyptic RPG scores critical acclaim will go on to win numerous awards.

Wii Sports

"TARA, PLEASE DON'T BREAK THE TV"

RETROREVIVAL

» WII » 2006 » NINTENDO

I'm so glad that I was at university when the Wii came out. It was really the perfect environment for the system – we had plenty of guests for the multiplayer games, our living room was spacious enough to make motion controls enjoyable, and honestly, swinging stuff around is even more fun when you're a little bit tipsy. I know what you're thinking – 'What got broken?' Given all the stories of Wii remotes being thrown through TVs, it was amazing that nothing did, though I do shudder whenever I remember a good friend narrowly missing the TV during a heated game of bowling on *Wii Sports*. The clatter when my controller hit the wall… ouch.

That friend wasn't exactly a big gamer, but then very few of the people I played *Wii Sports* with were. That was the beauty of the game, and more broadly the Wii's motion controls – anyone could understand it, from your eight-year-old nephew to your 80-year-old nan. All you needed to do was hold the nonthreatening remote control and *do the thing*. *Wii Sports* was the perfect game to demonstrate that. Boxing? Make punching motions. Playing tennis? Swing that thing like a tennis racquet. When you got it out for that first time on Christmas day, everyone wanted a go.

The Noughties, as we like to call them in this magazine, was the decade where breakthroughs in game control meant that everybody became a gamer. Casual audiences loved the *EyeToy*, but they weren't picking up PS2 consoles to get them. Today's casual gaming market is largely cordoned off from the 'serious' games machines, confined to the smartphones that gained popularity later in the decade – and, arguably, picked up the audience that used to poke at *Dr Kawashima's Brain Training* on the DS. But the Wii was the bridge between the two worlds – motion control technology offered exciting possibilities for hardcore gamers and experiences compelling enough to convince casual players to buy dedicated gaming hardware. It didn't matter how interested you were in games beforehand – *everyone* played *Wii Sports*, making it a true cultural phenomenon.

2008 NOVEMBER *Mirror's Edge* offers a fresh take on the first-person shooter genre by choosing free-running over accurate shooting.

2009 Markus Persson forms Mojang AB in Stockholm, Sweden. He soon starts working on an ambitious project that becomes known as *Minecraft*.

2009 MARCH *GTA: Chinatown Wars* hits DS. It makes great use of the touchscreen and offers a cool drug empire minigame.

2009 MAY PopCap Games releases *Plants Vs Zombies*, a cute spin on the tower defence genre which ends up becoming a huge hit.

2009 MAY Remember that *Minecraft* project we spoke about? Well, it's surfaced on the TIGSource forums. Exciting!

2009
JULY
Battlefield 1943 fires up Xbox Live and PSN thanks to its excellent graphics, well-designed maps and chaotic action.

2009
AUGUST
The first Gamescom starts in Cologne, Germany. It's visited by 245,000 people and sees Sony reveal the PlayStation 3 Slim.

2009
SEPTEMBER
Dead Space: Extraction reinvents lightgun shooters thanks to a solid story, excellent voice acting and great plot twists.

2009
OCTOBER
Naughty Dog releases *Uncharted 2: Among Thieves*. It's a big hit for the PS3 and solidifies Nathan Drake as a hero.

2009
DECEMBER
Angry Birds is released by Rovio and it becomes a huge hit. Sequels, movies and theme parks soon follow.

INSIDE THE XB

MICROSOFT MAESTROS

The developers who dared to think outside the box

SEAMUS BLACKLEY
Xbox CTO

ED FRIES
VP of games publishing, Microsoft Game Studios

OX

MICROSOFT IS ONE OF THE TITANS OF TODAY'S GAMING WORLD, BUT IT WASN'T ALWAYS THIS WAY. WE SPEAK TO THE MEN BEHIND THE MACHINE AND ITS GAMES TO FIND OUT HOW THE WINDOWS COMPANY INVADED THE LIVING ROOM...

Words By Nick Thorpe

"The idea of Microsoft making a games console in 1999 was fucking ludicrous!" Seamus Blackley's recollection isn't wrong, but such a notion seems like ancient history today. Microsoft is now established in the console gaming industry, with a tenure that is soon to match the likes of Sega and Atari's hardware ventures, so it's easy to forget a time when journalists openly questioned how such a "terminally uncool" company could make a successful incursion into an entertainment business. But the Xbox did succeed thanks to a band of committed gamers, a forward-thinking approach to development and a boatload of cash – and there's never been a better time to get into the console than today, thanks to its cheap games.

The Xbox story begins with Seamus Blackley, who in the late Nineties was at Microsoft and in charge of entertainment graphics on Windows – essentially, getting multimedia and gaming applications working nicely. "Sony announces the PlayStation 2, and they say it's going to replace the PC," recalls the industry veteran. "I had the roadmaps of all the graphics card manufacturers – 3DFX, Nvidia, ATI. I was visiting my girlfriend who was at that point living in Boston, flying there, and I realised that the roadmap for graphics from the guys making cards for the PC was going to far exceed the performance of what PlayStation

XBOX

▶ was going to do." The only problem for Seamus was the PC platform itself. "I'd been making PC games at that point for many years. You have to pander to the lowest common denominator, so you can never make a game that actually uses the full performance of any of these things, whereas on console you can because obviously you've got a single hardware target."

The appeal of a single platform was somewhat rooted in Seamus' recent development history. "I had nothing to lose but I was also passionate, because I had this titanic and horrible failure with the game *Trespasser*," notes Seamus. The *Jurassic Park* tie-in was ambitious – its environments, physics engine and rendering techniques were far beyond what most games had to offer in 1998, but it was shoved out of the door early and required a monstrously powerful PC to run acceptably. Together with fellow DirectX engineers Kevin Bachus, Ted Hase and Otto Berkes, Seamus drew

» [Xbox] Instead of porting PC properties, existing Microsoft developers like FASA Studio worked on new games, like *Crimson Skies*.

"When it was looking bad, people called it 'Coffin Box' - Your career's in the coffin if you work on that!"
Seamus Blackley

up a plan for a "DirectX Box" console. "Our entire goal was to make a box for developers, because we were all developers," Seamus explains.

Rather than using the custom components of its competitors, the team chose to employ largely off-the-shelf PC parts in the hardware design. "At that time, everybody made games on the PC. All the PlayStation games – even Nintendo, the PC was the development platform. They would have a target, and then they would compile it for this other platform, because the PC had all the tools," explains Seamus, explaining the philosophy behind this choice. "So the basic, simple thought is why don't we just have the target platform also employ that architecture? Then it's super trivial and nothing gets in your way. If we can do that, then we should have a huge advantage in making better content, and in a content business that's the win."

To get that content, the DirectX team would have to work with Microsoft's established gaming division. "I'm someone who loves games, and I had left the Office side of the company to run Microsoft's game business because of that," remembers Ed Fries, former vice president of game publishing at Microsoft. "I had worked for about four years to grow Microsoft's game business on the PC and we had done well there, so we were just starting to think about how we could grow more and faster. That involved thinking about getting into the console world, where we hadn't really done anything yet. So that was what was in my head when the guys from the DirectX team first walked into my office and proposed the original Xbox." Ed would soon find himself as part of that team, managing Microsoft's internal Xbox software development efforts, and after launch he became responsible for third-party relations, too.

Selling the Xbox vision was easier said than done, in part because the Xbox as a consumer entertainment device didn't fit the company culture of selling business software. "One of the huge problems we had was that we were at the Windows company," Seamus explains. "We said, 'Hey, we want to make this games console,' and every Microsoft guy who had been steeped in operating systems said, 'Oh yes, Windows for the living room – it'll run Windows and we can upgrade it,' and we would freak out and say, 'No, it's fixed, that's not how this business works.' We had to explain to them that the console business was a business in which you sold content, and made money from the content, not from the operating system." Seamus and the Xbox team would have to fight an uphill battle against corporate caution, and soon learned that the best way to fight it was to make out that there was no battle at all. "There were a lot of people who said it should be Windows for the living room, and we surfed on that – we let people believe that because it helped us. Members of our tiny little rogue tribe, we understood that the end result was going to have to be no operating system."

While an internal political battle is no surprise, what comes as a shock is that despite being aware of the company's power and resources, the games industry was also sceptical of Microsoft's chances

» Seamus Blackley credits Bill Gates, seen here unveiling the Xbox, as being a key internal supporter of the console.

» [Xbox] *Halo 2* generated an enormous $125 million in sales on launch day.

in the console market. "For the first six months, Xbox was me and Kevin going around and giving a presentation for developers," recalls Seamus. "We had a meeting with the president of one of the big Japanese game companies. He proceeded to tell me that Xbox was going to fail, that no American console could succeed, and that I was going to be unable to get Microsoft to do it, and that nobody was going to believe that Microsoft would carry through." That wasn't the only hostile response Seamus endured, as another incident at a large publisher's Canadian studio illustrates. "The guys who ran that office took me aside and told me I couldn't speak there because they didn't believe Microsoft would do a console, and that I could pull it off. The whole audience was waiting for 40 minutes while they grilled me."

Right up until the green light was given, other people wanted to have their say, and the Xbox team found itself fending off attempts to turn the project into Web TV, a tablet and other such things that were closer to Microsoft's comfort zone – as well as attempts to kill it stone dead. "When it was looking bad, people called it 'Coffin Box'," remembers Seamus. "Your career's in the coffin if you work on that! People would say this to me and I'd say 'No, it's going to succeed' and then I'd drive home crying."

What ultimately kept the project from failing was the support of the company's old guard, from the early Windows days. "A few people who were around from that era, and remembered what it was like, were reminded of it by what we were

» [Xbox] Rare utilised the power of Xbox to make Conker look fluffier than ever before.

Q&A: PHILIP OLIVER & ANDREW OLIVER

The men in charge of Blitz Games look back at the creation of the first published Xbox game

» [Xbox] Designed as the Xbox's answer to party games like *Mario Party*, *Fuzion Frenzy* sold enough to warrant a sequel.

How did you get the job of producing *Fuzion Frenzy* for Microsoft?

Philip: When Microsoft decided to enter the console market they sensibly decided to contact many major developers around the world. Blitz Games was growing fast and gaining a great reputation for mass market, fun character-based games. They wanted to launch with a variety of first-party games that appealed to different player types and one of the slots they were trying to fill was a party game. This fitted our profile well and we were invited to pitch.

What were the advantages and disadvantages of the Xbox hardware compared to the competition?

Andrew: It really was a standardised PC in box. This meant it was extremely familiar and easy to develop for, especially for any developers that came from PC development. In fact, Microsoft told developers to just get on and write the games, ASAP, with high-spec PCs and console-style controllers.

How long did development of *Fuzion Frenzy* take?

Philip: We learnt Microsoft was planning a console in summer 2000 and pitched *Blitz Party* in the Autumn. November and December saw us getting the team together and getting the project underway. To win the contract, not only did it need to be a great compelling game, we had to agree to have the game mastered by the end of August 2001. Microsoft assured us things would move fast from their side and so we immediately put developers on making minigames, as we only had ten months of development time.

How did you come up with the minigames found in *Fuzion Frenzy*?

Andrew: We had a team of about 35 people on the game and split them into three subteams. Within these subteams, we paired artists with programmers and each had to create a prototype game a week for the first two months. Then, working with our Microsoft Producer, Gordon Hee, we picked the ones that were working best and dropped those that looked problematic or just weren't fun. The next phase was to work up the chosen prototypes to more polished games, with depth, AI and fitting the chosen art style. It was massive parallel development and it worked really well and resulted in 45 minigames and the metagame. *Fuzion Frenzy* was completed on schedule and was the first mastered game for Xbox, in fact it appeared on shop shelves a week ahead of the Xbox itself!

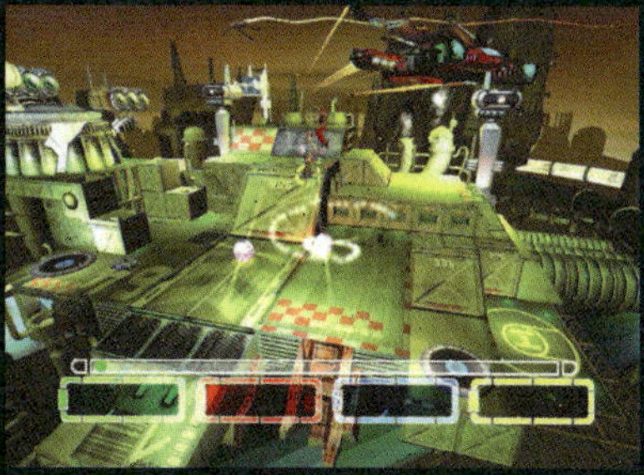

» [Xbox] *Fuzion Frenzy* will is backwards compatible on the Xbox One and Xbox Series X/S.

What audience was the setting and cast of *Fuzion Frenzy* designed to appeal to?

Philip: We wanted to ensure there was a consistent style running through all the games, even though they were all very different in gameplay. So, whilst designers and programmers were prototyping fun minigames, the art team were working on characters and art styles that would bind everything together coherently. They took inspiration from the skaters and boarders scene and then we decided to give it a strong futuristic sport arena look, taking inspiration from films like *Blade Runner* and *The Running Man*. We worked with JD Alley, the Microsoft art consultant to finalise the style.

How did you feel about *Fuzion Frenzy*'s sales and critical reception?

Andrew: I think the reception and sales, around half a million copies for the opening selling quarter, were all pretty reasonable and justified. Obviously, we'd hoped for more, but the small install base, and cost of additional controllers limited its potential. The development team continued development with *Fuzion Frenzy 2* with online play, as we knew that in the new year Microsoft would be launching the Live service and *Fuzion Frenzy* would make an obvious launch title for the service. Sadly, slow sales on the original boxed version meant they halted development of this version.

Later, sales continued to rise and over a million copies were sold. We were in constant contact with our producer and we convinced them it was worth making a sequel. However, due to internal politics at Microsoft, whilst they agreed to a sequel, they put the game out to tender and we had to bid competitively to win the rights to develop it. Hudson Soft was chosen as the developer of the sequel and they used a lot of our concepts.

We are extremely proud of *Fuzion Frenzy* and the team that built it. Those ten months were a pretty intensive time for all involved, but it was fun to develop and we so pleased that so many people found it fun to play and still fondly remember it.

BARGAIN HUNT

IF YOU WANT TO GET YOUR XBOX COLLECTION OFF TO A FLYING START, CHECK THESE OUT…

AMPED.................... £2.00
■ This is an enjoyable snowboarding game, featuring free-roaming action that wouldn't become commonplace until later in the decade.

CHRONICLES OF RIDDICK: ESCAPE FROM BUTCHER BAY...... £2.00
■ This first-person adventure is a fantastic prison break tale, which allows you to both attack from the shadows and enjoy brutal brawls.

DEAD OR ALIVE 3....... £3.00
■ This fast-paced fighting game boasts phenomenal graphics and multitiered arenas to smash your opponents through.

FABLE: THE LOST CHAPTERS................. £3.00
■ This Classics version of the ambitious Lionhead RPG has even more content than the original, with extra areas, quests and more.

HALO: COMBAT EVOLVED.. £2.50
■ The FPS which almost single-handedly propelled the Xbox to success is an essential purchase for this crazy price.

HALO 2.................. £2.00
■ It's the bestselling Xbox game ever! For this price, you might as well buy four copies and get a good old fashioned LAN party going.

NINJA GAIDEN........... £1.00
■ It's tough, but this 3D revival of Tecmo's classic franchise is a fast, stylish and very violent hack-and-slash adventure. Heads *will* roll.

PROJECT GOTHAM RACING 2................ £2.00
■ Bizarre Creations' sequel occupies the middle ground between arcade excitement and hardcore simulation.

TOM CLANCY'S SPLINTER CELL £1.50
■ This stealth classic is at its best on Microsoft's console, thanks to longer levels and a tougher challenge all-round.

TOP SPIN TENNIS........ £1.50
■ This doesn't let you give Tim Henman the Wimbledon victory he craved, but that's about all this excellent tennis game doesn't do.

TOTAL......... £20.50

» [Xbox] *Knights Of The Old Republic* was a big exclusive draw for *Star Wars* fans and RPG die-hards alike.

doing with Xbox and helped us out," Seamus recalls. "Chief amongst them was Bill Gates, but also Rick Rashid who ran Microsoft Research and Rick Thompson who ran the hardware group, and many, many others who loved the spirit of the thing, and backed us up politically in ways that I didn't even understand that we needed."

After getting the green light, Ed had less than two years to put together a launch line-up. As well as commissioning games from respected external studios, Microsoft employed what Ed calls an "all hands on deck" approach to game development internally. The teams that had been responsible for the company's successes in PC gaming were involved, but for various reasons didn't bring the old properties across. "It didn't really make sense to take *Flight Simulator* over, but it was certainly considered at times," Ed recalls. "The guys at Ensemble Studios looked at *Age Of Empires* and had multiple Xbox prototypes that they were developing, but none of those ended up turning into something real. The FASA group had a lot of contributions, *Crimson Skies* is a well-loved original Xbox game, and that came out of a PC game that the group had developed a few years earlier." While not a conscious choice, this ultimately gave the Xbox an identity distinct from Microsoft's PC gaming heritage.

For all of the gaming expertise that already existed within Microsoft, the team that would ultimately make the biggest impact was a new acquisition, Bungie. The team had a good reputation from the *Marathon* and *Myth* games,

» [Xbox] *Ninja Gaiden* put the Xbox to great use, displaying a number of impressive graphical effects.

> “As far as Bungie goes, I definitely bet everything on Halo… All was going to get was the team and Halo”
>
> Ed Fries

but had hit financial trouble and was up for sale. “As far as Bungie goes, I definitely bet everything on *Halo*,” says Ed. “I had to do a deal with [minority Bungie owners] Take-Two, and basically the way we put the deal together was they got the back catalogue, all the old work and brands from the past, and all I was going to get was the team and *Halo*.” The promising first-person shooter had already been revealed for PC and Mac, but Microsoft decided it'd be a great Xbox exclusive.

“**Did I know then that *Halo* would be the killer app?** In a lot of ways, we didn't really know what we were doing,” confesses Ed. “We had never done a game in the console world before. We were getting a lot of mixed feedback – a lot of people looked at *Halo* and thought it looked like a PC game, they thought it wasn't colourful enough, the characters weren't cartoony enough. There was a nagging feeling that because we had come from a PC heritage, that this was the game that appealed to us, but it wouldn't to the regular console audience.” Knowing that the office favourite might not be universally appealing, the team made sure to back a safer bet too. “At the same time we were working with Lorne Lanning, who is a super talented guy with his *Oddworld* franchise which had been proven successful on the PlayStation,” Ed explains. “That was another game we were excited about, so we launched both games with a pretty similar amount of marketing support.”

What helped every team was that the system was easy to work with. This was the biggest goal for the system, and by all accounts the team delivered on this front. Chris Sutherland was at Rare as the company transitioned from GameCube to Xbox, and remembers the move being relatively painless. “As you'd expect with Microsoft, there was plenty of documentation so it wasn't too tough to move over,” the programmer recalls. Former Bizarre Creations developer Stephen Cakebread was also impressed with the developer support, particularly when it came to tools. “They were a significant step up from the tools on other platforms, and eventually they even surpassed what was available on the PC,” he explains. “Even though the Xbox had better raw performance numbers over the competition, I think the improved environment for devs is what made the most difference.” It was a big win for the team, and one which Seamus considers to be a signature achievement for the platform. “Sony and Nintendo got away with treating their developers terribly,” he says of the pre-Xbox years. “The thing that I'm most proud of, that I think everybody can be most proud of, was that Sony suddenly had to do developer support.”

It also didn't hurt that as a piece of hardware, the Xbox was a beast. The system packed a 733MHz Intel Pentium III CPU, a custom Nvidia GeForce 3-based GPU, 64MB shared RAM and a DVD drive. The machine also included an 8GB hard disk – a first in console gaming. This was a big advantage, as former Bizarre Creations programmer Stephen Cakebread explains: “The HDD was faster than a DVD, so if you copied files from the DVD to the HDD you could load them much faster next time around, with the additional bonus that you could load from both the HDD and DVD at the same time! (eg, loading levels from one and streaming music from the other).” Overall, the Xbox had the specification of a decent PC of the time (which still would have cost twice as much as an Xbox on launch), but as the Xbox wasn't burdened with the task of running Windows and its developers didn't have to worry about supporting lesser systems, its gaming performance was astonishing.

When the press finally got their hands on the Xbox, reception was broadly positive though there were some reservations about the console's look, as well as the enormous joypad nicknamed the ‘Duke’ by players. “You should ignore

» Richard Branson sells the UK's first Xbox at the Virgin Megastore on Oxford Street.

Q&A: MARTYN CHUDLEY

The man who was in charge of the Project Gotham Racing series remembers the start of the series

» [Xbox] *Project Gotham Racing* was warmly received on its debut, netting 8/10 scores from *Edge*, *Game Informer* and *Eurogamer*.

What did the Xbox offer over the competition in terms of performance? What was it like to code on?

The Xbox was a dream to develop for. The PS2 was crazy powerful for the time, but you had to work so hard to get access to that power – with the Xbox, it was all abstracted, allowing our coders to get far more of the raw power with much less effort. We also had a stable development environment through Microsoft's pre-existing Windows development tools. We (Bizarre) also had direct access to the Microsoft guys and gals who were 100% responsible for the hardware and software, so this support was amazing.

How did your exclusivity deal on *Project Gotham Racing* come about?

The deal for *PGR* came about as a result of Sarah (my other half) and Brian (Woodhouse – our development director) doing a pitch to Microsoft for an 'F1-style game in cities', as way of a follow-up to *Metropolis Street Racer*. We 'knew' at that point that Dreamcast was effectively dead and that Sega would be going to become a multiplatform publisher, but they refused to acknowledge this to us. Ideally, we would have taken *MSR* to both PS2 and Xbox with Sega, but they just couldn't admit their situation to us in time for us to recoup some of our losses. Upon doing the 'F1-ish' pitch, the chaps at Microsoft saw a near-complete demo version of *MSR* and simply said, 'Why not give us *that*?'

Upon examining our contract with Sega, it transpired that we (Bizarre) owned all the code and data, whereas Sega just owned the IP – essentially just the name *Metropolis Street Racer*. This meant that we could do a 'homage' game, using all of the cities and any new cars that Microsoft would license, just as long as we didn't call it *Metropolis Street Racer*!

Was there much stress getting the game ready for launch?

Oh yeah – it was mega stressful for the entire production. We basically had well under 12 months from start to finish. Our original plans for development started at the tail end of 2000, targeting console release of November 2001. This was a stupidly tight schedule given that we were doing a complete code rewrite, remodel of all the cars, had to hire new staff, working with a brand-new set of production people and to cap it all had multiple revisions of (usually underpowered) preproduction hardware and libraries to aim at.

» [Xbox] We hope that one day *PGR* will be announced as a supported title on Xbox's backward compatibility list.

How did you end up choosing the four city locations you went with?

The original locations (San Francisco, London and Tokyo) were chosen in conjunction with Sega as they were absolutely iconic, fit the key console territories and were all visually (and layout-wise) unique. New York was, again, chosen for its worldwide recognisability and also it was relatively easy for us to perform the research trips. In fact, the cover art of the game was to feature the Ferrari F50 in front of the Twin Towers, but due to the catastrophic events of 9/11 we had long discussions with Microsoft about whether to keep (as a tribute) or remove the towers from the game (which we eventually did).

What improvements did *Project Gotham Racing* make over *MSR*?

As far as I can remember, the biggest improvements over *MSR* included the addition of New York, and higher 'perceived value' cars – Ferrari, TVR etc. Ultimately, the game was a complete rewrite from the Dreamcast code – everything, not just the engine. Physics, gameplay, UI, you name it. From a technical perspective Xbox gave us an order of magnitude more polygons (in the cars at least, the cities were just upscaled where it made most sense given our time pressures), shader effects (mainly reflections in both car rendering and circuit, and improved weather) and a doubling of the framerate to 60fps. I think we also made a conscious effort to make the game more 'mainstream' than what we perceived as a pretty hardcore *MSR* experience.

Why do you think Microsoft have never created a fifth game?

I'm guessing that basically Microsoft felt they could cover all bases with both the *Forza* and *Forza Horizon* brands – they didn't need a *PGR* hanging around in between, not quite a simulator, not quite an arcade experience. I think that if we had stayed with Microsoft (and not been acquired by Activision) then a *PGR5* could have happened, but alas it was not to be…

Finally, on a personal note I'd like to add that *PGR* couldn't have happened without our coder Edmund Clay, who sadly passed away in 2013. Edmund joined us to work on *PGR*, and I don't think there was an area of the game that he didn't touch – physics, rendering, AI, shaders - you name it, he was a massive influence.

> **"I think the improved environment for developers is what made the most difference"**
> Seamus Blackley

▶ the naysayers and doom merchants who have ignorantly dismissed Xbox out-of-hand," opined *Edge* after taking delivery of the finished product. "It's expensive, corpulent and the joypads aren't entirely ergonomic – but by the gods is it powerful." What's more, the software accompanying the machine delivered. In particular, *Halo* was hailed as "the most important launch game for any console, ever" by *Edge* and received the magazine's fourth 10/10 score. Other reviewers were similarly impressed, as evidenced by its score of 97 on review aggregator Metacritic.

The first territory to receive the system was North America, on 15 November 2001. Propelled by the popularity of Bungie's *Halo* and demand generated as a natural result of the holiday season, the Xbox sold an impressive 1.5 million units in the region before the end of the year. It was an encouraging start for a system that had faced so much scepticism, and North America would remain the console's stronghold for the duration of its lifetime – for every Xbox sold in the rest of the world, Microsoft sold two on its home continent.

However, things weren't nearly so rosy in Japan. Microsoft brought 250,000 consoles into the country for launch, and attracted some very high-profile Japanese developers. Tecmo jumped in with both feet and provided some great exclusive

» People still love this alluring Xbox prototype – possibly because the production machine is no looker.

» [Xbox] Great Japanese games like *Panzer Dragoon Orta* failed to sell the Xbox to the Japanese public.

games, and Sega did the same while also building its Chihiro arcade platform around the console. However, others were more cautious. The likes of Capcom, Namco and Konami all jumped aboard, but didn't necessarily bring their big hitters with them – *Resident Evil* and *Tekken* didn't appear at all, for example. Companies like Square, Enix and Atlus stayed away completely. The Xbox never shed the perception that it was a product built by a foreign company for foreign audiences, and never gained a foothold in Japan as a result, selling a miserable 450,000 consoles over its entire lifetime.

Trading also proved difficult in Europe. The Xbox launched to great fanfare on 11 March 2002, but sales quickly dropped off and after just five weeks Microsoft announced that it would slash the price of the console by a third, cutting it from £299 to match the PlayStation 2's £199 price tag. The move understandably upset early adopters, who were offered two free games and an extra controller to make up for the unprecedented price drop, but it did serve to stabilise the system – during the week of the cut, Xbox sales were neck and neck with PS2 sales. The move also sparked a price war. Nintendo cut its GameCube price before even launching, and two subsequent price cuts brought the Xbox down to just £129 by April 2003. Cutting the price of the console by over 50 per cent in a little over a year did eventually convince European consumers to pick up the machine, but also ensured that Microsoft took heavy losses on every piece of hardware sold.

» [Xbox] The ease of porting from PC to Xbox ensured that the machine received versions of high-profile games, like *Doom 3*.

Microsoft also took other measures to ensure the success of the Xbox. A major one was the purchase of Rare, long considered to be one of Nintendo's key studios – a shock to players at the time, but something that had been brewing behind the scenes for some time. "I was equally shocked when they approached me and there was an opportunity to work with them," Ed reveals, surprisingly. "They had an interesting deal with Nintendo. Nintendo owned 50% of Rare, and when they put that deal together, it was done well. They didn't want to sell half of their company and never be able to sell the other half. So they had a deal where [Nintendo] buys half, and then has the option to buy the other half within a number of years – and if you do not buy the other half, then [Rare] has the right to buy back your half at fair market value." The deal had already expired by 2000, but Nintendo paid for a two-year extension and then declined to buy the company when the opportunity came around again.

Microsoft's $375 million purchase of Rare was made public on 24 September 2002, the day after Rare's only GameCube game was released. "I'd known there was a decision to be made between Activision and Microsoft," recalls Chris, who didn't perceive any shift in focus after the deal. "Rare wanted to carry on making the kinds of games it had been making and that would have been the wish of Microsoft too!" Ironically, though, Rare actually produced more games for Nintendo's Game Boy Advance than it did the Xbox during

» [Xbox] The *XSN Sports* range of games was key in the early years of the Xbox, before EA built Xbox Live support into its own sports games.

this time – only *Grabbed By The Ghoulies* and *Conker: Live & Reloaded* appeared on Microsoft's console, though it wasn't the only project Rare was working on. "*Kameo* was being built on the original Xbox, but it was brought over with a visual overhaul to the Xbox 360 as a launch title," explains Chris.

In November 2002 Microsoft launched its online gaming service, Xbox Live. The high-end service relied on broadband internet connections and required an annual subscription, but was far in advance of the decentralised online experience on PS2 and the near-total lack of online games on GameCube. Players enjoyed relatively lag-free and stable sessions, had a single username across all games, as well as systems for adding friends, sending messages and even voice chat. In

XBOX

November 2004, the service was extended to include downloadable game distribution via the new Xbox Live Arcade service, which allowed players to buy small, download-exclusive games such as *Bejeweled* and *Ms Pac-Man* for relatively low prices. As it arrived late in the life of the Xbox, this was a relatively short-lived service that hosted less than 30 games in total.

"If I had really known how powerful Sony and Nintendo were, I would have probably given up and there wouldn't be an Xbox"
Seamus Blackley

While players looking for online console gaming were undoubtedly best served by Microsoft, it's worth remembering that those customers were still a relatively small market – Xbox Live picked up a million subscribers by July 2004 and doubled that to 2 million by July 2005, but take-up of the service was never beyond ten per cent of the total Xbox user base at any given time. "I think Xbox Live truly took off with the 360," says Stephen, who points to the technical limitations of the era. "Having a wired internet connection to whatever room you had your gaming system setup in was a big ask for a lot of people, while Wi-Fi is ubiquitous now."

» [Xbox] *Dead Or Alive 3* looked absolutely astonishing in 2001, and holds up well today.

By 2004, the Xbox had gone from office punchline to legitimate knockout artist. The enormously popular *Grand Theft Auto* games made their way to the platform, as did Konami's *Pro Evolution Soccer*. EA launched its first Xbox Live compatible sports games, and in November, *Halo 2* became the biggest entertainment launch of all time. But despite its successes, the Xbox was not a tremendously long-lived console. On 12 May 2005, just three-and a-half years after the Xbox had initially gone on sale, Microsoft unveiled the next-generation Xbox 360 for release later that year. On the same day, Nvidia announced that Microsoft had ceased orders for the Xbox GPU and wouldn't be taking any more after 1 August – effectively shutting down production of the original console for good. Xbox owners would still enjoy a full slate of games into 2006 thanks to third party publishers, but releases dropped off following that year's holiday season, with just a handful of licensed games and annual sports updates arriving in 2007. The last Xbox game to be released was *Madden NFL 09*, in August 2008, and original Xbox Live shut down on 10 May 2010 (some weeks after its original 15 April termination date, thanks to some dedicated *Halo 2* players).

For all of Microsoft's clout as a company, and its considerable financial expenditure, the Xbox could only manage second place in its generation. "If I had really known how powerful Sony and Nintendo were, I would have probably given up and there wouldn't be an Xbox," admits Seamus. 24 million Xbox consoles were sold, scraping ahead of Nintendo's GameCube by just over 2 million units but falling massively short of the 155 million PlayStation 2 consoles that Sony sold. However, Microsoft gained many positive things from the original Xbox. It successfully established itself as a major player in the console market, building consumer recognition and developer relationships that would pay dividends for the Xbox 360. What's more, the Xbox allowed Microsoft to influence the wider console market, as the console shaped the future development of games consoles on a technical level. Every major console released since the Xbox has included some form of mass storage, built-in broadband internet support and support for downloadable software.

If you missed out on the system first time around, now is a great time to catch up as the Xbox is one of the best value platforms in retro gaming right now. Few games are anywhere near their original price, and most are ridiculously cheap – even the best on the platform. Original hardware isn't too hard to come by, and if you're stuck for that the Xbox 360 will run certain games (be sure to check before you buy). Microsoft also supports original Xbox backwards compatibility on the Xbox One and Series X/S consoles.

Looking back at the impact of the Xbox, Chris feels it comes down to the skills transferred from Microsoft's other business. "This was really Microsoft's first sizeable foray into gaming

» [Xbox] Big new western gaming franchises, such as *Splinter Cell*, got their big break on Xbox.

» In 2000, Raven and her giant robot buddy danced together to introduce the Xbox to the world.

entertainment; yes, they'd had *Flight Simulator* before and had built joysticks, but creating their own console was in many ways an unexpected move for a company that was more associated with operating systems and business software," he explains. "Their experience with working with developers on those more conventional products would have helped them build a system that would also be easy to develop for by game studios." But that's far from the only factor, as Stephen reminds us. "*Halo* defined the Xbox," the coder states. "There were plenty of other good games, but *Halo* was why you bought one in that first year after launch."

However, the last word must go to Seamus, for whom all of the political battles and the frustrated car journeys home were worthwhile because of the players themselves. "There are all of these times in my life when, wandering around, I meet somebody who tells me that Xbox stopped them from killing themselves during their divorce, or was the only reason they could survive as a kid in some horrible situation, or got them interested in studying science and now they have a PhD in chemistry. Every time that happens I choke up because I see a person in front of me whose life is better, and there's really nothing like that. That's what it's about." And he's right – the Xbox made an impact on the gaming industry and on Microsoft, but the real legacy of the Xbox lies in every *Halo* LAN party, your moral choices in *Fable*, and all those times you stayed up a little *too* late on Xbox Live.

Special thanks to Seamus Blackley, Ed Fries and everyone else who contributed to this article.

» [Xbox] With games like *Project Gotham Racing 2*, the Xbox brought the dream of photorealism closer than ever before.

SPECS BOX

Take a look at how the guts of the Xbox compared to other machines of its era

DREAMCAST

RELEASED: 27 November 1998
CPU: 200MHz Hitachi SH-4
GPU: 100MHz VideoLogic PowerVR2
MEMORY: 16MB RAM, 8MB video RAM, 2MB audio RAM
MEDIA: 1.2GB GD-ROM
STORAGE: Up to two Visual Memory Units per connected controller (128KB each, optional)
NETWORKING: 56k dial-up modem (standard) / Broadband adapter with Ethernet port (optional)
CONTROLLER PORTS: 4

PLAYSTATION 2

RELEASED: 4 March 2000
CPU: 295MHz 'Emotion Engine'
GPU: 147.5MHz 'Graphics Synthesizer'
MEMORY: 32MB RAM, 4MB video RAM, 2MB audio RAM
MEDIA: 8.5GB DVD-ROM
STORAGE: Up to two memory cards (8MB each, optional), 40GB hard disk (optional)
NETWORKING: i.LINK port for local networking (standard on pre-2003 models), Network adapter with dial-up modem and Ethernet port (optional), Ethernet port (standard on slimline models)
CONTROLLER PORTS: 2

GAMECUBE

RELEASED: 14 September 2001
CPU: 485MHz IBM 'Gekko'
GPU: 162MHz ATI 'Flipper'
MEMORY: 24MB RAM, 3MB video RAM, 16MB audio/DVD cache
MEDIA: 1.5GB miniDVD-based 8cm disc
STORAGE: Up to two memory cards (512KB – 8MB each, optional)
NETWORKING: 56k dial-up modem (standard), Broadband adapter with Ethernet port (optional)
CONTROLLER PORTS: 4

XBOX

RELEASED: 15 November 2001
CPU: 733MHz custom Intel Pentium III
GPU: 233MHz Nvidia NV2A
MEMORY: 64MB shared RAM
MEDIA: 8.5GB DVD-ROM
STORAGE: 8GB hard disk (standard), Up to two memory units per connected controller (8MB each, optional)
NETWORKING: Ethernet port (standard)
CONTROLLER PORTS: 4

THE

2 0 1 0 s

two zero one zero s

THE DECADE WHERE SEEMINGLY EVERYONE BECAME A GAMER

Was this the decade where gaming truly went mainstream? It could well be. Mobile gaming continued to grow in popularity, and the traditional gaming market grew bigger than ever. Sony's PS4 soared past 100 million units, Microsoft began to pivot towards a new multitiered console approach and launched its Netflix-style subscription service, Game Pass, while Nintendo bounced back from its Wii U failure with the Switch. PC gamers were also laughing thanks to the introduction of Epic's new store, which led to fierce competition in the market. And let's not forget the rise of VR, which finally began realising the promises first made in the early Nineties.

GAMES OF THE DECADE

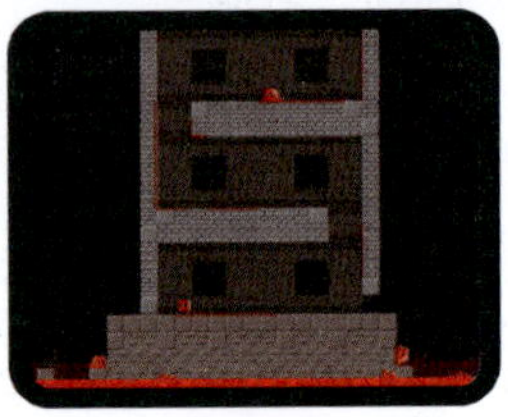

2010
SUPER MEAT BOY

There's been a noticeable trend for unashamedly hard games this decade, and Team Meat's indie 2D platformer is an early example of that. *Super Meat Boy* is the sequel to a popular flash game, and it caught the imagination of players thanks to its ultra-tough, but precise, fair and well-designed platforming gameplay.

2011
PORTAL 2

Valve's puzzling sequel improved on the original game, greatly enhancing the puzzle-solving of your portal gun and introducing the Stephen Merchant-voiced Wheatley. Friends can also team up for the excellent co-operative mode, one of the few games of the time that allowed PC and PS3 owners to play online together.

2012
THE WALKING DEAD

Before its downfall, *The Walking Dead* helped cement Telltale Games as one of the most important developers of the last decade. Replays will reveal you don't have as much agency on the episodic adventure as you're initially led to believe, but the strong character arcs and gripping story keep you hooked.

2013
THE LAST OF US

Naughty Dog's apocalyptic adventure remains a brilliantly brutal experience on PS3 and PS4. A moving story, satisfying combat mechanics, engaging characters and its gripping horror elements ensure it remains one of the greatest games of the decade. Hell, it could well be the greatest game ever made.

2014
HEARTHSTONE

Blizzard's decision to move into the digital card game market proved a sound one. Its freemium model is surprisingly flexible, it's easy to play on any device and the huge selection of available cards allows for countless strategies. Little wonder that card game rival Wizards Of The Coast has hit back with *MTG: Arena*.

2010
Niantic Labs is formed in San Francisco by John Hanke. It will eventually go on to make huge strides in augmented reality gaming.

2010 FEBRUARY
Developer The Coalition forms. It consists of Zipline Studios, Black Tusk Studios and Microsoft Game Studios Vancouver.

2010 APRIL
Respawn Entertainment is founded by *Call Of Duty* veterans Jason West and Vince Zampella in Beverley Hills.

2010 APRIL
After Midway Games closes, NetherRealm Studios is formed and overseen by *Mortal Kombat*'s Ed Boon.

2010 OCTOBER
Super Meat Boy is launched by Team Meat on Xbox Live Arcade and captures the glory days of 16-bit platformers.

THE TENS... AS TOLD BY DAVID DARLING

THE COFOUNDER OF CODEMASTERS NOW FOCUSES ON MOBILE DEVELOPMENT WITH KWALEE. HERE HE REVEALS WHY HE MADE THE MOVE

The previous decade saw a huge boost in technology improvements, greatly enhancing modern consoles and PCs. Other technological advancements have also benefitted the mobile sector that David shrewdly moved into in 2011 with his company Kwalee. "[There have been] amazing improvements to the speed of broadband and the increases to the speed of mobile cell signal data speeds," he tells us. "With 4G pretty commonplace nowadays it really makes downloading apps very quick and also enables multiplayer games on-the-go. And mobile phone screen sizes are so big and bright, great for gaming and watching videos."

It's no surprise, then, that David feels that mobile devices are the things that have defined the industry this past decade particularly when he tells us that 3.8 billion sales are projected by 2021. "They have developed so quickly, improving with each new version and before you know it, they have spread around the globe on a truly massive scale and enabled an international market for games so much bigger than anything that has come before. For game designers, this provides a huge audience." That huge audience has led to developers like Nintendo muscling in on the mobile industry and titles like *Fortnite* being easily accessible. "Casual gaming has exploded," David excitedly tells us. "People seem to like to multitask. They play games in the Starbucks queue, they play games during ad breaks whilst watching TV. They play games on the bus, train, at airports, etc. Casual gaming fits into this kind of lifestyle."

While home consoles like the PlayStation 4 and Switch are keeping the hardcore gamers happy, developers like David realise that they're just one source of potential income. As great as epics like *The Witcher 3* and VR experiences like *Resident Evil VII* are, there are plenty of people out there who simply aren't interested. They don't even consider themselves gamers, but they'll happily play titles like *Candy Crush* when they're at a loose end. These casual gamers have helped facilitate the creation of even simpler games, many of which have become gigantic hits. "Hyper-casual games have sprouted up to fill even smaller gaps in peoples lives, and they have become huge," confirms David. "Kwalee's games have been

downloaded hundreds of millions of times, and some of my favourites are *Jetpack Jump*, *Looper* and *Go Fish!*."

While triple-A games continue to be a huge driving force of the industry in 2021, big budget developers and publishers are only part of the reason why the previous decade was so successful for games. "Indie games are where huge innovation is happening," concludes David. "Lots of small studios making games quickly, using their creative talents. Big studios and big games have pressure to de-risk and produce sequel after sequel. This stifles innovation and creates an opportunity for indie games."

2015 THE WITCHER 3: WILD HUNT

CD Projekt's RPG powerhouse won numerous awards on release and it remains one of the most absorbing adventures you can play right now. Relatable characters, epic monsters and a strong narrative thread will keep you hooked on the Path'. And let's not forget the excellent in-game card game, Gwent.

2016 POKEMON GO

What's better than hunting for Pokémon in the Viridian Forest? Hunting for them in the world *you* inhabit. Niantic's GPS-enabled spin on the classic monster battle RPG allowed players to hunt for Pokémon on their phones, generating true social interaction as players ran into each other while seeking rare critters.

2017 FORTNITE: BATTLE ROYALE

PlayerUnknown's Battlegrounds popularised the 'battle royale' last-man-standing template, but Epic's decision to bolt it to a building system and a free-to-play business model unleashed a monster. Every playground in the country has seen kids imitating the dances of this online multiplayer phenomenon.

2018 SUPER SMASH BROS ULTIMATE

This party fighting series has long offered tight game design and massive amounts of content. But the latest entry truly transcended the series' roots as a Nintendo crossover project, and became a celebration of Japanese gaming history as a whole, with just about every major company you can think of represented.

2019 TETRIS 99

Applying the 'battle royale' concept to the world's most beloved puzzle game was a stroke of genius – it's a fantastic example of an old game being revitalised with modern concepts and technology. More than that, it's a great example of a free-to-play game that doesn't take advantage of its players.

2011 FEBRUARY Nintendo releases its 3DS console in Japan. It's an innovative device that doesn't require the use of 3D glasses.

2011 MARCH Julian Gollop's *Shadow Wars* launches alongside the UK 3DS launch. It's a superb strategy game for the handheld.

2011 APRIL Valve releases its superb cerebral sequel, *Portal 2*. It features the voice talents of Stephen Merchant and JK Simmons.

2011 AUGUST Imangi Studios' *Temple Run* reimagines the endless runner on iOS by utilising an into-the-screen perspective.

2011 OCTOBER *Skylanders* kicks off the toys-to-life craze. It launches as a *Spyro* game, but the cute dragon will soon take a step back.

"THE PS4 WAS THE MARKET LEADER THROUGHOUT THIS GENERATION AND HAD A ROSTER OF QUALITY FIRST-PARTY TITLES"

AGE OF THE GIMMICK

In some ways, the previous decade wasn't a surprise – anyone could have foreseen continued increases in hardware power, as well as the increased level of integration that online functions have been afforded. But what's striking is how manufacturers tried to maintain consumer interest. Every console has had a gimmick, from 3D displays to motion-detecting cameras. Few became integral parts of games on their home formats, and some were detrimental to commercial performance. But the success of the Nintendo Switch, which takes a simple idea and realises it well, proves there's still room for hardware innovation.

1 PLAYSTATION 4 — SONY • 2013

Sony's fourth mainline system is a triumph of evolution over revolution, a solid gaming-focused console that offers little in the way of innovation. The DualShock controller was given a full overhaul, with a new Share button allowing players to take screenshots and video clips of gameplay, as well as streaming straight from the console. The multimedia focus of the PlayStation 3 was discarded, but so too was its backwards compatibility. A mid-generation hardware refresh, the PS4 Pro, was aimed at improving 4K performance but was perhaps better suited to boosting 1080p games and those running on PlayStation VR. Despite a relatively barren first year, the PS4 was the market leader throughout this generation and had a roster of quality first-party titles. In 2019, it became the third Sony console to sell over 100 million units, tying Nintendo's record.

2 3DS — NINTENDO • 2011

The successor to the DS offers 3D visuals without any glasses – a bit of a gimmick in early models, and ultimately something that Nintendo felt comfortable dropping with its 2DS revision. However, the more powerful hardware is nice, as is the analogue 'Circle Pad' and cameras. After sluggish sales during its first few months, Nintendo slashed the price of the hardware dramatically in order to help establish an audience. The gamble paid off, and key 2011 releases *Mario Kart 7*, *Super Mario 3D Land* and *The Legend Of Zelda: Ocarina Of Time 3D* played their part too. Six different models were eventually released, including 'New' models with slightly more power and a handful of exclusive games, and combined they have sold 75.3 million units – a figure we don't see rising much further now the Switch has established itself on the scene.

3 PLAYSTATION VITA — SONY • 2011

Sony's successor to the PSP is a similar proposition to its first handheld, offering console-quality gaming on the go. The hardware's form factor was only slightly revised, however an array of new features were implemented – dual analogue sticks, a touchscreen, two cameras, a tilt sensor and games distributed on cartridge rather than disc. The high price of the system and its proprietary memory cards proved problematic, and sales were slow despite some great games. First-party game development soon stopped and the system quickly faded from the limelight outside of Japan, where it remained reasonably popular. Those that continue to treasure the system in the west largely exist on a diet of great indie games and distinctly Japanese titles. Estimates of sales are 15 to 16 million, and Sony appears to have no plans for a successor.

2011 NOVEMBER *The Elder Scrolls V: Skyrim* launches to huge critical acclaim. It will be bolstered by three pieces of excellent DLC.

2011 DECEMBER Sony launches the PS Vita in Japan. It's an incredibly powerful handheld with an amazing five-inch OLED screen.

2012 FEBRUARY The Chinese Room's *Dear Esther* is released on PC. It's an exploration game that helps popularise the 'walking simulator'.

2012 APRIL Telltale Games releases *The Walking Dead*'s first episode. It's praised for its excellent story and strong characters.

2012 MAY Blizzard launches dungeon-crawler, *Diablo III*. It's notable for selling 3.5 million copies in its first 24 hours.

4

"WHILE IT WON'T EVER CATCH THE PLAYSTATION 4, MICROSOFT HAS PERFORMED AN ADMIRABLE RESCUE JOB"

OTHER SYSTEMS FROM THE TENS

OnLive Onlive, 2010

An early attempt at a subscription-based 'cloud console' using remote servers. It was scuppered by issues with input lag and video quality.

Ouya Ouya Inc, 2013

This crowdfunded Android console aimed to provide a cheap, open console platform, but failed to retain consumer interest post-launch.

Amazon Fire TV Stick Amazon, 2014

This plug-and-play Android device supports controllers and gets the odd dedicated app, including a nice *Sega Classics* one.

Nvidia Shield Nvidia, 2015

This capable Android-based set top box has received some high-profile console ports, but has never attracted format-exclusive games.

Steam Machines Various, 2015

These devices, supported by Valve, were offered by various manufacturers and attempted to offer PC gaming in console form factor.

5

6

4 XBOX ONE MICROSOFT • 2013

Microsoft's strategy for this generation was to turn its console into an 'all-in-one' entertainment unit, hence the name – indeed, the system seemed to be about everything *but* games. This could have been forgiven, but Microsoft's policy of circumventing the sale of used games was a step too far. The loss of goodwill was permanent, despite Microsoft's prelaunch U-turn. This was compounded by the high price of the hardware, driven by the mandatory Kinect bundle, and the original hardware's weakness in cross-platform comparisons. While it won't ever catch the PlayStation 4 in sales, Microsoft has performed an admirable rescue job – backwards compatibility is great despite being partial, the Games Pass service has delivered an irresistible value proposition, and the Xbox One X upgrade beat the PS4 Pro when it came to raw power.

5 WII U NINTENDO • 2012

The key selling point of Nintendo's successor to the immensely successful Wii was a controller with a large touchscreen, which received video from the main unit wirelessly – a nod to the popularity of tablets. However, the system never quite seemed to get anything right. While the ability to play games without a TV was welcome, few compelling uses for the controller were found. The name and similar exterior design confused consumers, many of whom believed that the Wii U was simply an accessory for the Wii, rather than a new and considerably more powerful system. Early sales were abysmal and third parties quickly abandoned the format, leaving players with little to play between Nintendo's excellent first-party games, like *Super Mario 3D World* and *Splatoon*. 13.5 million consoles were sold worldwide, making it a notable flop.

6 SWITCH NINTENDO • 2017

Nintendo's latest console has a major unique selling point – it's a handheld and a home console, all in one package (well, unless you buy the recent handheld-only Switch Lite version). The ability to effortlessly take your games away from your front room allows the system to fit into busy lifestyles, and it is just powerful enough to fit into cross-platform development plans, albeit with some graphical cuts. The built-in multiplayer capability offered by the detachable Joy-Con controllers is popular, though the Joy-Cons themselves have suffered from engineering issues and 'analogue stick drift'. Aided by an astonishing first year of games including *The Legend Of Zelda: Breath Of The Wild*, *Splatoon 2* and *Super Mario Odyssey*, the system surpassed the Wii U's lifetime sales in less than a year, and is currently selling faster than the 3DS did.

2012 AUGUST
Amazon Game Studios is founded by Amazon and starts off by publishing a number of releases for the mobile market.

2012 SEPTEMBER
Klei Entertainment's indie stealth gem, *Mark Of The Ninja*, sneaks out on to the Xbox 360. Other versions will soon follow.

2012 NOVEMBER
Nintendo launches its Wii successor, the Wii U, in NA, nearly a month ahead of its Japanese December launch.

2013 JUNE
The Kickstarter-funded Ouya is released. It sells for a staggeringly low $99 and uses Android as an operating system.

2013 JUNE
Naughty Dog releases *The Last Of Us* to critical acclaim on PlayStation 3. It will go on to win numerous awards.

THE RETRO REVOLUTION

WORDS BY
NICK THORPE

THE PREVIOUS DECADE SAW INCREDIBLE DEVELOPMENTS IN EVERY ASPECT OF RETRO GAMING, FROM NEW EVENTS AND VENUES TO THE RISE OF YOUTUBE STARS, AND OF COURSE THE INCREDIBLE TECHNOLOGIES THAT GIVE A NEW LEASE OF LIFE TO OUR OLD GAMES. WE TAKE A LOOK AT HOW THINGS HAVE DEVELOPED, AND WHERE THEY MIGHT BE GOING NEXT

YOU'VE GOT REISSUES

MAJOR CORPORATIONS ARE STILL GETTING THE CLASSICS OUT THERE, ALBEIT INCONSISTENTLY

The last decade was a bit of a mixed bag as far as support from the major companies goes. The promise of a vibrant digital market where reissues could be picked up individually has fallen by the wayside, with only PC retailer GOG still championing it. Nintendo's Virtual Console programme appears to have been discontinued, and the vast library of digital PlayStation classics is still incompatible with the PlayStation 4. Microsoft's backwards compatibility technology is excellent, but its stop-start approach to expanding the programme is disheartening.

However, it's not all bad news. Retro compilations from the likes of Sega, Atari and Namco, though less common now, are still being produced for the major formats. The new Evercade handheld console is even dedicated to hosting such compilations. Subscription services are increasingly prevalent, too – Nintendo allows subscribers to its Switch online service to access a library of NES and SNES games, and PlayStation Now offers streaming access to older games. On the PC, Antstream cuts across systems and companies to offer hundreds of games via remote streaming.

Perhaps most excitingly, there has been a growing trend for companies to produce officially licensed reprints of classic games on their original formats, ranging from common games like *Street Fighter II* to expensive, sought-after games like *R-Type III*. These have come courtesy of Retro-Bit, iam8bit, Piko Interactive and Limited Run Games in the west, and Columbus Circle in Japan. As we take our first steps into the new decade, we are expecting to see even more frequent and high-profile cartridge reprints.

MINI MADNESS

PLUG-AND-PLAY CONSOLES HAVE BEEN ELEVATED FROM CHEAP DIVERSIONS TO MULTIMILLION SELLERS

Although plug-and-play retro consoles have existed since the early Nineties, one of the biggest market shifts over the last decade has been the emergence of those consoles as highly desired retro products. The Nintendo Classic Mini: NES was the key release in the field, as it offered the authenticity you'd expect of a first-party product and an excellently curated 'greatest hits' library. Demand outstripped supply for a long time, and the SNES-themed follow-up was even better.

Since then, many companies have been driven by the renewed interest that Nintendo's efforts have brought to the field, and tried to create definitive nostalgia packages at low prices – and that's not just original manufacturers, as products like Retro-Bit's Super Retro-Cade have also entered the market. However, devices have experienced mixed fortunes. While The C64 Mini did well enough to inspire the creation of the high-end Capcom Home Arcade, the PlayStation Classic fell short of expectations due to emulation issues and a game roster that missed big names and ended up discounted.

Expect more of these machines in the decade to come – Konami has debuted the PC Engine Mini, and we're sure companies have more exciting projects on the way. We're hoping for a true follow-up to Sega's Mega Drive Mini.

2013 SEPTEMBER
Rockstar releases *Grand Theft Auto V* on PS3 and Xbox 360. It goes on to make $1 billion in its first three days on sale.

2013 NOVEMBER
Sony launches the PS4 in America and Japan. Microsoft releases the Xbox One shortly afterwards.

2014 JANUARY
Sony Interactive Entertainment announces PlayStation Now, a cloud streaming subscription service, at CES.

2014 FEBRUARY
Capcom Osaka Studio teams up with Double Helix Games to release a brand-new *Strider* game... which makes fans happy.

2014 MARCH
Warcraft spin-off, *Hearthstone* is launched by Blizzard. The digital card game soon becomes extremely popular.

ATTACK OF THE CLONES

HOW THIRD-PARTY MANUFACTURERS ARE CREATING MODERN MANIFESTATIONS OF TIMELESS TECHNOLOGY

Christopher Taber

© Viola Gaskell

While it's always an incredible thrill, playing classic games on the original hardware may not be the best option for everyone today. Even if you don't suffer from component failures as your hardware ages, there's another big problem. "Classic videogame systems were designed to be used on CRTs," says Christopher Taber of hardware developer Analogue. "When you hook a game system using analogue video to a HDTV, it looks terrible, has enormous lag and in general proves to be a poor-quality experience." Today's clone consoles must bridge that gap, making classic games viable on modern TVs.

Of course, cheap old-style Famiclones and their ilk are still out there, but you get what you pay for. The first HD-capable machines that became popular over the last decade used software emulation to offer compatibility with a variety of formats, such as Hyperkin's RetroN 5 and Cyber Gadget's Retro Freak, but questions over the licensing for emulators used mired those machines in controversy. A new software emulation system – the Polymega – arrived in 2020 and provides support for systems such as the Saturn and PlayStation. It comes at an eye-watering starting price of $399, though.

However, the most interesting new development in the clone hardware field has been the appearance of FPGA-based systems. "An FPGA (Field Programmable Gate Array) is, in essence, a special chip that can be configured to be, well, basically any other chip. Whatever an FPGA is configured to be, it can operate identically to, in real time. This can translate into 100% accuracy," explains Christopher. "The downsides are that FPGAs are expensive (the FPGA in Mega Sg is a $53 chip) and it takes an incredible amount of time and talent to achieve this (our engineers spent over 5,000 hours engineering Mega Sg). Fortunately, we've got the best guy to do it," he continues, referring to Kevin 'Kevtris' Horton.

Analogue is the only company selling FPGA-based consoles at present, and Christopher asserts, "FPGA is the future of preserving videogame history and we are the only company putting the time, money and effort into this." While they are premium consoles targeted at enthusiasts, it's hard to argue with the results. The SNES-compatible Super Nt and Mega Drive-compatible Mega Sg offer perfect video over HDMI, no added lag and a variety of features. With even more consoles like the Pocket and Duo, this new market becoming is supremely exciting.

» Analogue has established a reputation of being a producer of excellent retro-themed hardware.

ACCESSORISE ME!

MODERN DEVICES ARE TAKING OLD HARDWARE TO NEW HEIGHTS

If you're still clinging on to your old hardware, it's been a bountiful decade. Hobbyists have led the way on this front. New accessories are becoming available all the time, from simple quality-of-life enhancements like HDMI cables and adaptors to modern wireless controllers from 8bitdo and Krikzz – Retro-bit has even produced officially licensed Sega controllers. There are solid state replacements for magnetic and optical drives like the Commodore 64 SD2IEC, Spectrum DivMMC and Dreamcast GDEMU, and at the extreme end of the scale, devices like Terraonion's Mega SD cartridge can replace whole add-ons like the Mega-CD using FPGA technology.

Matt Cope

OLD DOG, NEW TRICKS

WHY TODAY'S CODERS ARE BRINGING NEW GAMES TO CLASSIC SYSTEMS

While we've long had new releases for old formats – just ask the likes of Cronosoft and Psytronik Software – the field has changed over the last decade. The most noticeable development is the increased production of cartridge games, which allowed for the likes of Broke Studio's NES games and Big Evil Corp's impressive *Tanglewood* for the Mega Drive. Still, this isn't easy, as Bitmap Bureau will tell you. "We've had to take this aspect in-house – Sega haven't manufactured any Mega Drive cartridges in a little while," says Matt Cope, part of the team that released the overhead shoot-'em-up *Xeno Crisis* in late 2019. "It's taken a huge hit on our time. In the future we'd like to just stick with the software development and hopefully find someone to handle the manufacturing and hardware logistics."

Fortunately, *Xeno Crisis* is a labour of love for the team. "It's certainly easier to develop a game for modern platforms, particularly thanks to game engines such as Unity and Unreal Engine, but we had spent many years previously making games with retro aesthetics, and felt that it was time to have a go at making a genuine Mega Drive game, rather than games that looked like they could be of that 16-bit era," says Mike Tucker. "For myself, gaming peaked in the Eighties and Nineties. What we're trying to do is recreate the feel of those classic titles (Capcom, Konami, Toaplan and Taito are big influences) and give gamers new titles to get excited about."

The team has some big advantages over those who developed its games in the Nineties, too. "There is definitely access to more shared knowledge and there have been a number of incremental steps within the Mega Drive homebrew scene over the years," says Matt. "We also benefit from much faster computers, so processing all the assets and compiling the code is very fast. I shudder to think what it would have been like waiting 20 minutes or so for each compile on a Nineties PC versus a few seconds today." As cooperation continues, look for ever more impressive games in years to come.

Mike Tucker

2014 APRIL
ZeniMax Online Studios releases *The Elder Scrolls Online*, an epic MMORPG seven years in the making, to mixed reviews.

2014 JUNE
Yacht Club unleashes the fun *Shovel Knight*, an excellent platformer that's styled to look like an old NES game.

2014 DECEMBER
Two years after its Kickstarter campaign, Frontier releases its sci-fi sequel, *Elite Dangerous*, on PC.

2015 APRIL
Retro Computers releases the ZX Spectrum Vega, a miniature games system that is preloaded with 1,000 Speccy games.

2015 MAY
The Witcher 3: Wild Hunt debuts on PC, Xbox One and PlayStation 4 and continues the amazing adventures of Geralt Of Rivia.

NEW DOG, OLD TRICKS

WHY MODERN SYSTEMS ARE SHOWING THE GRAPHICS OF YESTERYEAR IN NEW GAMES

Rob Hewson

If you play modern indie games, you're sure to have noticed the prominence of pixel art. Some, like *Fez*, offer a twist on an old style, while others adopt the style out of love for the past, like *Shovel Knight, Blazing Chrome* and *Undertale*. According to Rob Hewson of Huey Games, this is a matter of artistic expression and efficiency. "Sometimes less is more in game design and that can apply to visuals, too," he says. "If you can capture the feelings of a pixellated character with just a few frames of animation, then why have more complex art and animation to achieve the same result? Would *Stardew Valley* or *Fez* be more powerful with a modern aesthetic?"

As well as artistic benefits, Rob believes that there are game design benefits inherent to certain pixel art styles. "For a fast, manic game like *Hyper Sentinel*, readability of the visuals was paramount, so we chose an 8-bit style with high-contrast colours and clean, crisp graphics. For a slower paced game, you might go for a 16-bit aesthetic which offers more detail, but not so much that you begin to cross towards realism and lose that space for the player's imagination." Beyond that, Rob reminds us that 3D can be expensive. "Pixel art allows you to do a lot with little, which is obviously going to be attractive to indie developers operating on a smaller budget."

While some developers choose to imitate the limitations of a specific piece of hardware, many choose not to restrict themselves in such a way. "We did choose a specific default look, but the option to switch to different graphical styles was added because it was something our community was passionate about," says Rob. "The CRT and Commodore 64 styles were stretch goals which were reached in our Kickstarter campaign, and we subsequently added the ZX Spectrum style as an extra thank you to fans. These bonus styles are great fun from a nostalgia point of view, but I think most players would agree the default style, which is inspired by 8-bit but without the flaws and limitations, is the best way to play."

AUDIO VIDEO CONNECTION

WHAT GOES INTO THE CREATION OF A HIT YOUTUBE RETRO GAMING CHANNEL?

The internet has been amazing for the retro community, as podcasts like *Retronauts, The Retro Hour* and *Maximum Power Up* provide audio coverage, and YouTube hosts informative videos from the likes of Kim Justice, Game Sack and Classic Gaming Quarterly. My Life In Gaming has risen to prominence since its 2013 launch and has almost 200,000 YouTube subscribers. "During the conception phase of the channel, I spent a lot on my commutes listening to three podcasts: *WTF* with Marc Maron, *Retronauts* and *This American Life*," says Coury Carlson, who hosts along with Marc 'Try4ce' Duddleson. "I wanted to do something that combined the feel of these but focus on videogames, developers and such. But in order to get these types of interviews, we needed to build a body of work to show people what we could do." That breakthrough was a pivot towards technology, as a video on the popular Framemeister upscaler was shared on *Kotaku* and provided a clear path to pursue. The hosts have now realised their ambitions of creating documentaries. Some of the best ones include a 49-minute documentary on *Night Trap* and an hour-long feature on M2, each with brand-new interview content.

One of the things that helps to set the channel apart from others is the high quality of the presentation. Both men have professional backgrounds in video, but they've had to invest plenty of cash ("probably way too much", admits Coury) into equipment for both game capture and filming. However, aspiring video creators shouldn't be deterred. "Anyone can make a good-looking show with some pretty minimal equipment if they use it well," says Marc. "Learn about how cameras work – terms like aperture, shutter speed, ISO and white balance – and force yourself to learn to use manual settings! I know that can seem daunting, but it will make your show look so much more professional. Also, don't forget the lighting! You can find very inexpensive starter lighting kits for well under $100 online, and it is absolutely worth it."

The hosts acknowledge their place in the community – as their expertise is in production and hosting, they do require assistance from peers on technical issues. "Without the help of key people in the scene, we'd never be where we are now. People like Robert Neal of RetroRGB, Artemio Urbina, Ste Kulov, and many others fact-check our scripts, give additional info, and explain stuff that we don't understand," says Coury. "We're generally like most of our audience – we don't truly understand this stuff without help, so part of our methodology is to break it down to the point where we *do* understand it and present *that* for our audience."

Coury Carlson

Marc 'Try4ce' Duddleson

2015 JUNE
Sam Barlow's captivating *Her Story* breathes life into interactive FMV games and has players trying to unravel its mystery.

2015 JULY
Psyonix releases the excellent *Rocket League*, with its car football mayhem offering a new twist on esports.

2015 NOVEMBER
Valve's Steam Machines start appearing in the wild. Some come with a distinctive controller with haptic feedback.

2016 JANUARY
Dragon Quest Builders, a delightful infusion of RPG mechanics and *Minecraft*-styled creating, makes its debut.

2016 MARCH
Oculus VR releases the game-changing Oculus Rift, a VR device that promises a new way of experiencing games.

BOOK SMART

HOW DEDICATED PUBLISHERS HAVE RISEN TO MEET THE DEMAND FOR RETRO GAMING BOOKS

While traditional publishers have continued to take on retro gaming book projects from prominent gaming writers, the more exciting development for many is the emergence of dedicated gaming publishers such as Fusion Retro Books, Read-Only Memory and Bitmap Books. But what's drawing fans to the printed page? "I think it's because we all have strong memories of the old games and for me, the humble book is the ultimate way of archiving these memories. It can sit on your shelf and can be picked up for a nostalgia hit whenever required," says Sam Dyer, creative director of Bitmap Books.

Bitmap Books' titles take anywhere from six to nine months to produce. "That's from initial concept, through all the design and writing until print-ready files are ready. Print and production takes around three months, so you're looking at about 12 months in total per book," Sam explains. "I really enjoy the process of seeing a book coming together and get a real buzz from working with different writers, artists and designers." The publisher has gained official licences for some titles, such as *Sega Master System: A Visual Compendium* and *Metal Slug: The Ultimate History* – an approach Sam highly recommends. "Going official is always best, in my opinion. You get access to proper assets – some that maybe have not been seen before. I also believe that an official product has an extra level of kudos attached to it and is likely to be more collectable." Of course, there are drawbacks. "Being official means quite a bit of extra work and certain rules to adhere to. In balance, though, I think it's well worth it."

One of the keys to the emergence of so many retro gaming books in recent years – and what is likely to keep them popular in the Twenties – is the growing popularity of Kickstarter and crowdfunding in general. "Without it, Bitmap Books certainly wouldn't exist today. It essentially removes financial risk for a product because if not enough people 'back' your project, you've lost nothing, apart from the time creating the pitch," Sam explains. "Sadly, due to several failed products, confidence in crowdfunding is very low and comes with an increased level of scepticism nowadays. However, I don't believe that many of the retro gaming books out there would exist without crowdfunding, as commercial publishers simply wouldn't take a risk on such a potentially niche subject."

MEGA MAGAZINES

HOW FANS ARE KEEPING PRINT COVERAGE ALIVE FOR THEIR FAVOURITE FORMATS

Although games mags aren't as abundant as they once were, the retro gaming scene has produced a vibrant selection of indie magazines including *Fusion*, *Mega Visions* and Vinny Mainolfi's *Freeze64*. "From a very early age, I always wanted to produce my own independent Commodore 64 fanzine," says Vinny when asked why he launched the magazine. "With the current technology and print facilities available, and my vast knowledge and experience in marketing, design and publishing, I felt that it was the perfect time to produce something that C64 enthusiasts will enjoy."

Rather than using Kickstarter, *Freeze64* was a risky self-funded venture – "I'm very much from the old-school way of starting, funding and selling an idea," Vinny explains – but the magazine caught on and over 30 issues have now been published. "I've always put it down to the fact that the Eighties generation are now at an age where most of them have a disposable income and so they can start to buy and collect the items they always wanted and couldn't afford as kids," he tells us, regarding the ongoing popularity of his magazine and others like it.

Another factor in *Freeze64*'s success is its regularity, which is possible due to a quick production cycle. "A couple of weekends and an issue is complete," Vinny explains. "By the time one issue is being sent to print, the next issue is almost complete. The trick is to enjoy the process, and the rest just happens." Impressively, it's mostly a solo effort too. "It's just me working on each issue, which means research, interviews, writing, designing, page-setting, ordering, posting, packing, admin and finances… but saying that, there are currently two other famous C64 personalities kindly submitting regular columns, which account for five of the 36 pages of each issue. Those guys are Julian Rignall and Steve Collins. And let's not forget my best buddy Frank Gasking who spends a lot of time proofreading each issue."

RETRO RETREATS

RETRO GAMING NEED NOT BE A SOLITARY PURSUIT THANKS TO NEW EVENTS AND VENUES

While retro gaming events and venues have been around for a long time, this decade has seen them grow to another level. In the UK, the biggest example of that is Arcade Club. Although the venue in Bury contains modern PC, console and arcade games, it also contains plenty of retro consoles and a whole floor dedicated to retro arcade games. These range from early hits like *Space Invaders* and *Pac-Man* through to Nineties favourites like *Street Fighter II* and *Ridge Racer*, and even beyond to games like *Soulcalibur* and *Dancing Stage EuroMix*. The success of the original venue has seen a second, similarly packed venue open in Leeds this year. Elsewhere, venues like the Konbo gaming cafe in Edinburgh (which sadly closed in January 2020), the Four Quarters Bar in London and Timewarp Arcade in Bridgwater are flying the retro flag, too.

Then, there are the events. Play Expo events have run up and down the country, becoming a well-recognised brand in the retro community as they always feature plenty of arcade, console and computer games to play, as well as live discussions with the likes of Philip and Andrew Oliver, Matthew Smith and Archer MacLean. For those who would prefer to buy games rather than playing them, there are events like the Retro Games Fair which has taken place in Leeds and Nottingham, the Video Game Market in Doncaster, as well as the London Gaming Market and Bristol Gaming Market.

2016 MAY
Blizzard Entertainment releases its acclaimed multiplayer hero shooter, *Overwatch*. It sends cosplayers crazy.

2016 JULY
Pokemon Go is released by Niantic. It will become a gigantic mobile hit, raking in over $3 billion in revenue over the years.

2016 AUGUST
Team17's *Worms* reinvents itself with *Worms WMD*, allowing its iconic annelids to craft weapons and utilise vehicles.

2016 OCTOBER
Sony enters the virtual reality market with PSVR. Great launch games like *RIGS* and *Rez Infinite* show it off.

2016 NOVEMBER
Nintendo releases its NES Mini worldwide. Meanwhile, Sony releases the PlayStation 4 Pro, its enhanced PS4.

VIRTUAL REALITY BLOWS UP

WORDS BY DARRAN JONES

VIRTUAL REALITY ISN'T EXACTLY A NEW THING IN VIDEOGAMES AND WAS ATTEMPTED DURING THE EARLY DAYS OF THE INDUSTRY, BUT ITS RETURN IN THE TENS HAS SEEN IT EXCEED THE WILDEST EXPECTATIONS OF MANY GAMERS. ÉRIC CHAHI AND FELLOW DEVELOPERS REVEAL WHY

ÉRIC CHAHI
Another World creator, Éric Chahi has released the VR game, *Paper Beast.*

STEVE BRISTOW
Steve is Rebellion's assistant head of design and has worked on VR titles like *Battlezone.*

STEWART GILRAY
Just Add Water's CEO, Stewart Gilray is impressed with the progress VR is currently making.

If we were to sum up the most exciting thing to happen to videogames this past decade it would absolutely be the revival of virtual reality. Aside from giving us hilarious videos of people using VR devices for the first time, it has also allowed many of us to experience games in a new and exciting way.

"My first VR experience was during the Nineties with *Pterodactyl Nightmare*," remembers gaming veteran Éric Chahi, who has released his own VR game, *Paper Beast.* "The graphics were 3D flat polygons, and as far as I remember, the game was slow and very low-res. *Pterodactyl Nightmare* was really ahead of its time. It took almost 20 years to finally have good technology."

» Oculus' Rift headset was a forerunner in this new wave of virtual reality devices.

Rebellion's Steve Bristow, who is currently involved with *Sniper Elite VR* also remembers *Prerodactyl Nightmare* and those early days. "The thing is, that Virtuality pod headset was clunky and uncomfortable, and the hardware just wasn't up to the job. In retrospect, it set me up perfectly to be absolutely blown away by my first contact with a PlayStation VR dev kit because the technology and design had so utterly transformed the experience."

Oculus Rift, Vive and PSVR have all been instrumental in the success of VR in today's gaming environment, but it's worth remembering just how far we've come since Virtuality's arcade experiences of the Nineties. "A lot more thought has obviously gone into the design of the headsets and controllers to make them more comfortable for people to use for a longer period of time," explains Just Add Water's senior producer, Les Ellis. "And, of course, the sheer processing grunt we have now enables the graphics to be more realistic. The whole experience is so much more immersive, so much easier to get into and so much more accessible for everyone." Steve Bristow also remembers being wowed by VR in the Nineties came with a cost. "There's a massive difference in visual fidelity of course," he begins. "The old Virtuality headsets had 276x372 resolution screens and the framerates were… periodic. You also had to stand inside a large magnetic ring and lash a bunch of, as I recall, fairly heavy hardware to yourself." And then, of course, there's the price. "The cost has been a major factor," continues Éric about VR's inability to take off in the early days. "Sony's PSVR did an incredible move in this regard. They took advantage of the existing hardware: the Move and DualShock controllers, and the camera. By adding a headset they were able to provide a fully functional system with 3D controllers allowing it to be super ergonomic to the player. The headset is also very comfortable to use."

While plenty of advances have been made, there are still issues that stop virtual reality from becoming truly mainstream at the moment, namely lower display resolutions (particularly on PSVR) and motion sickness, which can affect gamers in a variety of ways. As a result, developers have plenty to think about when making games. "Performance is key, and in most cases the hardware providers have a minimum framerate we can't drop below," explains Just Add Water's Stewart Gilray. "As such, everything has to be optimised, the art, the

2016 DECEMBER
After nine years of development, Fumito Ueda's enchanting *The Last Guardian* is finally released on PS4.

2017 JANUARY
Capcom's seventh *Resident Evil* game features a first-person viewpoint and offers a scary VR experience.

2017 MARCH
Nintendo releases its hybrid console, the Switch, a neat little system that can be played on-the-go or on a TV.

2017 MARCH
Link wakes up from a deep sleep in *The Legend Of Zelda: Breath Of The Wild,* an epic adventure for the Wii U and Switch.

2017 SEPTEMBER
Nintendo follows up its miniature NES with the Nintendo Classic Mini: SNES. It becomes another hit for the company.

» The PSVR's 'halo' design helps distribute the weight away from the front of your face.

code… everything, to make sure the experience is smooth and fluid."

This is something Les echoes. "Keeping great visuals and a viable framerate is a constant battle throughout development," he says. "Controls are another thing. A player can't just look down at the controllers to see what button to press, so everything has to feel completely natural and intuitive. We've really enjoyed taking advantage of the PlayStation Aim controller in *Sniper Elite VR*, where it's an obvious match. The game plays great with regular control methods, but it's a nice bonus to have a rifle in your hands and feel yourself lining up a shot as you keep your aim steady."

While creating VR games can cause headaches, they also present exciting new opportunities for adventurous developers as Éric reveals. "We have, for the first time, an actual feeling of space and its real size, which is pretty unique to VR. So our design of *Paper Beast* takes advantage of this and allows us to play with confined spaces or a sense of scale. Tiny creatures or immense ones! And then there is the physical 3D manipulation. By manipulating entities through gestures, the VR world becomes more tangible. One thing that works super well in *Paper Beast* is this: the feeling of mass. A player can control entities with a flexible beam, which is influenced by the curve and resistance, allowing you to really feel the weight."

While advancements are being made all the time, everyone we spoke to was convinced that VR's current success is largely down to the hardware teams championing it. "The VIVE, Rift and PSVR have been massive for gaming," concludes Les. "Without these devices, VR would be a gimmick, but they have created a viable marketplace that will lead to more investment in new and even more powerful devices, which in turn will lead to even bigger and better gaming experiences."

"They've certainly brought it to the mainstream in terms of user pickup and acceptance," confirms Stewart. "Don't get me wrong, it's not mainstream yet, but certainly it's grown to be more popular than I think most people expected it to be," Steve agrees. "It's hard to understate," he concludes. "They are the pivotal moment in making VR an industry rather than a gimmick. I think in a few years we'll look back on them in a similar way as we do the Motorola DynaTAC phone; as the progenitors of a new medium." ★

VIRTUALLY BRILLIANT

ESSENTIAL VR GAMES TO EXPERIENCE

ASTRO BOT RESCUE MISSION

While everyone was praising *Super Mario Odyssey*, it was *Astro Bot* which really shook up the platformer genre in 2018. While it's very conventional in some ways, VR gives it a tangibility and sense of scale that no other game within the genre can match. It's a real game-changer.

RESIDENT EVIL VII

Capcom's reboot of its premier survival horror series also happens to be a terrifying showcase for virtual reality. The sense of scale is superb, while the atmosphere is second to none. We lost count of the times we were expected to enter a room and just went, "Nope!"

HALF-LIFE: ALYX

VR inspired the developers at Valve so much that they decided to return to the world of *Half-Life* with this astonishing first-person shooter. What stands out here is how intuitive interacting with the world feels, and how you can use your environment against your foes. One of the best experiences you can have in gaming right now.

BEAT SABER

There are a number of rhythm action games available in VR, but *Beat Saber* is by far the best. It works exceptionally well with motion controls, requiring you to strike incoming blocks from different directions (it's harder than it sounds), and like *Superhot* it ensures you get a real workout during play.

WIPEOUT OMEGA COLLECTION

While we were tempted to go with *Rez Infinite* or *Skyrim*, this is probably one of the best examples of converting an old game to the exciting new medium of VR. Just sitting in your cockpit during the game's opening is worth the entry price alone. This is truly a mind-blowing experience.

2017 SEPTEMBER
Epic Games showcases *Fortnite Battle Royale*, a free-to-play online game that quickly angers the *Daily Mail*.

2017 OCTOBER
Platforming gets reinvented by *Super Mario Odyssey*. Mario makes friends a sentient cap and can control enemies.

2017 NOVEMBER
Originally known in development as 'Project Scorpio', Microsoft releases the Xbox One X, an enhanced Xbox One.

2018 JULY
The Neo-Geo Mini is released in Japan. Unlike other mini systems, SNK has it designed like an arcade cabinet.

2018 AUGUST
Mega Drive platformer, *Tanglewood* is released (no, really) and introduces gamers to Nymn, a cute little fox.

Minecraft

IF YOU BUILD IT, THEY WILL COME

RETROREVIVAL

» VARIOUS » 2011 » MOJANG

Throughout this journey through time, the games we've showcased in our Retro Revivals largely share a common trait. They're the videogames that pierced through the gaming audience and broke out into the wider world. They're examples from our beloved medium that everyone has heard of (except maybe your nan) and anyone can enjoy. They're so well-designed that bar for entry is low yet each one appeals to the wider 'hardcore' gaming demographic thanks to their potential for high-skill play – sure, we can all play *Tetris*, but can we all beat Nick at it? I think not (trust me, I've tried). So now the sun has set on the Tens, we thought about what was the best example of that type of game for this decade… and of course, it's *Minecraft*.

It's effectively a toybox of boundless possibilities, and the premise is so simple. You're dropped onto a verdant world, and what you do is up to you. Want to build a house? Punch a tree until it breaks to build a log cabin. Want to adventure? Grab some stone, craft a sword and go on, be a murderhobo. Want to be a simple farmer? Sure, go gather some seeds and entice a chicken. I love *Minecraft* because I'll never get bored of it, and I find it just so relaxing to build myself a house or go down into a cave in the search of diamonds or Redstone. Mojang trusts that you can make your own stories, and to be honest I have more memories playing *Minecraft* than, say, *The Legend Of Zelda* or *Apex Legends*.

So, yes, *Minecraft* is special. It deserves its place between *Pong*, *Tetris*, *Super Mario 64* and *Wii Sports*… but I think there's something about this modern classic that makes it go one step beyond. It's a tool for education, for one, there's a dedicated '*Educational Edition*' which can teach kids about tons of stuff from history, through to chemistry and coding. *Minecraft* can also be used to help people with developmental challenges such as autism. I genuinely welled up at a story I read about how *Guardian* journalist Keith Stuart discovered that *Minecraft* helped his son communicate and integrate himself with his school peers. Until I became an adult (around the time *Minecraft*'s release, actually), I never really gave much thought that games can be a force for good, but Mojang's magnum opus proves that they can. There's truly no other game out there that has potential like *Minecraft* does, and sure, it's not for everyone, but anyone can appreciate the good it has done during its time on this planet. ★

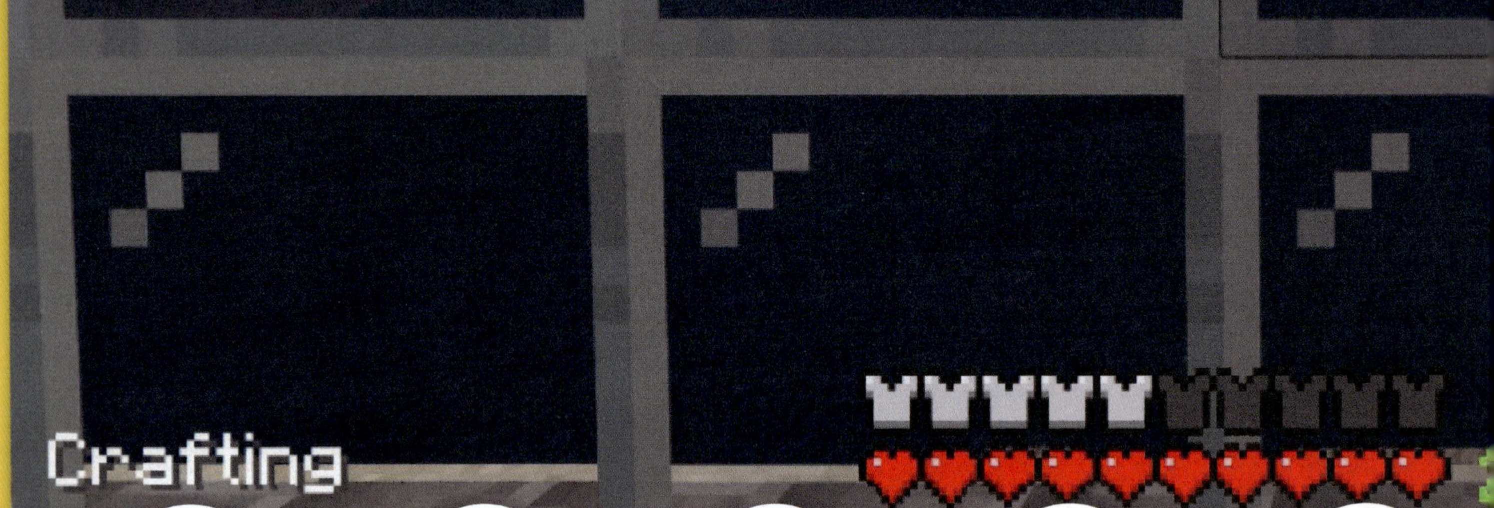

2018 OCTOBER
Astro Bot Rescue Mission gives platformers a shot in the arm and highlights just how incredible VR gaming can be.

2018 DECEMBER
Sony enters the 'mini console' market with the PlayStation Classic. It fails to impress and will soon lines bargain bins.

2018 DECEMBER
Super Smash Bros Ultimate arrives, it's an ambitious entry that features every fighter that's appeared in the series.

2019 FEBRUARY
Respawn Entertainment's *Apex Legends*, a game set in the *Titanfall* universe, comes out of nowhere to take on *Fortnite*.

2019 FEBRUARY
Tetris reinvents itself with *Tetris 99*, a fun battle royale-styled Switch exclusive designed for up to 99 competitors.

2019
MARCH
FromSoftware's *Sekiro: Shadows Die Twice* debuts and becomes a success with consumers and critics alike.

2019
JUNE
The Kickstarter-backed *Bloodstained: Ritual Of The Night* arrives to a warm reception... unless you're playing on Switch.

2019
AUGUST
World Of Warcraft Classic launches and mimics the original *WOW* before *The Burning Crusade* was released.

2019
SEPTEMBER
The M2-developed Genesis Mini is released in North America. It's a big hit and includes 42 preinstalled games.

2019
NOVEMBER
Hideo Kojima's first post-Konami game, *Death Stranding*, is released. Its unique gameplay loop proves divisive.

retrogamer.net

THE 2020s

A GREAT YEAR FOR GAMES… BUT BAD FOR EVERYTHING ELSE

We've only seen one full year of the Twenties pass us by so far but it felt like an entire decade. In the wake of the global COVID-19 pandemic, gaming has felt more important than ever. Stay-at-home orders left us restricted in how we find enjoyment in our lives, and videogames were there to pick many of us up when we were down. And then the George Floyd protests started, forcing many big-name publishers to look introspectively at themselves and pledge to do better when it came to representation and philanthropy. 2020 also saw the beginning of a brand-new generation of consoles, ushering in the PlayStation 5 and Microsoft's Xbox Series S/X systems, all launching in November.

GAMES OF THE DECADE (SO FAR)

FEBRUARY '20
DREAMS

Media Molecule's ambitious title is more like a creation system than your typical game. It enables users to devise all sorts of creations, from 3D sculptures to experiments and even fully fledged games. Its community has produced some jaw-dropping feats, including a remake of *PT*, a *Seinfeld* horror game, crazy platformers, racers, shooters and more.

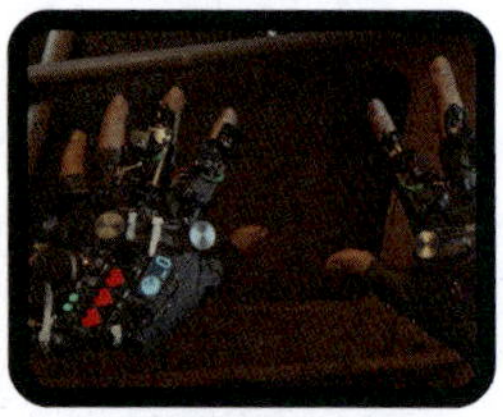

MARCH '20
HALF-LIFE: ALYX

12 long years after the cliffhanger in *Half-Life 2: Episode 2*, we finally have a follow-up. Here, Valve brings its legendary skill to the world of virtual reality in this first-person prequel/sort-of-sequel, placing you directly in the eyeballs of Alyx Vance as she looks to help fight off the oppressive alien Combine forces.

MARCH '20
ANIMAL CROSSING: NEW HORIZONS

Nintendo managed to deliver this wonderful package of positivity just in time to see us through lockdown. *New Horizons* gives you an entire island to manage, hundreds of cute animals to befriend and tons of activities to get stuck into. Also new to the series is a terraforming system, enabling you to shape your paradise as you see fit.

APRIL '20
FINAL FANTASY VII REMAKE

A full remake of *Final Fantasy VII* has been requested by fans for decades, and it finally arrived in 2020… well, the first part did. Set entirely in the dystopian city of Midgar, the debut title in this remake series is an incredible reinvention of the PlayStation classic. A new action-packed combat system delivers satisfying battles in style.

JUNE '20
THE LAST OF US PART II

Following up on a success like the first *The Last Of Us* is a tough task, however Naughty Dog pulled it out the bag. This is an unflinching story about revenge, anger and how far you'd go for the people you love. It looks absolutely astonishing, the action-packed gameplay is better than ever and the new infected enemies are truly terrifying.

2020 JANUARY
The inaugural season of the *Call Of Duty* League launches, pitting pro North American *COD* teams against one another.

2020 FEBRUARY
Sonic The Hedgehog is released in movie theatres worldwide. It stars Ben Schwartz, James Marsden and Jim Carrey.

2020 FEBRUARY
Saber Interactive is acquired by Embracer Group. It joins Koch Media, Nordic Games and DECA Games as a subsidiary.

2020 FEBRUARY
Game developer Kazuhisa Hashimoto passes away at the age of 61. He was best known for creating the famous Konami Code.

2020 MARCH
Rockstar cofounder Dan Hauser leaves the company after an extended break. He had a hand in writing many successful games.

THE TWENTIES... AS TOLD BY DEREK YU

THE CREATOR OF SPELUNKY 2 TALKS TO US ABOUT A DIFFICULT YEAR FOR US ALL, AND WHAT IT'S LIKE TO LAUNCH A GAME IN A PANDEMIC

Releasing a game is difficult at the best of times, but this year saw a slew of complications thanks to the COVID-19 pandemic. Despite that, Derek Yu and his team managed to ship the indie roguelike *Spelunky 2* earlier in September 2020. "I feel lucky, because the *Spelunky 2* team, which has always worked remotely (from the US, Spain, and Norway), didn't have to make too many adjustments to keep working," he tells us. "In some ways, the pandemic simplified the final stretch of development because there wasn't much to do but work and spend time with family at home."

Once the game was out, though, Derek had mixed feelings. "It was a strange mix of emotions," he says. "Launching a game always feels strange, though, so maybe it's more accurate to say it was extra strange. Here we are, releasing a videogame, which feels like a frivolous thing when the world is struggling with a pandemic and other serious problems. And yet, releasing *Spelunky 2* was really important to us – we'd worked hard on it for many years – and it was important to our players, who were also stuck at home and excited about having it to play. Overall, I'm glad we released the game when we did – it gave me something positive to focus on when I needed a break from the news. And perhaps the news put into perspective all the little annoying hiccups that inevitably arise when you ship a videogame!"

When looking back on 2020, Derek thinks gaming has been a force for good. "I think people are playing a lot more games this year and using games to connect with each other more," he explains. "I've been meeting up with friends once a week to play *WebLiero* and it's been a great way to hang out and catch up now that we can't meet face-to-face. For my young daughter, a lot of special occasions felt more normal this year thanks to games like *Animal Crossing*, where we dressed up and celebrated."

This year has reframed the way we look at so many different things, and Derek is keen to talk about how the games industry fits in that discussion. "I think that, as videogames continue to evolve as an art form and become more integrated into everyone's lives, the games industry needs to both hold its head up high and be proud of its achievements, while also realise that there's a lot of responsibility that comes with it," he tells us. "We need to keep working on improving the lives of both players and developers. 2020 showed that a lot of things are possible that were previously thought to be too difficult, like allowing everyone to work from home, creating more learning and networking opportunities online, etc. Hopefully, in the future, it doesn't take another disaster to get us to make these sorts of changes that benefit us all in the long run."

AUGUST '20
FALL GUYS: ULTIMATE KNOCKOUT

Ever think the likes of *Takeshi's Castle* and *Total Wipeout* would make a good videogame? Well, Mediatonic thought the same thing and produced this adorable spin on the battle royale genre. Here you guide your cute bean-person through a series of elimination matches against other players online. It's easy to pick up, and funny as hell.

SEPTEMBER '20
HADES

This roguelike action RPG hacked and slashed its way out of early access to critical acclaim. In this hellish Greek epic, you take control of Zagreus, the son of Hades, as he looks to high-tail it out of the Underworld and scale Mount Olympus. While you will die, many times, you can purchase upgrades to improve your chances.

JUNE '21
CHICORY

This painterly indie adventure game casts you as a dog in a monochromatic world. Using a paintbrush to solve puzzles and interact with the world, *Chicory* offers a distinctive take on the genre and proves the adage that independent developers like Greg Lobanov are the beating heart of creativity within the gaming industry.

SEPTEMBER '21
DEATHLOOP

Think *Groundhog Day* meets *Dishonored* in the screening of a Seventies grindhouse double-feature. Sound awesome? That's because *Deathloop* is nothing short of magnificent. Placed in the shoes of the surly assassin Colt, you are tasked with eliminating a cadre of targets before the sun sets... or you're offed by rival killer Julianna.

OCTOBER '21
METROID DREAD

In one of the most anticipated revivals in recent memory, Samus Aran dons her power armour once again in this side-scrolling adventure. MercurySteam's sequel demonstrated that there's still life in the galaxy's most badass bounty hunter, and hopefully provoked an appetite for more arm cannon blasting in the future.

2020 MARCH Crowbar Collective releases its *Half-Life* remake, *Black Mesa*. This concludes a 15-year development period.

2020 MARCH Microsoft unveils its Xbox Series X. Early reports from *Digital Foundry* say that it's at least twice as powerful as the Xbox One X.

2020 MARCH This year's Game Developers Conference is held virtually, due to the rising dangers surrounding the COVID-19 pandemic.

2020 MARCH Due to the high infection rates of COVID-19, the UK goes into full lockdown to help combat the virus.

2020 MARCH Capcom launches its *Resident Evil 3* remake. While it's praised, this reimagining doesn't hit the highs of the *RE2* remake.

retrogamer.net

THE DECLINE OF THE DISC

Sony and Microsoft have both flirted with disc-free consoles in the past – the former with the PSP Go and the latter with the Xbox One S All-Digital Edition. However, 2020 proved to be the year where both manufacturers felt that enough consumers would be comfortable with an all-digital future to offer consoles without disc drives, right at the beginning of the generation rather than as a low-cost option later on. While neither of them was bold enough to abandon optical media completely, it's clear to see where console manufacturers wish to lead players. Time will tell whether they follow.

1

2

1 EVERCADE

BLAZE ENTERTAINMENT • MAY 2020

With the popularity of retro gaming continuing to rise, Blaze Entertainment has introduced this low-cost handheld console dedicated to running classic games. Recognising that building a collection is much of the fun of collecting for older consoles, Blaze adopted cartridges for the Evercade, with each multi-game collection containing up to 20 titles from a variety of formats including the NES, SNES, Mega Drive and Atari 2600. The initial line-up of ten cartridges from the likes of Namco, Atari, Interplay and Data East offered over 100 games, and eight more cartridges have since been announced, including *Xeno Crisis & Tanglewood*, *The Oliver Twins Collection* and *Worms Collection 1*. The hardware has proven solid for the price and firmware updates have resolved initial teething troubles with control schemes, and *Piko Interactive Collection 2* will introduce the system's first attempt at PlayStation emulation. The future could be bright for this handheld – especially if some more big names sign up to provide software.

2 XBOX SERIES X

MICROSOFT • NOVEMBER 2020

Traditionally chunky, yet understated compared to Xboxes past, the Xbox Series X is a high-performance system bearing the 'X' designation established when Microsoft took the performance lead over Sony in the last console generation with the Xbox One X. The AMD Jaguar CPU cores in the Xbox One were relatively weak and proved to be a constraint on complexity, and Microsoft is hoping that AMD's new CPU means that Xbox Series X won't have the same problem. AMD's new Radeon RDNA2 GPU offers hardware ray tracing, which should make for improved lighting effects in games that use it. Unlike Sony, Microsoft is aiming for a soft transition, and first-party Xbox games will also appear on Xbox One consoles for the time being. This means that rather than selling the console based on exclusive games, Microsoft will be banking on the value proposition of services like Game Pass, as well as enticing previous customers with the prospect of extensive backwards compatibility with older Xbox games.

2020 APRIL
Riot debuts its card game, *Legends Of Runeterra*. It's based on *League Of Legends* and hopes to steal *Hearthstone*'s crown.

2020 JUNE
Sony reveals its striking new PS5 design, along with a roster of games, at its livestreamed 'Future Of Gaming' event.

2020 JUNE
French videogame publisher Focus Home Interactive picks up *The Surge* developer Deck 13 Studios.

2020 JULY
Sucker Punch launches its swan song for the PS4, the open-world Samurai epic, *Ghost Of Tsushima*.

2020 AUGUST
Epic updates *Fortnite* on Apple's and Google's stores to bypass their payment systems. They remove the game entirely.

3 XBOX SERIES S
MICROSOFT • NOVEMBER 2020

After struggling to attract players to the expensive Xbox One in 2013, Microsoft decided to take a different approach for the next generation. The Xbox Series S is essentially a variant of the Xbox Series X – the CPU is the same but with a slightly lower clock speed, and it has less RAM, a less powerful GPU and no Blu-ray drive. Despite this, it runs the same games as the Series X, just with less intensive graphical settings, targeting a 1440p resolution rather than 4K. The benefit to the consumer is that the Xbox Series S is a considerably smaller and cheaper console, launching at a much more palatable £249.99 compared to the hefty £449.99 of its bigger brother. It's evidence that Microsoft views the Xbox as a continuous family of platforms akin to Apple's iPhones, rather than a series of discrete devices – something also seen in its commitment to backwards compatibility for original Xbox and Xbox 360 games, and its vision of supporting the Xbox One systems past the launch of the Xbox Series consoles.

4 PLAYSTATION 5
SONY • NOVEMBER 2020

The PlayStation consoles have always been designed for high performance, and the PS5 is no different. As such, while the aesthetic design of the console is an interesting departure, under the hood it's business as usual and the system has a similar performance profile to that of the Xbox Series X. Sony has chosen to stick with AMD for its key components too, allowing it to include backwards compatibility at a lower cost than it had in previous generations, and while support is less than perfect, it is a key step towards ensuring that PS4 owners upgrade. The main differentiating factor is storage speed – Sony's engineers targeted high data transfer rates, utilising custom SSD technology to achieve them. Additionally, the newly designed DualSense controller offers novel features such as haptic feedback on the L2 and R2 triggers. The PlayStation 5 is available both with and without a Blu-ray drive, but there are no other differences between the two models.

5 POLYMEGA
PLAYMAJI • FEBRUARY 2021

While multiformat emulation devices have existed before, such as the RetroN 5 and Retro Freak, none of them has done everything that the Polymega does – nor have they cost quite as much. The Polymega supports original PC Engine CD, Neo Geo CD, Mega-CD, 32X CD, Saturn and PlayStation games as standard, but with plug-in modules can also accept NES, SNES, Mega Drive and PC Engine HuCard games and controllers. Games can be installed to internal storage, allowing you to reduce usage of your original media. The emulation is very good and the user interface is clean and simple, allowing you to browse your library of installed games with ease. The system is very good at what it does, but its European price is very close to that of the PlayStation 5 and Xbox Series X. It will be interesting to see how many players will pay that kind of premium to relive old favourites when new experiences are also within reach.

3

4

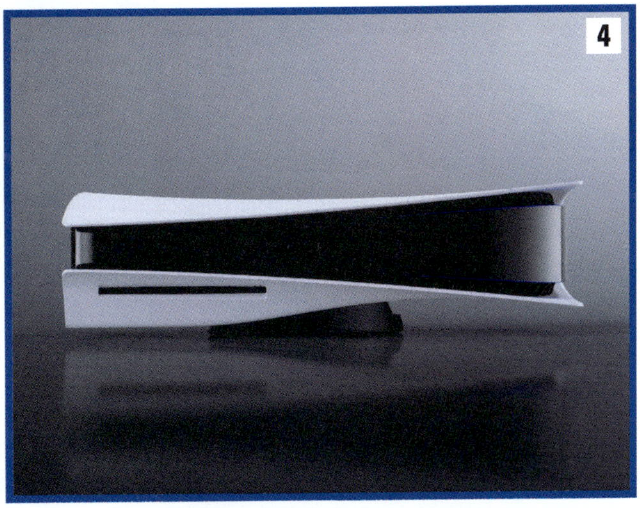

5

OTHER SYSTEMS FROM THE TWENTIES

PC Engine Mini • Konami, June 2020

M2's solid emulation and a well-chosen game selection make this a perfect introduction to a legendary piece of hardware.

Game Gear Micro • Sega, October 2020

These Japanese-exclusive handhelds are almost impractically small and have tiny game selections, but novelty value does the heavy lifting.

Game & Watch: Super Mario Bros • Nintendo, November 2020

Celebrating both *Super Mario Bros* and Game & Watch anniversaries, this special release offers *Super Mario Bros* and *The Lost Levels*.

Astro City Mini • Sega, December 2020

This mini cabinet offers 36 arcade games, from established favourites to deep cuts, plus TV output and USB controller support.

2020 AUGUST Dlala Studios and Rare unleash the Battletoads for PC and Xbox in a brand-new cartoon-like beat-'em-up reboot.

2020 SEPTEMBER *Tony Hawk's Pro Skater 1+2* is released. It's a remake of the first two *THPS* games and reignites interest in the Birdman.

2020 SEPTEMBER Microsoft announces plans to acquire ZeniMax Media (with its subsidiaries Bethesda, Arkane, id and more) for $7.5 billion.

2020 SEPTEMBER Mossmouth launches its roguelike sequel, *Spelunky 2*. You can read more from creator David Yu over on page 139.

2020 NOVEMBER Microsoft launches its new Xboxes. If you like a bargain, go for the Series S, if you want power, get a Series X.

GAMING IN A PANDEMIC

WE TAKE A LOOK AT SOME OF THE WAYS THE GAMING COMMUNITY PULLED TOGETHER TO TAKE THE STING OUT OF ONE OF THE WORST CRISES IN LIVING MEMORY

WORDS BY DREW SLEEP

It started out like any other year, but by March we all soon realised that 2020 was going to be anything but 'normal'. A new strain of coronavirus, called COVID-19, soon took over the entire planet, and many countries issued stay-at-home orders to help prevent its spread. By the end of March, the UK was in full lockdown. Offices and factories closed, and people started working from home wherever possible. We weren't allowed to meet friends or family, however we were allowed to go outside to shop for essentials and exercise, but that was it: other than that brief reprieve, we were trapped in our homes.

Losing the ability to go out, see movies, attend gigs and so on can limit your options when it comes to entertaining yourself, but considering you're browsing a book entitled '*History Of Videogames*' it's safe to say that you're a fan of picking up a controller and taking part in some good old virtual entertainment, and that's what many of us did. Gaming provided comfort to many during lockdown, and our hobby began acting as a surrogate for staying in touch with loved ones.

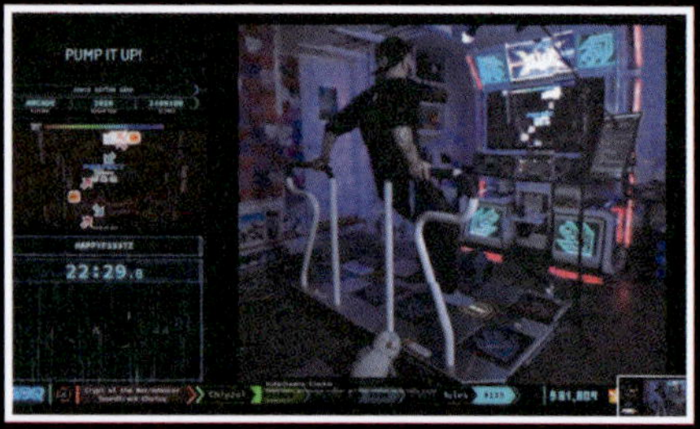

» Corona Relief Done Quick was held entirely online, and allowed for runners to play rhythm action games like *Pump It Up!*.

The first event that appeared to mark this trend was the arrival of *Animal Crossing: New Horizons* on 20 March. Its low-stress gameplay, ability to visit other players' islands and undeniable charm provided escapism for the millions who bought it on launch day, and word of mouth began to catch on, turning the life sim into a runaway success. People got creative with how they interacted with the game – couples hosted unofficial weddings and celebrations, a whole sub-community formed over turnip (basically stocks) advice, and a digital talk show, called *Animal Talking*, even popped up.

The gaming goodwill which was spreading across the internet didn't stop at cultivating a feeling of togetherness. Games Done Quick was due to host its annual Summer Games Done Quick charity speedrunning event in June, however the pandemic prompted its creators to have a rethink. They cancelled SGDQ and launched Corona Relief Done Quick, an event where contestants would stream speedruns from their homes. The team moved quickly, scheduling the event to run from 17 to 19 April. CRDQ was a success, raising over $400,000 for Direct Relief. "Since the event was held online, the risks and impact of the pandemic were greatly reduced," explains GDQ director of operations Matt Merkle. "We also have some experience with quickly assembling an event […]. It was stressful, but the staff and speedrunning community were really behind the idea.

"In pure numbers alone, it was the most successful emergency fundraiser we've ever held!" Matt continues. "I think one of the standout showings during the event was the *Pump It Up!* showcase. We had shied away from dance games in the past because it can be difficult to set up on stage at our main events, but as the online nature allowed the performance to occur at the runner's home, it was a much easier choice."

While *Animal Crossing* dominated the mainstream gaming headlines throughout the first half of 2020, it was toppled in August by a new launch, *Fall Guys: Ultimate Knockout*, developed by Mediatonic. This multiplayer title's premise will feel similar to those who enjoy *Takeshi's Castle* or *Total Wipeout*, tasking up to 60 jellybean-like humanoids to save themselves from elimination throughout a series of ridiculous events. This feel-good battle royale was another breath of fresh air, and it became a huge success – by November, *Fall Guys* had reached over 10 million sales on Steam alone. "I'd always imagined us all sat around together as a team and pressing the 'big red button' to send the servers live to a huge fanfare, so it felt incredibly odd to just be sitting on my own in my bedroom watching the player count go through the roof!" Joe Walsh, the game's lead designer tells us. "I do think the game launched at the perfect time, though – people needed something joyful and funny in their lives this year, so being able to help bring a bit of happiness to everyone is probably the thing I'm most proud of."

A major part of *Fall Guys*' appeal is how accessible it is. "I'd always had confidence in the idea of a giant physics game show, ever since we put together the first pitch," Joe says. "Everyone

2020 NOVEMBER Sony releases the PS5. Its design is divisive, but gamers agree that its controller and launch games are excellent.

2020 DECEMBER After many delays, CD Projekt releases its RPG *Cyberpunk 2077* in a borderline unfinished state. CDPR promises patches.

2021 JANUARY Lucasfilm Games is revived, acting as a brand guardian for all gaming adaptations of Lucasfilm properties.

2021 FEBRUARY Electronic Arts completes its purchase of racing specialist Codemasters. The deal went down to the tune of $1.2 billion.

2021 MAY Horror fans are treated to a new instalment of *Resident Evil* with *Village*. This thriller continues the story of Ethan Winters.

» [Switch] *Animal Crossing* gave us an opportunity to forget the about the wider world and bury our heads in the sand.

» [PC] *Among Us'* popularity received a shot in the arm in September, thanks to streamers and AOC.

» [PC] "We're figuring out how far we can go with *Fall Guys* now that we have this momentum behind us," Joe says.

we showed it to has had this 'oh my God, I'd play that' reaction to it, but I'd never imagined we'd end up selling over 11 million copies on PC, let alone becoming the most downloaded PS Plus game of all time! Now we're in this amazing position where we get to build on this phenomenon and push *Fall Guys* into areas we'd only really dreamed about before."

Speaking of bean-like characters, InnerSloth's *Among Us* was the talk of September. In this survival sim, you and up to nine other players must repair a ship but some players take the role of the 'imposter', sabotaging the efforts of the crew and murdering them one by one. Although it debuted in 2018, streamers began broadcasting the game during lockdown and its popularity resurged. In October, *Among Us* drew the attention of US Congresswomen Alexandria Ocasio-Cortez and Ilhan Omar, who broadcast themselves playing the game to help encourage young people to vote in the US elections.

Despite being a crapshoot of a year, the world wised to the fact that gaming can offer a reprieve to a bad situation in many different ways. "To a degree, I think [gaming] has helped people not just keep their sanity, but also to support each other," Matt explains. "I think the lockdown and subsequent isolation would have been much more brutal without it. It provides the opportunity to hang out and 'de-stress' with your friends in ways no other medium really allows for." *

SURVIVAL KIT

The essential games that saw us through lockdown

ANIMAL CROSSING: NEW HORIZONS

1 Nintendo's latest life sim is just so damn cosy. You find yourself as the newest resident of a deserted island, and guided by the ever-capitalistic hand of Tom Nook you'll gather all sorts of flora and fauna to help make money and turn your lovely slice of land into a personal paradise.

AMONG US

2 Building on the concept popularised by tabletop games like *Werewolf*, *Among Us* is a game of deduction where you must 'out' the imposter hiding in your group. Things are made difficult when the villains in your crew start killing off the good guys. Warning: playing this could ruin friendships.

FALL GUYS: ULTIMATE KNOCKOUT

3 This mean bean elimination machine took over everyone's 'currently playing' lists during the summer. It pits 60 players against one another across a series of elimination challenges, from madcap races to perilous platforming courses. Its deliberately janky physics make for brilliant slapstick comedy.

JACKBOX

4 Everyone loves a good party game, but it's difficult to play them when you're not allowed to have gatherings. Enter *Jackbox*, a series of virtual toyboxes that you can stream to your friends, who can take part using their phones. The series offers a bunch of great games that are sure to cater for all tastes.

MINECRAFT

5 We've already sung *Minecraft*'s praises on page 136, but its open-ended sandbox game design and multiplayer capabilities offer all kinds of possibilities which suits it perfectly for lockdown gaming. The only limit to what you can do in this modern classic is your imagination.

2021 JULY Activision Blizzard is the subject of a lawsuit asserting that its leadership perpetuated a frat boy culture.

2021 SEPTEMBER Sir Clive Sinclair, inventor and founder of Sinclair Research, passes away at the age of 81 after a battle with cancer.

2021 SEPTEMBER Netflix makes moves into the videogame sphere by purchasing Night School Studio, developer of *Oxenfree* and *Afterparty*.

2021 OCTOBER Interest in Samus Aran resurges after *Metroid Dread* launches. Developed by MercurySteam, it's a side-scrolling hit.

2021 DECEMBER Speaking of suited space heroes... Master Chief returns in *Halo Infinite*. This new adventure places more focus on John-117.

Get great savings when you buy direct from us

1000s of great titles, many not available anywhere else

World-wide delivery and super-safe ordering

THERE'S A BOOKAZINE FOR EVERYONE

Whether you're a film buff, an avid gamer, or love all things sci-fi, we've got you covered with our range of entertainment titles

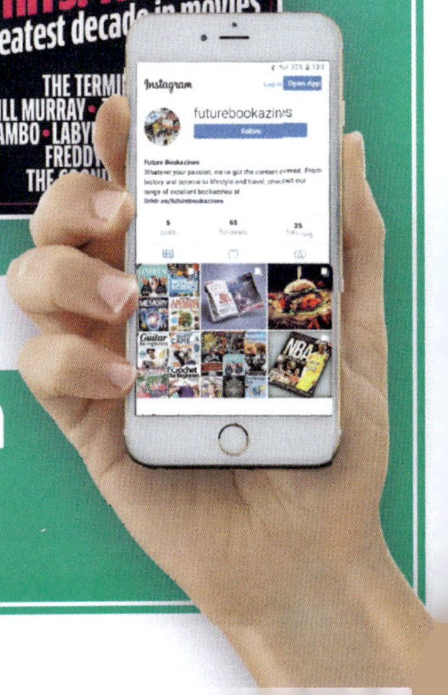

Follow us on Instagram @futurebookazines

FUTURE

www.magazinesdirect.com

Magazines, back issues & bookazines.

SUBSCRIBE & SAVE UP TO 61%

Delivered direct to your door or straight to your device

Choose from over 80 magazines and make great savings off the store price!

Binders, books and back issues also available

Simply visit www.magazinesdirect.com

No hidden costs · Shipping included in all prices · We deliver to over 100 countries · Secure online payment

FUTURE

magazinesdirect.com
Official Magazine Subscription Store

commodore 64
RESTORE
RETURN
SHIFT
HIT & RUN
4 MB
0226
TUROK
EVOLUTION
NINTENDO
GAMECUBE
PAL
CRISIS CORE
SONY
SLES-53702
PAL
CAPCOM
res-evil.com/re4

Printed in Dunstable, United Kingdom

91226142R10085